STRENGTH AND CONDITIONING

Strength and Conditioning offers a concise but comprehensive overview of training for athletic performance. Introducing essential theory and practical techniques in all of the core areas of athletic training, the book clearly demonstrates how to apply fundamental principles in putting together effective real-world training programs.

While some established textbooks rely on established but untested conventional wisdom, this book encourages students and professionals to think critically about their work and to adopt an evidence-based approach. It is the only introductory strength and conditioning textbook to properly explain the interdependence of aspects of training such as needs analysis, assessment, injury, competition level, athlete age, and program design, and the only book to fully explain how those aspects should be integrated.

No other textbook offers such an accessible, engaging, and reflective introduction to the theory and application of strength and conditioning programs. Including clear step-by-step guidance, suggestions for further reading, and detailed sport-specific examples, this is the perfect primer for any strength and conditioning course or for any professional trainer or coach looking to refresh their professional practice.

John Cissik is the Director of Fitness and Recreation at Texas Woman's University and a human performance consultant to track and field programs. He has authored six books, produced four videos, and written more than 70 publications on strength and speed training. He also serves as an associate editor for the *Strength and Conditioning Journal*.

STRENGTH AND CONDITIONING

A CONCISE INTRODUCTION

JOHN CISSIK

Routledge
Taylor & Francis Group

LONDON AND NEW YORK

First published 2012
by Routledge
2 Park Square, Milton Park, Abingdon, Oxon OX14 4RN

Simultaneously published in the USA and Canada
by Routledge
711 Third Avenue, New York, NY 10017

Routledge is an imprint of the Taylor & Francis Group, an informa business

British Library Cataloguing in Publication Data
A catalogue record for this book is available from the British Library

Library of Congress Cataloging in Publication Data
Cissik, John M.
Strength and conditioning : a concise introduction / John Cissik.
p. cm.
1. Physical education and training. 2. Muscle strength. 3. Physical fitness—Physiological aspects. 4. Athletes—Training of. I. Title.
GV711.5.C56 2011
613.71—dc22
2011013940

ISBN: 978-0-415-66664-0 (hbk)
ISBN: 978-0-415-66666-4 (pbk)
ISBN: 978-0-203-80714-9 (ebk)

Typeset in Zapf Humanist and Eras
by FiSH Books, Enfield

Printed and bound in Great Britain by
TJ International Ltd, Padstow, Cornwall

CONTENTS

ACKNOWLEDGEMENTS

While my name is on this book as the author, a lot of people provided help and support. My wife, Ewa, and our children were very supportive and patient with me during this process. Simon Whitmore and Joshua Wells at Routledge had great suggestions and were very easy to work with. I would also like to thank the models, Allison Meguro and Shigeaki Meguro, for their patience and hard work.

INTRODUCTION

The field of strength and conditioning is a rich field consisting of application, theory, philosophy, and scientific foundation. This book is meant to tie all those aspects together for the student and practitioner. Quite simply, this book will cover the "hows" of the various aspects of strength and conditioning and will incorporate many of the modern training implements and training approaches that are widely used but not yet widely researched.

Strength and conditioning is a broad field that attracts athletes, parents, the general fitness population, researchers, rehabilitation professionals, sports medicine professionals, fitness professionals, sports coaches, and strength and conditioning coaches. As a field, strength and conditioning consists of a number of tools. These include strength training, plyometrics training, speed training, agility training, conditioning, and sport-specific training.

Strength training refers to overcoming some external resistance to make the muscles stronger, larger, and more explosive. Typically, this is the first thing that one thinks of with regards to strength and conditioning. While important, it is only part of an athlete's training.

Plyometric training involves jumps or throws to make the athlete more explosive. It became very popular about 20 years ago but still is not very well understood today.

Speed training refers to training athletes to run faster. Speed is a critical component to athletics, though overemphasizing this can make it difficult to apply the qualities developed to the sport.

Agility training teaches the athlete to change direction quickly while maintaining his or her balance. It is one of the most difficult areas to coach.

Conditioning gets the athlete in shape for the sport. It can involve running sprints with little recovery, but can involve much more than just running.

Sport-specific training is what the athlete does on the field or on the court to directly prepare for the game. It is an area that many strength and conditioning professionals are deficient in and this makes linking the strength and conditioning to the sport challenging.

This book is going to cover most of these important parts of strength and conditioning and will also address injuries; age differences and its impact on training; how level of competition impacts training; how to put everything together into a program; long-term periodization; and will provide a number of examples using various sports. To my knowledge, no other book addresses these subjects this comprehensively.

There are 12 chapters in this book. The chapters are organized around the following topics:

- Adaptations from training: Why is strength and conditioning important? What exactly happens as a result of it? This section breaks down what we "know" as a result of science on the impact of strength and conditioning.
- Techniques: What are the major tools used to train *athletes*? This section covers the major exercises, but this is not an exhaustive look at exercises – other books do this already. The focus will be on the major ones, how/why they are performed, and safety relative to each exercise.
- Assessments: How do we evaluate athletes to assess their needs and to assess the effectiveness of training? Major assessments under each area (strength, power, speed) are described with an emphasis on assessments that are common to many sports.
- Components of a training session: Each component is covered in isolation. What types of exercises are used in each component? Why? Are the components organized a specific way?
- Principles of training: These are the guidelines for strength and conditioning. They are defined and examples of using them are provided.
- Needs analysis: The needs of the sport, combined with the needs of the athlete, should drive the designing of the training program. However, we often forget this step and jump straight into the program.
- Program design: This is covered on a micro level and a macro level. At the micro level, training for different goals (strength, speed, power, etc.) is described. At the macro level incorporating multiple goals/training modes are presented in a step-by-step manner.
- Periodization of training: With athletes, there is a need to take the long-term view of training and to prepare them to be at their best during a specific moment in time. This is one area that lends itself to being overly complicated. A simple, methodical approach is used to teach the concept.
- Injuries: Unfortunately, this is a common occurrence in athletics. The major ones are described from the standpoint of what is occurring, how they can be accommodated in training, and how they are "fixed."
- Age and training: Most books are typically written for the 18–30-year-old population. Most athletes do not fall into this group. Based upon their age, they are going to have different training needs and are going to respond to training differently.
- Level of competition and training: Many books are typically written for university and elite athlete populations. Most athletes don't fall into these populations and will have different needs.

■ Putting it all together: Soccer is used to help illustrate the concepts in the book.

Each chapter includes a "key readings" section, which provides articles and books that are important for understanding some of the concepts covered. Some are controversial, some are outdated, but they are all important for giving the reader a perspective on why things are the way they are today.

At the end of this book is a glossary to help with key concepts and terms, an exhaustive bibliography so that the reader can research concepts in more detail, and an index to assist the reader with locating key concepts.

As a field, strength and conditioning is part science and part philosophy. As this book, hopefully, demonstrates, there is a prodigious amount of research on strength and conditioning. Yet, there are significant holes in the research and these gaps form the foundation of many of the key beliefs held in strength and conditioning. Despite decades of research, our evidence-based knowledge of core beliefs such as the efficacy of core training, hypertrophy, the neural effects of strength training, periodization, plyometrics, and velocity specificity is extremely limited. This means that much of the practice of strength and conditioning is based upon tradition, marketing, and logic.

Approaching strength and conditioning in this manner isn't necessarily a negative. The philosophy frequently drives the science (i.e. we try something and science later verifies it). American track and field coach, William Freeman (1994), in a wonderful article, wrote that "Athletes improve because their training evolves – it changes as they improve. We must try new ideas, new approaches. Most of these will come from unsubstantiated theory."

It is important to highlight and acknowledge where there are gaps in our knowledge of strength and conditioning. Without acknowledging these gaps, they can never be addressed. This book addresses where there are gaps, where the research is inconclusive, where there are conflicting results, and where the applicability of our knowledge is limited. To the author's knowledge, no other book addresses evidence-based strength and conditioning this comprehensively.

This book is appropriate for many audiences. The student, fitness professional, and coach will find a wealth of information about the hows and whys of strength and conditioning. The parent, fitness enthusiast, and athlete will be able to find exercises and programs that can be applied to their situation. The sports medicine professional can read this book and get a sense of what the coach is trying to accomplish. The researcher can read this book and take out of it the wealth of opportunities for advancing our knowledge in this field.

KEY READINGS

Freeman, W. (1994) Coaching, periodization, and the battle of artist versus scientist, *Track Coach*, 127: 4054–7.

William Freeman in this article addresses the debate of art versus science with regards to coaching. He points out that science is important; after all, biology is the basis of movement. However, as he points out, the science has limitations and is frequently behind the practice of coaching. In other words, the art of coaching often drives the science, not the other way round.

CHAPTER ONE

ADAPTATIONS FROM TRAINING

The human body's physiology determines what kinds of adaptations are made from training and drives why training is performed the way that it is. Understanding how and why the body responds to exercise allows one to more effectively perform exercises and design programs.

OUTLINE

Background

- Muscle structure and function
- Muscle fiber types
- Neural structure and function
- Fueling movement

Neural adaptations

Muscular adaptations

- Changes in muscle size
- Changes in pennation angle
- Changes in fiber typing

Hormonal adaptations

Bone/connective tissue adaptations

Energy system adaptations

Key readings

BACKGROUND

Muscle structure and function

The skeletal muscle that lies under the skin is surrounded by a layer of connective tissue called the *epimysium*. Under that layer are bundles of muscle fibers, each bundle called a *fasciculus*. Each fasciculus is surrounded by a layer of connective tissue called the *perimysium*. Each fasciculus is made up of many *muscle fibers*, which are the cells of the muscle.

Muscle fibers run the entire length of the muscle and have multiple nuclei. Each muscle fiber is surrounded by a layer of connective tissue called the *endomysium*. The endoymsium consists of two parts: a *basement membrane*, which is on the exterior, and a *plasma membrane* (also known as the *sarcolemma*), which is on the interior. Located between the two parts of the endomysium are *satellite cells*.

The muscle fiber has the appearance of alternating light and dark bands, which is why skeletal muscle is called *striated muscle*. These alternating light and dark bands are the *sarcomere* of the muscle fiber, which is the contractile unit of the muscle fiber.

Sarcomeres consist primarily of two protein filaments, *actin* and *myosin*. Actin filaments are also known as the thin filaments and there are many of them in a sarcomere. Myosin filaments are also known as the thick filaments. There are fewer in a sarcomere and they are surrounded by actin.

Surrounding the sarcomere are a series of interlocking tubular channels called the *sarcoplasmic reticulum*. The lateral ends of the sarcoplasmic reticulum terminate at the end of each sarcomere and contain vescicles that store calcium. Adjacent to the sarcoplasmic reticulum are t-tubules that run into the muscle fibers.

During a muscular contraction, an electrochemical signal (called the *action potential*) is sent from the brain, down the spinal cord, to a motor nerve, to all of the muscle fibers that the motor nerve innervates.

The action potential changes the charge of the nerve and the muscle fiber. At rest, muscle and nerve fibers are negatively charged inside. As the action potential moves down the nerve and muscle fiber, this changes and the fibers become positively charged inside, which is called *depolarization*. As the action potential travels across the muscle fiber, it also travels down the t-tubule, depolarizing it. This depolarization causes the sarcoplasmic reticulum to release calcium into the t-tubule. The calcium travels down to the actin filament and causes it to shift its structure, allowing myosin to reach out and attach to the actin. This attachment is known as a *cross-bridge*.

Once the cross-bridge is formed, myosin will expend energy and flex the cross-bridge, causing actin to shorten. When this happens on a big-enough scale, the muscle fiber will shorten, causing movement. As long as calcium and energy are present, cross-bridges will continue to be formed. The more cross-bridges that can be formed, the more force can be exerted.

When it is time for movement to stop, repolarization changes the charge of the muscle and nerve fibers back to resting values, halting the release of calcium. Without calcium the cross-bridges cannot form.

Muscle fibers attach to bone via *tendons*. All the layers of connective tissue that are present in the muscle (epimysium, perimysium, and endomysium) run into the tendon, so that when the muscles shorten they are able to move bone.

Muscle fibers either run parallel to the tendon's line of pull or obliquely to it. When they run parallel they are said to be *in series* and they shorten more quickly than fibers that run obliquely to the line of pull. When they run obliquely they are referred to as *pennate muscle fibers* (Narici, 1999). Pennate muscle fibers allow for more sarcomeres to be located in parallel, allowing for more cross-bridges to form and more force to be generated (Kawakami *et al.*, 1995; Komi, 1979; Narici, 1999).

Muscle fiber types

Muscle fibers have several different classification systems depending upon the textbook or article that describes them. This can make interpreting literature challenging. According to Staron (1997), muscle fibers may be classified according to:

- Contraction speed: *Fast-twitch muscle fibers* can generate a large amount of force, quickly, for a very short period of time. *Slow-twitch muscle fibers* can generate a smaller amount of force, at a slower speed, but can maintain it for long periods of time.
- Color: Muscle fibers can be red or white. Red muscle fibers have a better blood supply due to the presence of more capillaries and would also be known as slow-twitch muscle fibers. White muscle fibers do not have as many capillaries and would also be known as fast-twitch muscle fibers.
- Enzymatic properties and speed of contraction: With this classification system, muscle fibers can be slow oxidative (SO), fast oxidative glycolytic (FOG), or fast glycolytic (FG). SO muscle fibers have a slow contraction speed and produce small amounts of force, but are difficult to fatigue. FOGs have a faster contraction speed and produce moderate amounts of force, but maintain it for a shorter period than SOGs. FGs have the fastest contraction speed and produce the greatest amounts of force, but fatigue very rapidly.
- Myofibrillar ATPase sensitivity: Differences in pH sensitivity are correlated with myosin heavy chain content and contractile properties. There is a gambit of muscle fiber types ranging from Type I (slow-twitch muscle fibers) to Type IIb (fast-twitch

7

adaptations from training

muscle fibers) to fibers with characteristics of both, to greater or lesser degrees (IIa, IIab, etc.).

Muscle fiber types are a limiting factor in athletic potential. Individuals are all born with a certain percentage of slow- and fast-twitch muscle fibers. It appears that the percentage of fast-twitch muscle fibers cannot be increased as a result of training, though it can be decreased. This means that an individual that is born with a higher percentage of slow-twitch muscle fibers will be limited in their success at events requiring speed, explosivity, or great strength.

Strength and conditioning programs develop different types of muscle fibers depending upon the exercise selection, speed of movement, loading, and rest/recovery. Programs that emphasize heavy weight training, explosive exercises, or sprints develop fast-twitch muscle fibers. Those that emphasize endurance training develop slow-twitch muscle fibers.

Neural structure and function

The brain controls movement via the motor cortex. *Neurons*, or cell bodies, located in the motor cortex extend into the spinal cord and terminate in the spinal cord's gray matter at the motor neuron. This is known as the *corticospinal tract* or the *pyramidal pathway*.

Some reflexes exist outside this pathway and allow for faster control, freeing up the higher centers of the brain for more important matters; for example, jerking one's hand away when touching a hot stove.

Once a command has reached the spinal cord, a motor neuron transmits the message to the muscle fibers. The body of the motor neuron is located in the gray matter of the spinal cord. The axon extends from the neuron to the muscle fiber, where dendrites receive the impulses and conduct them to the muscle fiber. A motor neuron and all the muscle fibers that it innervates is called a *motor unit*. Motor units innervate the same classification of muscle fiber. In other words, motor unit A will consist of all slow-twitch muscle fibers or all fast-twitch muscle fibers.

Fueling movement

At the most basic level, the body uses a compound called *adenosine triphosphate* (ATP) to fuel movement. The body uses three different energy systems to find and break down ATP for fuel. While these energy systems are all presented in isolation, they do not operate that way. The energy systems are:

8

- Phosphagen energy system: Fuels six to ten seconds of high-intensity movement. ATP that is present in the muscles is broken down for fuel. As ATP is broken down for fuel, it can be resynthesized using *creatine phosphate* (CP). The amounts of CP limit the performance of this energy system. Fast-twitch muscle fibers contain 15–20 percent more CP than slow-twitch fibers (Sahlin *et al.*, 1998). This energy system provides the fuel for activities such as a vertical jump, a maximal lift, and short sprints.
- Glycolytic energy system (also known as anaerobic glycolysis): Fuels up to two to three minutes of exercise. Stored carbohydrates in the form of glucose (which circulates in the blood stream) or glycogen (which is stored in the muscles and liver) are broken down to generate ATP. This process takes several seconds to warm up, so it is not available immediately. As glucose and glycogen are used for fuel, the intensity of the exercise means that oxygen is not available to assist with this process. This means that a waste product, lactic acid, is produced. Lactic acid is believed to produce hydrogen ions, which interfere with enzymatic reactions and muscular contractions. In other words, the presence of lactic acid is often the limiting factor in this energy system. The glycolytic energy system fuels activities such as a 200-meter sprint or performing push-ups to failure.
- Oxidative energy system (also known as aerobic glycolysis) fuels movement lasting longer than two to three minutes. Glucose and glycogen stored in the muscles or liver, or found in fat, is broken down to generate ATP in the presence of oxygen. In extreme examples even protein will be used for fuel (Howarth *et al.*, 2010). Theoretically, if the intensity remains constant and glucose/glycogen is available, exercise could be fueled indefinitely. This system provides a large amount of ATP, but it does so very slowly. Because it requires oxygen, if the intensity of the exercise increases, the activity can no longer be fueled through this energy system and the athlete will begin producing ATP via anaerobic glycolysis.

The energy systems limit performance. Understanding how they work and how they limit performance allows for strength and conditioning programs to be designed to train those systems. If programs do not address the proper energy system, they are going to be ineffective and may be counterproductive.

NEURAL ADAPTATIONS

Strength training is thought to train the nervous system. This can be seen best in how it effects the untrained. When an individual begins strength training, their strength improves rapidly. This is despite the fact that increases in muscle mass are much slower. This is thought to be from neural adaptations. For example, Kubo *et al.* (2010) performed a study looking at the effects of training and detraining. After two months of isometric strength training, untrained individuals experienced an almost 30 percent strength increase on isometric knee extensions while there was no accompanying increase in muscle size during that time.

According to some authors, there is a moderate relationship between muscle size and strength. Knight and Kamen (2001) report a correlation of 0.5 between muscle size and strength. If true, this means that only 25 percent of the variations in strength are explainable by muscle size. Izquierdo *et al.* (2001), when examining the effects of training on older individuals, found that after 16 weeks of training the cross-sectional area of the rectus femoris increased by an average of 12 percent. However, knee extension strength increased by an average of 27 percent.

Research on neural adaptations is challenging to conduct. While one can measure strength, power, and speed, researching what the nervous system is doing is difficult. Most research involves surface electromyography (EMG), which has limitations. The pads that measure the EMG signals pick up ambient electricity. They move on the skin, they require equations to smooth out the data that may or may not be accurate, and they may not be positioned correctly to measure what is intended. Direct measures are likely to interfere with performance.

If neural adaptations occur, one result is that the excitability of the corticospinal tract should increase. Research on this is mixed. Carroll *et al.* (2009) found that four weeks of strength training of the wrist extensors led to a gain in corticospinal transmission to the muscles acting on the wrist. Jensen *et al.* (2005), however, did not find an effect of four weeks of biceps brachii strength training on corticospoinal excitability.

In theory, several additional neural adaptations are possible from training:

- increased number of muscle fibers recruited;
- decreased antagonist activation;
- increased co-activation of the antagonist and synergists;
- increased frequency of muscle fiber recruitment;
- bypassing the size principle.

When a muscle fiber contracts, it does so maximally. In order to generate more force, one has to recruit more muscle fibers. A possible adaptation from a strength and conditioning program is to learn how to recruit more muscle fibers in order to generate more force (Cormie *et al.*, 2010a; Follard and Williams, 2007; Gollhoffer, 2007).

The muscle that performs a movement is called the *agonist*, sometimes known as the prime mover. Agonists have muscles that oppose, or perform the opposite movement. These are known as the *antagonist* muscles. Untrained individuals have trouble quieting the activity of the antagonist muscles, which limits their ability to exert force during movement. This is something that is trainable with time and helps the untrained to increase their strength rapidly (Behm, 1995; Carroll *et al.*, 2009; Follard and Williams, 2007).

There is a debate in the literature over whether an increase in agonist activation is possible (Follard and Williams, 2007). According to Behm (1995), untrained individuals can already fully activate their muscles, though he concedes that the trained may be able to do so better during conditions of fatigue. This would seem to be supported by Knight and Kamen (2001) who found that untrained older adults (mean age of 77) could already recruit 97 percent of their knee extensors prior to beginning a six-week strength-training study.

Not all authors agree with this. Kubo et al. (2010) found that after three months of strength training, younger subjects (mean age 22) improved their ability to activate their rectus femoris by 27 percent.

A number of joints and movements have muscles that neither act as the agonist nor as the antagonist. These muscles serve a stabilizing or synergistic role. With training, one learns to have better control of these stabilizing muscles to allow for more force to be generated during movements.

Another feature of many movements is the fact that there is co-activation of many muscles through the entire range of motion. For example, during the squat exercise, one lowers oneself into the bottom position and then stands up from the squat. While standing up, the knee is extending so that the quadriceps are acting as the agonists to extend the knee. The hamstring muscles oppose the quadriceps and are therefore the antagonists. However, while standing up, the hip is also extending. The hamstrings are the agonists during hip extension; the quadriceps serve as the antagonists. The reverse is true during the descent in the squat. In other words, the hamstrings and quadriceps are active through the entire range of motion of the exercise. This takes practice to do in a manner that allows for a great deal of force to be generated (Behm 1995; Carroll et al., 2009).

As a result of training, muscle fibers may be recruited more quickly (Cormie et al., 2010a; Gollhofer, 2007). This is known as increasing the rate of force development. This would be an important adaptation for athletic events that require speed or explosivity.

A final possible adaptation is to bypass the size principle. According to the size principle, during movement, motor units are recruited according to their size; the smaller (and slower) motor units are recruited first and the larger (and faster) motor units are recruited last. It's possible that with training this could be bypassed so that one recruits the larger, stronger, faster units more quickly. Komi (1979) suggests that the size principle may be movement-specific. According to him, during fast voluntary movements the size principle may not be valid.

MUSCULAR ADAPTATIONS

Changes in muscle size

Muscles can become larger as a result of a strength and conditioning program. This is thought to be through the process of *hypertrophy*. When muscle fibers undergo hyper-trophy, individual fibers become larger. Hypertrophy involves an increase in the number of myofibrils (i.e. actin and myosin) (Follard and Williams, 2007; Spangenburg, 2009). In the initial phases of hypertrophy, this seems to be governed by an increase in protein synthesis rates (Spangenburg, 2009). As training progresses, hypertrophy seems to occur from an increase in the RNA content in the muscle fibers via the incorporation of satel-lite cells (Follard and Williams, 2007; Spangenburg, 2009). These suggest two possible important genetic limitations to hypertrophy: the number of nuclei in the muscle fiber (and thus the amount of RNA) and the number of satellite cells.

Hypertrophy takes eight to twelve weeks to occur (Follard and Williams, 2007). Upper-body muscles may have a greater hypertrophic response than lower-body muscles, due to the anti-gravity nature of the lower-body muscles.

When looking at the whole muscle, its growth is going to vary due to the extent of the loading and the activation of the constituent muscle fibers. This is going to be governed by the mechanics of each muscle in relation to the exercise. Hypertrophy may not occur at a uniform rate throughout a muscle as a result of exercise (Follard and Williams, 2007).

An alternative explanation to hypertrophy is called *hyperplasia*. During hyperplasia, muscle fibers split into more fibers. In other words, instead of getting larger muscle fibers, an athlete would develop more of them. There is not a lot of evidence of hyperplasia in humans and it seems to be largely confined to the extremes (i.e. professional body-building combined with performance-enhancing drug use). There is some evidence for this in research on cats, but their physiology is so different from humans that it is very possible that this could be present in cats and not in humans.

It is expensive for the body to increase the size of the muscles and to maintain that increased size. It requires more protein and it increases the body's resting metabolic rate. It is also a slow process because protein synthesis must be greater than protein break-down for an extended period of time (i.e. weeks and months) (Hawley, 2009).

Changes in pennation angle

Strength and conditioning programs can change the pennation angle of muscle fibers (Cormie et al., 2010c; Follard and Williams, 2007; Narici, 1999). This allows for more contractile material to be packed into the muscle, allowing it to generate more force (Kawakami et al., 1995, Narici, 1999). Kawakami et al. studied the effects of 16 weeks

12

of unilateral French presses on the triceps brachii. As a result of 16 weeks of training, increases in the angle of pennation for the triceps brachii ranged from 9.4 to 39.3 percent in subjects.

According to Follard and Williams (2007), there is an optimal angle of pennation for the generation of force: 45 degrees. Most muscle fibers are far below this. For example, in studies looking at the influence of pennation angle on speed, Abe et al. (2000) and Kumagai et al. (2000) report values of 14 to 24 degrees for the vastus lateralis and gastrocnemius muscles.

This adaptation, while important for improving force production, should be viewed with caution in certain situations. While it is true that muscle fibers with a greater pennation angle generate more force, muscle fibers with a smaller pennation angle shorten faster. Two studies in particular make a link between pennation angle and speed. Abe et al. (2000) compared sprinters to distance runners and found that sprinters had a statistically significantly smaller pennation angle at the vastus lateralis and gastrocnemius muscles. Kumagai et al. (2000) compared slower sprinters with faster ones and found that the faster sprinters also had statistically significantly smaller pennation angles at the vastus lateralis and gastrocnemius. This suggests that there may be a trade-off between increasing the size of the muscles and the speed with which they can shorten, which is an important consideration in some athletic events.

Changes in fiber typing

Strength-training programs can increase the size of existing slow-twitch and fast-twitch muscle fibers, but they do not increase the number of fast-twitch muscle fibers.

HORMONAL ADAPTATIONS

As chemical messengers, hormones play an important role in adaptations to strength training. The remodeling of muscle tissue begins to occur after a strength-training session. If the stress was too great there will be a *catabolic* (i.e. tissue degradation) response. If the stress is just right there will be an *anabolic* response resulting in an increase in the synthesis of actin and myosin coupled with a reduction in protein degradation.

Testosterone is the primary anabolic hormone and has both direct and indirect effects on protein synthesis. It promotes the growth hormone responses from the pituitary gland. It acts on the nervous system through interacting with neuron receptors and increasing the amount of neurotransmitters, both of which increase force production. It can also bind to the nuclei of skeletal muscle fibers resulting in protein synthesis (Buresh et al., 2009; Kraemer, 2000).

Growth hormone increases cellular amino acid uptake and protein synthesis, resulting in hypertrophy (Buresh *et al.*, 2009; Kraemer, 2000). Its other main roles include decreasing glucose utilization, decreasing glycogen synthesis, increasing the utilization of fatty acids, and increasing collagen synthesis.

Insulin-line growth factor (IGF) is produced by the liver and is thought to have a role in regulating hypertrophy, though this is controversial (Spangenburg, 2009). The presence of growth hormone stimulates the liver to release IGF, and IGF is thought to mediate the effects of growth hormone (Buresh *et al.*, 2009).

Cortisol is the primary catabolic hormone. In reality, it is the primary signaling hormone for carbohydrate metabolism. When through starvation, stress, or overtraining the body perceives that there are not enough carbohydrates present, cortisol will increase protein degradation. Cortisol converts amino acids to carbohydrates and inhibits protein synthesis (Buresh *et al.*, 2009; Kraemer, 2000).

Hormones are affected acutely and chronically by training. Acute effects refer to those that happen during and just after training; chronic ones are long-term adaptations from training.

In terms of acute effects, high-volume strength training seems to produce the greatest change in hormone levels. Several studies have found that high-volume training raises testosterone levels, human growth hormone levels, IGF-1, and cortisol levels acutely (Buresh *et al.*, 2009; McCall *et al.*, 1999; Smilios *et al.*, 2003).

Chronic adaptations are more problematic to find in the literature. Buresh *et al.* (2009) note that in as little as five weeks, exercise stops having a hormonal response. This suggests the need for regular variety in a strength-training program. Research looking at the effects of 12 weeks of strength training (McCall *et al.*, 1999) and 16 weeks of strength training (Izquierdo *et al.*, 2001) finds no changes in resting concentrations of testosterone pre- to post-study. In addition, McCall *et al.* (1999) found no changes in resting concentrations of IGF-1 or human growth hormone after 12 weeks of training. Both authors did find that resting cortisol levels decreased after the training program.

The lack of chronic changes in resting testosterone, IGF-1, and human growth hormone levels may indicate several things. First, the training may not have been challenging enough. This is unlikely as in both studies participants made large gains in strength (25–45 percent across both studies) and cross-sectional area of the muscles (11–13 percent across both studies). Second, the training may not have lasted long enough. Third, there may not be changes to resting hormonal levels as a result of training. If that is true, it would suggest that the acute effects drive the muscle's response to strength training.

BONE/CONNECTIVE TISSUE ADAPTATIONS

Bone and connective tissue such as ligaments and tendons adapt to loading and unloading. In bone, this process is called *bone modeling*. During bone modeling, bone cells called osteoblasts move to the surface of the bone that is experiencing the load. The osteoblasts secrete proteins that are deposited in the spaces between bone cells. These proteins form the bone matrix, which eventually becomes mineralized and rigid. New bone formation occurs on the outer surface of the bone, which is called the *periosteum*. This process increases the diameter of the bone.

A number of factors are important for bone to adapt to an exercise program:

- The *minimum essential strain* (or the threshold that initiates new bone formation) must be reached. If the stimulus is not great enough, new bone formation will not occur.
- Bone formation as a result of exercise is site-specific. For new bone formation to occur, that bone must be loaded. For example, running would stimulate new bone formation for the tibia but not for the wrist.
- Structural exercises that direct the load through the bones are necessary to cause bone to form. Squats, cleans, deadlifts, presses, etc. will all cause bone to form if the minimum essential strain is reached. Leg extensions, leg curls, flies, and like exercises really do not direct the force through the bone.

Calbet *et al.* (1999) compared professional volleyball players to controls. They found that the volleyball players had 14 percent more *bone mineral density* (quantity of mineral deposited in a given area of bone) at the lumbar spine and 20–27 percent more at the hip. With the jumping that volleyball players do, these results are not surprising. Sabo *et al.* (1996) looked at national-caliber weightlifters, boxers, cyclists, and controls and compared the bone-mineral density of the lumbar spine. They found that weightlifters had 24 percent greater bone-mineral density at the lumbar spine than controls, boxers 17 percent greater, and cyclists 10 percent less. This study serves to illustrate the site-specific adaptations with regards to bone formation. Weightlifters with their focus on cleans, jerks, snatches, pulls, and squats, directly load the lumbar spine. Boxers perform and train on their feet using a combination of skill work, running, conditioning, and weight training and also directly load the lumbar spine. Cycling unloads the lumbar spine.

Just as bone can become stronger, it can also lose mass and strength as a result of unloading. Bed rest, immobilization, space flight, and disease such as osteoporosis are all things that can cause bone to lose content and become more brittle.

Tendons attach muscle to bone. The various layers of connective tissue that surround the muscle, fascicle, and muscle fiber converge at the end of the muscle to form the tendon. Strength training can increase the tendon's ability to withstand greater tension.

15

Ligaments, which attach bone to bone, seem to heal faster as a result of exercise. It would seem logical that ligaments would become stronger as a result of strength training, but research on humans is lacking.

ENERGY-SYSTEM ADAPTATIONS

Strength and conditioning programs offer several adaptations with regards to energy. These include enhanced energy stores, increases in enzymes, and a shift in substrate utilization.

The process of exercising depletes energy stores. If the strength and conditioning program allows the athlete to recover, and if the athlete eats properly, the body's response to this depletion is to increase the energy stores to meet the demand. This takes the form of increased CP stores and increased glycogen stores (Perry et al., 2008; Yeo et al., 2008). Aerobic exercise increases the size and number of mitochondria, which improves the muscle's ability to produce ATP during oxidative metabolism (Hoyt, 2009).

Studies have found that exercise increases the enzymes involved in anaerobic and aerobic metabolism. For example, Greiwe et al. (1999) trained six untrained individuals for ten weeks, six times per week, on a cycle ergometer and jogging (alternating workouts). After ten weeks, maximal oxygen consumption improved by an average of 22 percent, GLUT-4 content by an average of 127 percent and citrate synthase by an average of almost 20 percent. In the presence of insulin, GLUT-4 allows the transport of glucose into muscle fibers to be stored as glycogen. Citrate synthase is a rate-limiting enzyme in oxidative metabolism. In other words, in the Greiwe et al. study, ten weeks of exercise improved the ability to store glycogen and the ability to produce energy aerobically.

Perry et al. (2008) examined the effects of six weeks of interval training on six untrained individuals. Subjects trained three times per week on a cycle ergometer. The exercise protocol involved performing ten exercise intervals, each lasting four minutes, at 90 percent of maximal oxygen consumption. Subjects rested on the ergometer for two minutes between each interval. After six weeks of training, citrate synthase levels had increased by 26 percent and resting glycogen stores by 59 percent.

At least in terms of aerobic exercise adaptations, training produces a glycogen sparing effect. This means that instead of relying on muscle glycogen for fuel, trained athletes will spare the glycogen to use fat as a fuel source. Hoyt (2009) attributes this, at least partially, to the increase in mitochondrial content.

Coyle et al. (1988) studied two groups of male endurance athletes. The first group (H) had a more training experience, a slightly higher maximal oxygen consumption, and reached a higher percentage of maximal oxygen consumption at lactate threshold that the other group (L). Both groups exercised to exhaustion on a cycle ergometer at 80 percent of maximal oxygen consumption. Group H exercised for more than 60 minutes, group L for almost 30. What is most interesting is that group H, even though they exercised longer, used less glycogen for fuel than Group L. This study serves to demonstrate that the group with the higher fitness was able to spare muscle glycogen during exercise.

KEY READINGS

Cormie, P., McGuigan, M.R. and Newton, R.U. (2011) Developing maximal neuromuscular power: Part 1, biological basis of maximal power production, *Sports Medicine*, 41(1), 17–38.

Cormie *et al.* (2011) is a review article looking at the state of knowledge with regards to power training. In it, they review the state of the research with regards to how training impacts the nervous system. Their findings include a lack of support for recruiting more muscle fibers as a result of training and a lack of support for preferentially recruiting fast-twitch muscle fibers (i.e. rate coding) as a result of training.

Abe, T., Kumagai, K. and Brechue, W.F. (2000) Fascicle length of leg muscles is greater in sprinters than distance runners, *Medicine and Science in Sports and Exercise*, 32(6): 1125–29.

Kumagai, K., Abe, T., Brechue, W.F., Ryushi, T., Takano, S. and Mizuno, M. (2000) Sprint performance is related to muscle fascicle length in male 100-m sprinters, *Journal of Applied Physiology*, 88(3), 811–16.

Both of these studies are important because they suggest that differences in muscle architecture may explain differences in sprinting performance. Basically, they reveal that muscle-fascicle length and pennation angle have a relationship with speed.

CHAPTER TWO

TECHNIQUES

This chapter will cover the techniques that are fundamental to a number of exercise modes used in a strength and conditioning program. These modes will include strength training, sprinting, agility skills, and core training.

OUTLINE

Strength-training techniques

- Power clean
- Power snatch
- Split jerk
- Squats
- Hip-extension exercises
- Presses
- Rows and pulls

Speed techniques

- Head/trunk
- Arm swing
- Lower-body mechanics

Agility techniques

- Starting
- Stopping
- Shuffling
- Back-pedaling
- Running curves
- Cutting

Core training

Key readings

STRENGTH-TRAINING TECHNIQUES

There is an almost infinite variety of strength-training exercises. This book is going to focus on those that are most important for the athlete and do not require a great deal of specialized equipment. These are the exercises that provide the greatest return on investment for the athlete's time and energy. This chapter will cover the following exercises and their variations:

- power clean;
- power snatch;
- split jerk;
- squats;
- hip-extension exercises;
- presses;
- rows and pulls.

Power clean

The power clean is a total-body exercise that develops strength and explosivity. The power clean has five phases: the start, the first pull, the second pull, receiving the bar, and the finish.

To perform the start of the power clean:

- The barbell will be on the floor. Approach the bar.
- Feet should be hip-width apart.
- Stand up tall, pull the shoulders back and stick the chest out (this is called *setting the back*). Maintain this position throughout the lift.
- Squat down and grip the bar. Feet should be flat.
- Grip the bar with an overhanded (or *pronated*) grip. Hands should be shoulder-width apart.
- Drawing a line from the shoulders to the floor, the shoulders should be in front of the bar. Adjust the height of the hips to allow this to happen (see photo 2.1).

The *first pull* is the period of the lift from the start until the barbell reaches mid-thigh. To perform the first pull:

- Keeping the back set, arms straight, and the shoulders in front of the bar, extend the knees and hips to lift the barbell off the floor.
- Begin the first pull slowly.
- Keep the barbell close to the body as the knees and hips are extending.
- As the barbell passes the knees, pull it close to the body.
- When the barbell reaches mid-thigh (i.e. at the end of the first pull), the shoulders should still be slightly in front of the bar (see photo 2.2).

19

Photo 2.1 Power clean, start.

Photo 2.2 Power clean, first pull.

techniques

The *second pull* is the explosive part of the lift. To perform the second pull:

- Once the barbell has reached mid-thigh, quickly dip with the hips and knees.
- Extend the hips, knees, and ankles powerfully while shrugging the shoulders.
- This extension will move the shoulders from being in front of the bar to being slightly behind the bar.
- The extension will drive the barbell up along the body (see photo 2.3).

Photo 2.3 Power clean, second pull.

As the barbell moves up along the body, drop down into a half- or quarter-squat to meet the barbell. If this is done correctly the barbell will be received on the front of the shoulders. In this position:

- The back is set.
- The barbell is on the front of the shoulders and the upper arms are almost parallel to the floor.
- The hips are pushed back and the knees are flexed.
- The feet are flat on the floor (see photo 2.4).

Photo 2.4 Power clean, receiving the barbell.

From this position, finish the movement by standing up with the barbell on the front of the shoulders. To finish the movement:

- Maintain the back set.
- Keep the elbows high so that the upper arms are almost parallel to the floor.
- Keep the feet flat on the ground.

There are several variations of the power clean that are valuable to athletes. These include hang cleans, split cleans, pulls, and dumbbell cleans.

Hang cleans

Hang cleans are performed from a starting position other than the floor. It may be with the bar beginning at mid-thigh (called hang cleans, mid-thigh), at knee height (hang cleans, knees), or from a position just below the knees (hang cleans, below the knees). These lifts have several uses:

1. they help teach the power clean as they break the movement down into its parts;
2. they are less complicated than the full-power clean while still including the explosive part of the lift, which makes it easier to use these lifts with large numbers of athletes;
3. they require athletes to develop a great deal of back strength in order to control the bar during the beginning of the lift.

To perform hang cleans, mid-thigh:

- Take a power clean grip on the barbell.
- Stand up with the barbell.
- Set the back.
- Push the hips back and unlock the knees. Allow the barbell to slide down the thighs until it is at mid-thigh level. The shoulders should be slightly in front of the barbell (see photo 2.5).
- Perform the second pull, receive the barbell, and finish the lift as described in the power clean description.

To perform the hang clean, knees:

- Take a power clean grip on the barbell.
- Stand up with the barbell.
- Set the back.
- Push the hips back and unlock the knees. Allow the barbell to slide down the thighs until it is at knee level. The shoulders should be slightly in front of the barbell (see photo 2.6).
- Extend the hips and knees so that the barbell is lifted along the thighs until it reaches mid-thigh.
- Perform the explosion, receive the barbell, and finish the lift as previously described.

Photo 2.5
Hang clean,
mid-thigh, start.

Photo 2.6
Hang clean, knees,
start.

To perform the hang clean, below the knees:

- Take a power clean grip on the barbell.
- Stand up with the barbell.
- Set the back.
- Push the hips back and unlock the knees. Allow the barbell to slide down the thighs until it is at a point just below the knees. The shoulders should be slightly in front of the barbell (see photo 2.7).
- Extend the hips and knees so that the barbell is lifted along the thighs until it reaches mid-thigh.
- Perform the explosion, receive the barbell, and finish the lift as previously described.

Photo 2.7
Hang clean, below the knees, start.

Split cleans

Split cleans allow for the exercise to focus more on one side of the body. This is a very useful exercise with soccer players, sprinters, jumpers, throwers, and pitchers, all of whom either use one side of the body at a time or lever off one side of the body to perform their event.

Split cleans may be performed from any of the starting positions described for the power clean or hang cleans. The split clean is exactly like the power clean through the second pull. As the bar moves up the body during the second pull, rather than move into a squat to receive the bar, the feet should be moved forward and back (i.e. they should be split). If this is done properly, the receiving position will look like:

- The barbell will be on the front of the shoulders.
- The upper arms will be almost parallel to the floor.
- The back will be set.
- The front leg will be flexed at the hip and knee. The front foot will be flat on the floor and will be well in front of the hips.
- The rear leg will be extended behind the body, with the knee slightly flexed. The back foot will not be flat on the ground but will be in plantarflexion with the front of the foot in contact with the ground (see photo 2.8).

Photo 2.8
Split clean.

Pulls

Pulls involve performing parts of the power clean, but the barbell is never received on the front of the shoulders. They may be performed from the floor or from any of the hang positions. Pulls are performed just like the power clean except that they are finished at the top of the second pull (i.e. the athlete never moves under the barbell).

Dumbbells

If an exercise can be performed with a barbell, it can also be done with dumbbells. Any of the exercises described above can also be performed with dumbbells. These exercises are easier to teach and have the benefit of making both sides of the body work independently.

Power snatch

The power snatch is another total-body explosive exercise. It requires the barbell to be lifted to a greater height than the power clean, so it requires more power from the athlete. It is a more technically demanding exercise than the power clean. Like the power clean it can be broken down into the following phases: the start, the first pull, the second pull, receiving the barbell, and finishing the lift.

To perform the start of the power snatch:

- The barbell will be on the floor. Approach the bar.
- Feet should be hip-width apart.
- Set the back. Maintain this position throughout the lift.
- Squat down and grip the bar. Feet should be flat.
- Grip the bar with a pronated grip. Hands should be much wider than shoulder-width apart.
- Drawing a line from the shoulders to the floor, the shoulders should be in front of the bar. Adjust the height of the hips to allow this to happen (see photo 2.9).

Photo 2.9
Power snatch, start.

To perform the first pull:

- Keeping the back set, arms straight, and the shoulders in front of the bar, extend the knees and hips to lift the barbell off the floor.
- Begin the first pull slowly.
- Keep the barbell close to the body as the knees and hips are being extended.
- As the barbell passes the knees, it should be pulled close to the body (see photo 2.10).
- When the barbell reaches mid-thigh (i.e. at the end of the first pull), the shoulders should still be slightly in front of the bar. Note that the bar will contact the thigh at a higher position than during the power clean.

Photo 2.10
Power snatch,
first pull.

To perform the second pull:

- Once the barbell has reached mid-thigh, quickly dip with the hips and knees.
- Extend the hips, knees and ankles powerfully while shrugging the shoulders.
- This extension will move the shoulders from being in front of the bar to being slightly behind the bar.
- The extension will drive the barbell up along the body (see photo 2.11).

Photo 2.11
Power snatch,
second pull.

As the barbell moves up along the body, drop down into a half- or quarter-squat to meet the barbell. If this is done correctly the barbell will be received overhead. In this position:

- The back is set.
- The barbell is held on fully extended arms.
- A line drawn from the barbell down should have the bar over the hips.
- The hips are pushed back and the knees are flexed.
- The feet are flat on the floor (see photo 2.12).

From this position, the movement is finished by standing up with the barbell held overhead on straight arms. To finish the movement:

- Maintain the back set.
- Keep the elbows locked.
- Keep the barbell in line with the hips.
- Keep the feet flat on the ground.

There are also several variations of the power snatch. These include hang snatches, split snatches, pulls, and dumbbell snatches.

Photo 2.12
Power snatch,
receiving the
barbell.

Hang snatches

As with hang cleans, hang snatches are performed from a starting position other than the floor.

To perform hang snatches, mid-thigh:

- Take a power snatch grip on the barbell.
- Stand up with the barbell.
- Set the back.
- Push the hips back and unlock the knees. As this is done, allow the barbell to slide down the thighs until it is at mid-thigh level. The shoulders should be slightly in front of the barbell (see photo 2.13).
- Perform the second pull, receive the barbell, and finish the lift as described in the power snatch description.

Photo 2.13
Hang snatch,
mid-thigh, start.

To perform the hang snatch, knees:

- Take a power snatch grip on the barbell.
- Stand up with the barbell.
- Set the back.
- Push the hips back and unlock the knees. Allow the barbell to slide down the thighs until it is at knee level. The shoulders should be slightly in front of the barbell (see photo 2.14).
- Perform the second pull, receive the barbell, and finish the lift as described in the power snatch description.

To perform the hang snatch, below the knees:

- Take a power snatch grip on the barbell.
- Stand up with the barbell.
- Set the back.
- Push the hips back and unlock the knees. Allow the barbell to slide down the thighs until it is at a level below the knees. The shoulders should be slightly in front of the barbell (see photo 2.15).
- Perform the second pull, receive the barbell, and finish the lift as described in the power snatch description.

31

techniques

Photo 2.14
Hang snatch,
knees, start.

Photo 2.15
Hang snatch,
below the knees,
start.

Split snatches

Split snatches may be performed from any of the starting positions described for the power snatch or hang snatches. The split snatch is exactly like the power snatch through the second pull. As the bar moves up the body during the second pull, rather than move into a squat to receive, the feet should be split. If this is done properly, the receiving position will look like:

- The barbell will be held overhead, on locked arms, in line with the hips.
- The back will be set.
- The front leg will be flexed at the hip and knee. The front foot will be flat on the floor and well in front of the hips.
- The rear leg will be extended behind the body with the knee slightly flexed. The back foot will not be flat on the ground but will be in plantarflexion with the front of the foot in contact with the ground (see photo 2.16).

Photo 2.16
Split snatch.

33
techniques

Pulls

Pulls are performed just like the power snatch except they are finished at the top of the second pull (i.e. the athlete never moves under the barbell).

Dumbbells

Any of the exercises described above can also be performed with dumbbells. These exercises are easier to teach and have the benefit of making both sides of the body work independently.

The split jerk

The split jerk is a total-body, explosive exercise. After the initial phases of the lift, it loads each side of the body differently, which is useful for the same type of athletic movements that split snatches and split cleans are useful for. It can be divided into the following phases: the start, the dip, the drive, the split, and the finish.

The split jerk begins with the bar on the front of the shoulders (it begins where the power clean ends):

- The bar is gripped with a pronated, shoulder-width grip.
- The back is set.
- The upper arms are held at a level that is slightly below parallel to the ground.
- The feet are hip-width apart.

The next phase, the dip, needs to be executed very quickly. From the starting position:

- Keep the back set.
- Keep the feet flat on the ground.
- Keep the bar on the shoulders.
- Flex the hips and the knees quickly. The hips should be pushed backwards slightly.
- Aim for a quarter-squat; a squat that is too deep will defeat the purpose of the dip (see photo 2.17).

There should be no pause between the dip and the next phase, the drive. From the dip:

- Keep the back set.
- Extend the hips, knees, and ankles quickly and explosively.
- If this is done properly the lower body drive will force the barbell off the shoulders. Once the bar reaches eye level, the next phase begins (see photo 2.18).

Photo 2.17 Split jerk, dip.

Photo 2.18 Split jerk, drive.

As the barbell reaches eye level, the split should begin:

- One foot should move forward, one foot should move back. This will allow the bar to be received overhead.
- As the feet contact the ground, the arms should be locked out with the barbell overhead.
- If a line is drawn from the barbell down to the ground, it should run through the hips.
- The back should be set.
- The front foot should be flat on the ground, in front of the body, with the front hip and knee flexed.
- The rear foot should be plantarflexed with the ball of the foot on the ground. The rear knee should be slightly flexed (see photo 2.19).

Photo 2.19
Split jerk, the split.

After the split, finish the lift by standing up with the barbell held overhead:

- The front foot should move back half the distance.
- Then the rear foot should move forward.
- As the feet move, the arms need to remain locked and the barbell should remain in line with the hips.
- Keep the back set.

There are two variations of the split jerk. These are push jerks and dumbbell jerks.

Push jerks

Push jerks are less complicated than split jerks. They are also a total-body, explosive exercise, so they are a great tool for most strength and conditioning programs. This exercise is also used as a teaching progression for the split jerk. The push jerk begins exactly like the split jerk and includes a dip and a drive. Think of it as a military press that uses the legs. After the dip and drive, there are differences between this lift and the split jerk:

- Once the barbell reaches eye level, let the heels come back to the ground (i.e. the feet should be flat).
- As the barbell reaches eye level, it should be pressed until the arms are locked out.
- The barbell should end up in line with the hips.
- The back should be set.

Dumbbell jerks

Split jerks and push jerks can be performed with dumbbells. This has the benefit of making the athlete coordinate between both arms and adds a level of complexity to the exercises.

It is frequently recommended that the Olympic lifts (variations of the snatch, clean, and jerk) be included in the strength-training programs of athletes. There are several reasons for this: first, even with heavy loads, they are performed very quickly. To be successful the Olympic lifts have to be performed in around a second. Second, they involve large power outputs. According to Garhammer (1981), world champion weightlifters are generating between 31 and 37 watts of power per kilogram of bodyweight when performing the snatch, clean, and jerk. This is superior to other strength-training exercises. For example, it is estimated that performing the squat and deadlift requires the athlete to generate around 12 watts of power per kilogram of bodyweight (Garhammer, 1993). Third, the Olympic lifts and their variations are similar to athletic movements, particularly jumping (Garhammer and Gregor, 1992).

Applying the research on power generation and movement similarities presents some challenges. First, these studies have challenges in terms of the subjects. The study that established the power-generating capability of the Olympic lifts was examining the winners of the various weight classes in the 1978 world championships. In other words, these data are based upon elite athletes who may be put together differently than athletes in other sports. The Garhammer and Gregor (1992), study which sought to establish a link between the snatch and the vertical jump, only studied 11 athletes, which makes generating broad conclusions impossible.

A second challenge is that the conclusions of the studies are not always supported adequately by the study results. For example, Garhammer and Gregor (1992) compared the force-velocity profiles of four athletes performing the snatch lift and nine athletes performing the vertical jump. Two athletes performed both activities. The study provides three sample force-velocity curves of both a snatch lift and a vertical jump. In each curve, there is an unweighting phase. In the snatch lift, it is in the transition from the first pull to the second. In the vertical jump, it is in the quarter-squat. However, there is not enough information provided to draw any conclusions from this information in the paper. While there is an unweighting phase, the magnitudes, rates of force development, and moment in time when everything occurs appears to be different between the snatch and the vertical jump. In addition, attempts to standardize force measurements between the snatch and the vertical jump revealed differences. To compensate for the added mass that must be overcome with the snatch lift, the researchers compared the *thrust force* during the snatch and the vertical jump. This is the difference between the system weight (athlete in the jump, or athlete and barbell in the snatch) and the force generated. In the athletes that performed both activities, the thrust force was between 7 and 10 percent greater for the snatch lift. Based upon this information, the authors made the conclusion that based upon the '... qualitative and quantitative similarities between the lifting movements and the vertical jump ... it is reasonable to recommend the utilization of one or more of the classical weightlifting movements ... in the strength and power development programs of other athletes who need to improve jumping skills' (Garhammer and Gregor, 1992: 133). This conclusion really is not supported by the results of the study.

Are the Olympic lifts effective in the conditioning of athletes? Absolutely. However, care needs to be taken with the application of research results on limited populations with vague data to a larger pool of athletes.

Squats

Squats are one of the fundamental exercises for a strength and conditioning program. They develop the muscles of the trunk and lower body; they develop mobility about the hip, knee, and ankle; they increase the strength of the bones in the trunk and lower body; and they do all this in a way that has a great deal of transfer to athletics.

Variations of the squat that are relevant to the strength and conditioning coach include:

- back squats;
- front squats;
- split squats;
- pause squats;
- eccentric squats.

Back squats

The back squat is performed with the bar on the back of the shoulders. It has several phases; the start, the descent, and the ascent.

During the start of the lift:

- The bar is comfortably on the back of the shoulders.
- Grip the bar where it is comfortable. Use a pronated grip.
- The feet are between hip-width apart and shoulder-width apart, as is comfortable or sport-specific.
- Set the back.
- Look straight ahead or slightly up (see photo 2.20).

Photo 2.20 Back squat, start.

To perform the descent:

- Keep the back set.
- Keep the feet flat on the ground with the weight on the heels.
- Unlock the knees and push the hips back.
- Ideally, descend until the thighs are parallel to the floor unless there is a sport-specific or injury reason not to (see photo 2.21).

Photo 2.21
Back squat, descent.

To perform the ascent:

- Keep the back set.
- Keep the feet flat on the ground with the weight on the heels.
- Extend the hip and knees until standing back up.
- Make sure that the shoulders and hips travel at the same speed. If the hips travel up faster than the shoulders, this could be dangerous for the lower back and will make the barbell more difficult to control.

There are two extremes with regards to placement of the barbell during the back squat. It can sit at the base of the neck (called a high-bar squat) or it can sit on the rear deltoids (called a low-bar squat). Each style has advantages.

Wretenberg *et al.* (1996) analyzed high-bar versus low-bar squats for a number of national-caliber powerlifters and Olympic-style weightlifters. They found that the high-bar squatters remained more upright during the squat and had the moments of force more evenly distributed about the hip and knee. High-bar squatters had a greater moment of force at the knee than low-bar squatters, suggesting that this style is important for activities that require an upright trunk or a great deal of knee flexor/extensor recruitment. Low-bar squatters, by contrast, are less upright during the squat and have a greater moment at the hip joint. This means a great deal more lower-back and hip involvement in the squat than during a high-bar squat.

In theory, the low-bar squat allows for the bar to be moved a shorter distance and allows for the larger muscles of the hip to be involved in the lift, all of which combines to allow for more weight to be lifted than in high-bar squats. High-bar squats, on the other hand, have a more upright trunk and (in theory) allow for more development of the knee extensors and flexors, which is why they are favored by Olympic-style weightlifters and many bodybuilders.

Front squats

Front squats are squats that are performed with the barbell on the front of the shoulders. This exercise forces the trunk to be more upright than in back squats and is extremely sport-specific for the sport of weightlifting. Like the back squat, the front squat is organized into a start, the descent, and the ascent.

The start begins with the barbell on the front of the shoulders, just as if the athlete had finished a power clean:

- The barbell is on the front of the shoulders.
- Hands should grip the bar with a shoulder-width pronated grip.
- The upper arms should be parallel to the floor.
- The back is set.
- The feet are hip-width apart and flat on the floor (see photo 2.22).

During the descent:

- Keep the upper arms parallel to the floor or the barbell will fall forward.
- Set the back.
- Keep the feet flat with the weight on the heels.
- Unlock the knees as the hips flex.
- Ideally, the descent should be performed until the thighs are parallel to the floor, unless there is a sport-specific reason for a different depth (see photo 2.23).

41

techniques

Photo 2.22
Front squat, start.

Photo 2.23
Front squat, descent.

During the ascent:

- The upper arms must remain parallel to the floor or the barbell will fall forward.
- The back is set.
- The feet are flat and the weight is on the heels.
- Extend the hip and knees until standing back up.
- Make sure that the shoulders and hips travel at the same speed.

Front squats are a challenging exercise because they require more technique and more upper-body flexibility than back squats. For the bar to be controllable, the elbows must remain high and the trunk must remain upright. This position of the elbows is difficult for beginning athletes. If the elbows drop, then the weight of the barbell sits on the wrists, which results in wrist pain. If the elbows drop, the barbell begins to move forward making it more difficult to control. With this in mind, there are several strategies to address this:

- Narrow the grip: Frequently beginners take a grip-width that is too wide to allow them to get their elbows high on this lift. Narrowing the grip to shoulder-width or even narrower will help this problem.
- Open the hands: Opening the hands will help with getting the elbows higher. If the elbows remain high, and the trunk remains upright, the barbell will not move during the lift.
- Use a specific movement pattern to "rack" the barbell on the front of the shoulders: To rack the barbell on the front of the shoulders, grip the barbell and step underneath it. As this is done, the elbows should first be moved towards the midline of the body and then elevated. This, combined with the other two strategies mentioned above, will put the barbell in the correct position with the elbows high enough.

Split squats

Split squats focus on one side of the body more than the other. This is beneficial to athletic events that use running, throwing, kicking, or jumping. The split squat also aids with the development of balance.

When performing split squats, the barbell may be on the back of the shoulders or on the front:

- Set the back.
- Initially, the feet should be hip-width apart.
- Move one foot comfortably forward. The front foot should be flat on the ground.
- Move the other foot back about twice the length that the first foot moved forward. The back foot should be plantarflexed with the ball of the back foot on the ground (see photo 2.24).

- With the back set, flex the front hip and knee until the back knee is just off the ground (see photo 2.25).
- Do not touch the back knee to the ground.
- Extend the front hip and knee until resuming the starting position.
- After the desired number of repetitions, switch legs.

Photo 2.24
Split squat, start.

Photo 2.25
Split squat, descent.

Pause squats

Pause squats can be done with the bar on the back of the shoulders, front of the shoulders, or split style. Pause squats are more difficult than traditional squats and help to increase the strength of the lower body while developing explosivity.

Pause squats are performed just like any other version of the squat with two important differences. First, at the bottom of the descent, pause for a full count (i.e. "one one-thousand") before ascending. This makes the exercise much more difficult to perform. Second, after the count, focus on exploding out of the bottom position (i.e. come up as fast as possible). Most athletes should begin this exercise with around 60 percent of what they would have performed on the normal variation. With practice, athletes can comfortably work up to 85 percent of normal squats.

Pause squats are not meant to be a high-volume exercise. They are extremely fatiguing and are not forgiving of technique errors. As a result, performing these with sets of more than three or four repetitions is not recommended.

Eccentric squats

Eccentric squats can be done with the bar on the back of the shoulders, front of the shoulders, or split style. As the name implies, these types of squats develop eccentric strength and explosivity.

This squat is performed exactly like a normal squat with two differences. First, take ten slow seconds to descend into the bottom position. This is extremely challenging and athletes have to focus on maintaining good technique. Second, once the bottom position has been reached, immediately reverse directions and explode during the ascent.

Eccentric squats are not meant to be a high-volume exercise either.

In 1961, a study was published that said that the deep-squat exercise was bad for the ligaments of the knee. In this study, the deep-squat exercise was defined as being where the athlete squats all the way down until the hamstrings touch the calves. The researcher compared the knees of weightlifters (performing the deep squat as part of training) with a group that had never done the deep-squat exercise. He determined that almost 50 percent of the squatters had medial collateral ligament (MCL) instability, almost 70 percent of the squatters had lateral collateral ligament (LCL) instability, and almost 50 percent of the squatters had anterior cruciate ligament (ACL) instability. By comparison, an insignificant number of the non-squatters had MCL and LCL instability and approximately 40 percent had ACL instability. His conclusion was that the deep-squat exercise caused the instability in the squatting group. He had two recommendations as a result of his findings: first, the deep-squat exercise should be avoided; second, squats should only be done until the thighs are parallel to the floor (he called this a half-squat) (Klein, 1961).

45

techniques

This study formed the foundation of a lot of misconceptions regarding the squat exercise. Since the study was published, there have been a number of attempts to confirm the results, with no success (Chandler et al., 1989; Chang et al., 1988; Meyers, 1971).

Broadly speaking, the squat impacts the knees in one of three ways:

1. tibiofemoral compression;
2. cruciate ligament tension;
3. patellofemoral compression.

Tibiofemoral compression

Tibiofemoral (TF) compression refers to the compression of the femur on the tibia. To a point, this is important because it keeps the tibia from moving forwards or backwards relative to the femur (i.e. it protects the ACL and PCL). Too much, however, could be bad as it could damage the meniscus in the knee or the cartilage. According to Escamilla et al. (2001), TF compression increases as one descends in the squat and decreases during the ascent. It is also slightly higher for wide-stance (i.e. feet wider than shoulder-width) squats. This means that, theoretically, too much weight combined with a squat that is too deep/too wide could damage the meniscus and cartilage in the knee. In practical terms it means that if you have an injury to either area you need to avoid really deep/wide squats.

Cruciate ligament tension

The cruciate ligaments are important because they keep the tibia from moving forwards or backwards too far, relative to the femur. The squat does not appear to stress the ACL regardless of stance or depth (Escamilla et al., 2001). There are a number of reasons for this. First, the hamstrings take up a lot of the tension that would exist. The hamstrings are pretty much active throughout the entire squat exercise. Second, the gastrocnemius helps to take up some of the tension that the ACL might experience. Third, the fact that the squat is weight-bearing causes TF compression, which helps to reduce the tension that the ACL might otherwise experience.

The PCL is a different story entirely. The tension on the PCL increases during the descent of the squat and decreases during the ascent. This means that people with PCL injuries need to avoid squats deeper than 50–60 degrees at the knees (Escamilla et al., 2001).

Patellofemoral compression

Patellofemoral (PF) compression refers to the patella acting on the femur. Clearly, PF compression increases during the descent of the squat, the compression is greatest at around 50–80 degrees of knee flexion (i.e. above parallel). It decreases during the ascent (Escamilla *et al.*, 2001). This means that people with PF injuries should avoid squatting deeper than 50 degrees.

The squat exercise does not appear to be bad for the knees but, like any exercise, it could interact with certain injuries to exacerbate them.

Hip-extension exercises

These exercises are important because they develop the lower back, glutes, and hamstrings. This chain of muscles is necessary for sprinting, jumping, and agility. The main hip extension exercises are:

- deadlifts;
- Romanian deadlifts;
- good mornings;
- back raises;
- reverse hyperextensions.

Deadlifts

Deadlifts involve lifting the barbell off the floor. They are an excellent way to develop lower-body, hip, and lower-back strength. Deadlifts are done with a clean-width grip (i.e. shoulder-width apart and pronated), a snatch-width grip, a mixed grip (one hand is pronated, one hand is suppinated), with the feet hip-width apart, or with the feet greater than shoulder-width apart. The description below will focus on the feet being hip-width apart and this will be followed by thoughts on the greater-than-shoulder-width variation.

The deadlift begins with the barbell on the floor:

- Approach the barbell.
- Feet should be hip-width apart.
- Feet should be flat on the ground.
- Set the back. Maintain this position throughout the lift.
- Squat down and grip the barbell using one of the grip styles described above.
- The arms should be straight. They should remain locked out throughout the lift.
- A line drawn from the shoulders to the floor should have the shoulders in front of the barbell.

- Keeping the back set and the arms straight, extend the hips and knees to lift the barbell off the floor.
- The hips and shoulders should rise up at the same speed.
- As the barbell passes the knees, bring it in close to the body.
- When the barbell reaches mid-thigh, extend the hips to straighten the body out (see photo 2.26).
- Replace the barbell on the floor and repeat.

When the feet are wider than shoulder-width apart, this is called a sumo deadlift. The sumo deadlift is often preferred in the sport of powerlifting because the barbell travels a shorter distance during the lift. While the feet are wider, the lift is performed similar to how it has been described above. The wider stance means that the trunk will be more upright during the lift.

Photo 2.26
Deadlift.

Romanian deadlifts

Romanian deadlifts (or RDLs) focus on hip extension and train the hamstrings, glutes, and lower back. This exercise begins by standing up with the barbell in the hands:

- A clean-width grip should be taken on the bar.
- Keep the arms straight throughout the lift.
- Set the back.
- Keep the feet flat throughout the lift (see photo 2.27).
- Unlock the knees; they should be soft throughout the lift.
- Keeping the back set, push the hips back.
- As this is done, allow the barbell to slide along the thighs.
- Lower the barbell as far as flexibility allows, keeping the back set and the knees soft (see photo 2.28).
- Reverse directions until standing up straight again.
- Repeat.

Photo 2.27
Romanian
deadlift, start.

Photo 2.28
Romanian
deadlift, descent.

Good mornings

This is another exercise that focuses on the hamstrings, glutes, and lower back. It is similar to the RDL only the barbell is on the back of the shoulders:

- Stand with the barbell on the back of the shoulders.
- Feet should be hip-width apart and flat on the ground.
- Set the back.
- Knees should be soft.
- Keeping the back set, push the hips back.
- Lower the barbell as far as flexibility allows, keeping the back set and the knees soft (see photo 2.29).
- Reverse directions until standing up straight again.
- Repeat.

Note that good mornings can also be performed from a seated position. To do this variation, sit on a bench with the barbell on the back of the shoulders. Set the back. Keeping the back set, lean forward from the hips as far as flexibility allows. Reverse directions and repeat.

Photo 2.29
Good morning,
descent.

Back raises

This is another hamstring, glute, and lower-back exercise. These involve a special bench. In this bench, the athlete lays prone on the bench so that pads are located just inferior to the athlete's hips and support the ankles. The athlete's legs are straight and the upper body is hanging in space. To perform this exercise:

■ Set the back.
■ Put the hands where they are comfortable.
■ Lean forward from the hips as far as flexibility allows (see photo 2.30).
■ Keeping the back set, reverse directions until the upper body is parallel to the floor.
■ Lower and repeat.

This exercise can be made more difficult by holding weights (either across the chest or behind the neck/head), It can also be done with only one ankle supported by the pads (i.e. turning this into a one-legged exercise).

Photo 2.30 Back raise, descent.

Reverse hyperextensions

This exercise also develops the glutes, hamstrings, and lower back. To perform this exercise, use the same bench as the back raises. The difference is that the upper body is supported by the bench and the legs hang in space:

- Support the upper body on the bench.
- Keep the legs straight.
- Allow the hips to flex so that a 90-degree angle exists at the hip joint.
- From this position, keeping the legs straight, bring them up until they are parallel to the floor (see photo 2.31).
- Lower and repeat.

This exercise can be made more challenging by having the athlete hold dumbbells in between their feet to add resistance.

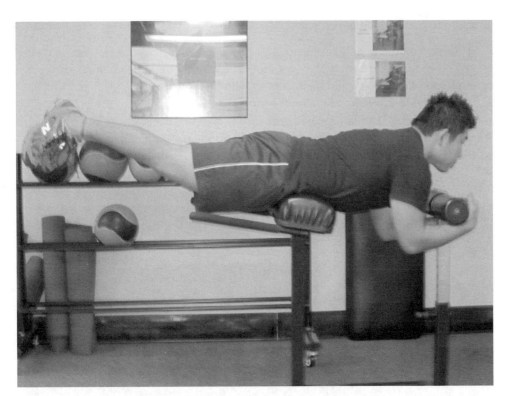

Photo 2.31 Reverse hyperextension, ascent.

Presses

Presses are fundamental exercises for developing the muscles of the upper body. This section will focus on the following presses and their variations:

- bench press;
- incline press;
- decline press;
- military press.

Bench press

The bench press develops the muscles of the chest, shoulders, and triceps. The bench press has several phases: set-up, descent, and ascent.

To set up to perform the bench press:

- Lie down on the bench, facing up.
- When lying on the bench, the eyes should be directly underneath the barbell.
- Shoulders and hips should be in contact with the bench.
- Ideally, the feet should be flat on the ground.
- Grip the barbell with a pronated grip.
- Grip width should be comfortably wider than shoulder-width apart.
- Lift the barbell off the rack and position it directly over the chest on extended arms

Photo 2.32 Bench press, start.

To perform the descent:

- Lower the barbell under control until it touches the lower half of the chest.
- As the barbell is lowered, keep the hips and shoulders in contact with the bench.
- Touch the barbell to the chest. Avoid bouncing the barbell as this can be bad for the ribs and sternum (see photo 2.33).

techniques

Photo 2.33 Bench press, descent.

To perform the ascent:

- Keeping the hips and shoulders in contact with the bench, press the barbell up until the arms are extended.
- Depending on an athlete's build, some athletes push the barbell in a straight line so that it ends up directly over the chest; some push it up at an angle so that it ends up in line with the eyes. Athletes are encouraged to experiment with both styles and to discover which works best for them.

Incline press

The incline press develops the muscles of the chest, shoulders, and triceps. It develops the part of the pectoralis major that attaches to the sternal-clavicular region of the chest. This variation is more difficult for most athletes as it is more of a shoulder exercise than the bench press, which means that, typically, less weight can be used.

To set up to perform the incline press:

- Lie down on the bench, facing up.
- Shoulders and hips should be in contact with the bench.
- Ideally, the feet should be flat on the ground.
- Grip the barbell with a pronated grip.
- Grip width should be comfortably wider than shoulder-width apart.
- Lift the barbell off the rack and position it directly over the chest on extended arms (see photo 2.34).

Photo 2.34 Incline press, start.

To perform the descent:

- Lower the barbell under control until it touches the chest.
- The barbell should touch the chest just below the clavicles.
- As the barbell is lowered, keep the hips and shoulders in contact with the bench.
- Touch the barbell to the chest. Avoid bouncing the barbell (see photo 2.35).

Photo 2.35 Incline press, descent.

To perform the ascent:

- Keeping the hips and shoulders in contact with the bench, press the barbell up until the arms are extended.

Decline press

This involves performing the press with the feet higher than the head. It can be easier for some athletes as the barbell does not travel as great a distance during the decline press as during the bench and incline presses.

To set up to perform the decline press:

- Lie down on the bench, facing up.
- Shoulders and hips should be in contact with the bench.
- Grip the barbell with a pronated grip.
- Grip width should be comfortably wider than shoulder-width apart.
- Lift the barbell off the rack and position it directly over the chest on extended arms (see photo 2.36).

Photo 2.36 Decline press, start.

To perform the descent:

- Lower the barbell under control until it touches the lower half of the chest.
- As the barbell is lowered, keep the hips and shoulders in contact with the bench.
- Touch the barbell to the chest. Avoid bouncing the barbell (see photo 2.37).

58

Photo 2.37 Decline press, descent.

To perform the ascent:

- Keeping the hips and shoulders in contact with the bench, press the barbell up until the arms are extended.

The bench press, incline press, and decline press also have several variations. First, they can be performed with dumbbells instead of the barbell. This requires the athlete to use each side of the body independently. Second, they can be performed with a pause. As with pause squats, this involves pausing with the barbell on the chest followed by an explosive ascent. Third, they can be performed eccentrically. As with eccentric squats, this means taking ten slow "seconds" to descend and ending the lift with an explosive ascent (note that this does not mean bouncing the barbell off the chest).

Military press

The military press develops the muscles of the shoulders and triceps. It is also a teaching progression for the split jerk as it teaches how to lift the barbell overhead. To perform the military press:

- Stand up with the barbell on the front of the shoulders.
- Take a clean-width, prontated grip on the bar.
- The upper arms should be at an approximately 45–degree angle with the floor.
- Feet should be hip-width apart.
- Set the back.
- From this position, push the barbell up and slightly behind the head.
- When the arms are fully extended, the barbell should be in line with the hips (see photo 2.38).
- Lower the barbell under control and repeat.

The military press can be performed from a seated position or with dumbbells.

Photo 2.38
Military press.

Rows and pulls

Presses develop the chest, shoulder, and triceps muscles. Rows and pulls develop the muscles of the upper back, shoulders, and biceps. Several variations of rows and pulls are important for a strength and conditioning program:

- bent-over rows;
- one-arm dumbbell rows;
- pull-ups;
- pull-downs.

Bent-over rows

To perform bent-over rows, stand up with the barbell:

- Grip the bar with a pronated grip. Hands should be shoulder-width apart.
- Feet should be hip-width apart and flat on the floor.
- Set the back.
- Keeping the back set, push the hips back so that the upper body leans forward.
- Allow the knees to flex slightly.
- Allow the bar to hang down below the upper body with the arms extended.
- The bar should be in line with the stomach.
- Keeping the back set and maintaining the trunk position, pull the bar up towards the stomach (see photo 2.39).
- As the bar is pulled up, focus on bringing the scapulae together.
- Lower and repeat.

Bent-over rows can also be performed with a dumbbell in each hand.

Photo 2.38
Bent-over row.

One-arm dumbbell rows

To perform one-arm dumbbell rows, you need a bench and a dumbbell:

- Support the right shin on the bench.
- Lean forward and place the right hand flat on the bench. The right arm should be extended.
- Reach down with the left hand and grip the dumbbell with a neutral grip.
- Set the back.
- The left arm should be extended.
- If a line is drawn from the body down to the floor, the dumbbell should line up with the left shoulder.
- Keeping the left arm close to the body, pull the dumbbell up towards the stomach (i.e. at an angle) (see photo 2.40).
- Lower and repeat. Switch sides after the desired number of repetitions have been performed.

Photo 2.40 One-arm dumbbell row.

Pull-ups

Pull-ups are a great exercise to develop the biceps, upper-back muscles, and muscles of the shoulder. They may be performed with a wide grip or with a close grip. To perform them with a wide grip:

- Grip the pull-up bar with a pronated grip.
- Hand width should be wider than the shoulders.
- Lower the body until the arms are fully extended. The feet should not be in contact with the ground.
- Flexing the elbows, pull the body up until the chin is higher than the pull-up bar (see photo 2.41). As this is done, concentrate on drawing the shoulder blades together.
- Lower and repeat.

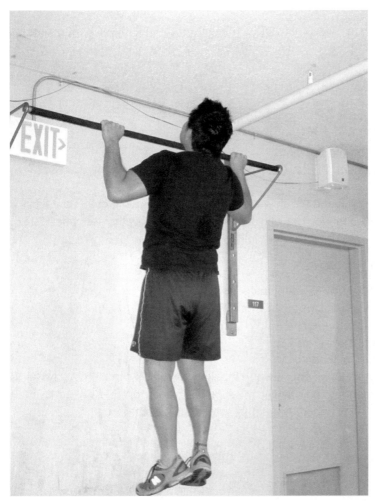

Photo 2.41
Pull-up.

The wide-grip pull-up is often more challenging for athletes. The close-grip pull-up (also known as a chin-up) provides the benefits of performing pull-ups but is easier to master. To perform it with a close grip:

- Grip the pull-up bar with a suppinated grip.
- Hand width should be narrower than the shoulders.
- Lower the body until the arms are fully extended. The feet should not be in contact with the ground.
- Flexing the elbows, pull the body up until the chin is higher than the pull-up bar. As this is done, concentrate on drawing the shoulder blades together.
- Lower and repeat.

Pull-downs

Pull-downs provide a way to get many of the benefits of the pull-up without possessing the skill that pull-ups require. Like pull-ups they may be performed with a wide grip or a close grip.

To perform wide-grip pull-downs:

- Grip the pull-down bar with a pronated grip.
- Grip width should be wider than shoulder width.
- Sit down with the bar in the hands.
- Secure the knees under the pad, this prevents movement during the exercise.
- Arms should be fully extended.
- Flexing the elbows, pull the bar down to a height just below the chin. As the bar is pulled down, concentrate on drawing the shoulder blades together (see photo 2.42).
- Allow the arms to relax until they are fully extended. Repeat.

To perform close-grip pull-downs:

- Grip the pull-down bar with a suppinated grip.
- Grip width should be narrower than shoulder width.
- Sit down with the bar in the hands.
- Secure the knees under the pad.
- Arms should be fully extended.
- Flexing the elbows, pull the bar down to a height just below the chin. As the bar is pulled down, concentrate on drawing the shoulder blades together.
- Allow the arms to relax until they are fully extended. Repeat.

Photo 2.42
Pull-down.

SPEED TECHNIQUES

Proper technique is important for running quickly. It minimizes the wasting of energy, prevents injuries, and helps to take advantage of the body's design to allow the athlete to be faster. The technique for sprinting at maximum velocity can be broken down into the following areas:

- head/trunk;
- arm swing;
- lower-body mechanics.

Head/trunk

When sprinting, the head should be in a neutral position with the eyes either fixed straight ahead or fixed at a point on the ground in the distance. The trunk should remain tall with the abdomen tight and the shoulders back. Failing to maintain this position results in slumping forward, which limits the ability to extend the hip during the sprint.

Arm swing

The arms swing in opposition to the legs. This helps to maintain balance while running. The elbows should be flexed to a comfortable angle (generally around 60 degrees), with the hands closed. The arms should swing from the shoulders. During the arm-swing motion, the focus should be on driving the arm backwards. If the arms are driven backwards with enough force, the stretch reflex at the shoulder and chest will kick in and the arm will automatically be brought forward. Utilizing the stretch reflex means that there are fewer things to think about while sprinting.

The arms should be kept against the sides and should move forwards and backwards. Avoid allowing the arms to cross the midline of the body as this causes the upper body to rotate while running.

Lower-body mechanics

During sprinting, the hips are moving forward. When the hips move over the right foot, the right ankle plantarflexes. After the hips pass over the right foot, the foot should break contact with the ground. The ankle is immediately dorsiflexed as the foot breaks contact with the ground. The knee and hip are then flexed as the right foot is brought up towards the hip. Ideally, the heel should touch the hip with the hip flexed at approximately 45 degrees. From this position, the knee is swung up. As this is done, the leg will unfold. As the leg unfolds, it should be driven down using the hip so that the outside of the fore-foot contacts the ground at a position just in front of the center of gravity. The body is then pulled forward.

The technique just described is not achieved until the athlete has had 10 to 15 meters to accelerate. Track and field events excepted, there are few sports where an athlete has ten to 15 meters to accelerate. While this is understood, the technique described is still the goal that the athlete is attempting to attain during any sprinting motion regardless of the distance.

66
techniques

AGILITY TECHNIQUES

There are several fundamental skills that are common to most athletic events:

- starting;
- stopping;
- shuffling;
- back-pedaling;
- running curves;
- cutting.

Starting

Possessing a fast explosive start gives an athlete the ability to arrive sooner than someone who starts slowly. Starting technique will be described from the classic ready position, but it can be modified to apply to all starting positions. In this example, the left leg will be the preferred leg to start with. If an athlete prefers to start with the right leg, modify the instructions accordingly:

- Feet are hip-width apart.
- Weight is on the balls of the feet.
- Back is tight.
- Head is neutral.
- Hips and knees are slightly flexed.
- Arms are at the sides with the elbows flexed to approximately 60 degrees and the hands open.
- Dorsiflexing the ankle, step forward by driving the left knee forward. As this is done drive the left arm backwards forcefully.
- Drive the right knee forward and the right arm backwards forcefully.
- Focus on staying low to the ground until stride length and stride frequency have increased to the point when running upright using the techniques described above is possible.

Stopping

Being able to stop suddenly is an important skill. When attempting to stop from a sprint, focus on three things:

- Keep the weight on the balls of the feet. This is important for maintaining balance.
- Drop the center of gravity. This is done by pushing the hips back. This allows one to brake while maintaining balance.
- Chop the steps. Begin taking very short steps while dropping the center of gravity.

Shuffling

Shuffling allows for movement in a lateral direction. To perform shuffling:

- Feet are hip-width apart.
- Weight is on the balls of the feet.
- The back is tight.
- The head is neutral.
- Hips and knees are flexed.
- Arms are at the sides with the elbows flexed to approximately 60 degrees and the hands open.
- To shuffle in the right direction, push with the left foot while stepping with the right foot.
- As the right foot steps out, bring the left foot back in so that the feet remain hip-width apart.

Back-pedaling

Back-pedaling allows for the athlete to run in a backwards direction:

- Feet are hip-width apart.
- Weight is on the balls of the feet.
- The back is tight.
- The head is neutral.
- Hips and knees are flexed.
- Arms are at the sides with the elbows flexed to approximately 60 degrees and the hands open.
- Keeping the weight on the balls of the feet and the hips flexed, pick up the feet and step backwards. Remember that the arms should act in opposition to the legs.

Running curves

There are instances where athletes must make sudden, tight runs. This is done by:

- lowering the center of gravity as the turn is entered;
- dropping the inside shoulder and (if possible) pointing the inside arm down; this allows for turning around the inside arm, helping to keep the turn tight and helping to maintain balance.

Cutting

Cutting involves making a sharp, sudden change of direction. If, for example, an athlete is sprinting and is going to make a cut in the right direction (for a cut in the left direction change the leg being described below):

- Flex the left hip and knee to lower the center of gravity.
- Push off the left leg, stepping into the new direction with the right.
- As the right foot makes contact with the ground, drive the left knee forward and start explosively in the new direction.

CORE TRAINING

Core training has exploded in popularity over the last ten years. Theoretically, it is emphasized because it improves athletic performance, prevents injuries to the lower back, and treats injuries to the lower back. Research, however, does not support these benefits of core training.

At least with how it has been studied, core training does not really impact athletic performance. It does not affect running mechanics, it does not affect rowing performance, and it has a minimal impact on the performance of strength and power tests (Nesser et al., 2008; Sato and Mokha, 2009; Stanton et al., 2004; Tse et al., 2004).

In terms of preventing injuries, this is challenging to prove because the medical literature divides lower-back injuries into two types: specific and non-specific (van Middelkoop et al., 2010). Specific low back pain is caused by a discernable event (for example, herniating a disc while deadlifting) and can be seen on imaging. This type of LBP impacts on about 10 percent of people with LBP, so while it exists, it is not all that prevalent. The other type, non-specific low back pain (NSLBP) impacts 90 percent of the people with LBP. This is not tied to an incident and cannot be found on MRIs or other images (van Middelkoop et al., 2010).

When we say that core training prevents injuries, what type of injury are we trying to prevent? This is an important question because researchers do not have a consensus on what causes NSLBP (Bakker et al., 2009; Balague et al., 2010; Heuch et al., 2010; Shirazi-Adl, 1989). Researchers think that an "event" related to loading causes SLBP but some feel that there is a gradual and insidious period of deterioration leading up to that event, while others do not agree (McGill, 2010; Shirazi-Adl, 1989; van Middelkoop et al., 2010).

The thinking in medical research seems to be that muscular fitness may help to prevent NSLBP but has little impact on SLBP. This is logical, but the research attempting to demonstrate this is very weak.

69

techniques

Core training is used to treat individuals with LBP, both SLBP and NSLBP. Research examining the effectiveness has mixed results. Some find a positive impact in terms of level of pain, function, and quality of life (Goldby *et al.*, 2006; Hides *et al.*, 2001; Kell and Asmundson, 2009; Kumar *et al.*, 2009). Others find that *all* treatments for LBP are as effective as no treatment. Some researchers question the clinical significance and applicability of the research findings and note that they are scarcely more effective than placebo (Deyo, 2004; Keller *et al.*, 2007).

One researcher, in an editorial, said that LBP is the price of walking upright and there isn't a lot that we can do about it (Weiner, 2007).

There is a need for more research on the injury prevention and treatment benefits of core training. It is possible that core training may prevent certain lower-back injuries (i.e. NSLBP) and not others. It is also possible that different types of core training have a different impact on treatment or on prevention.

KEY READINGS

Garhammer, J. and Gregor, R. (1992) Propulsion forces as a function of intensity for weightlifting and vertical jumping, *Journal of Applied Sport Science Research*, 6(3): 129–34.

Garhammer and Gregor (1992) is a ground-breaking paper that helped to establish using the Olympic lifts and their variations for the strength and conditioning of athletes. It also has flaws and limitations that need to be taken into account by the practitioner.

Klein, K.K. (1961) The deep squat exercise as utilized in weight training for athletics and its effect on the ligaments of the knee, *Journal of the Association of Physical and Mental Rehabilitation*, 15(1): 6–11, 23.

An extremely important article for the strength and conditioning professional to read, this article is why many feel that the back squat is dangerous for the knees. It is also one of the most misinterpreted articles in strength and conditioning, so it is important to read it to discover what it says and what the author actually recommends.

Cissik, J.M. (2011) The role of core training in performance improvement, injury prevention, and injury treatment, *Strength and Conditioning Journal*, 33(1), 10–15.

A review of the literature on the effectiveness of core training, the article concludes that there is no evidence that core training improves overall athletic performance and has conflicting results with regards to preventing and treating lower-back injuries. It indicates that there is a strong need for better definitions and more stringent research in this area.

CHAPTER THREE

ASSESSMENTS

Assessing the athlete is important because it provides the coach with objective feedback about what the athlete needs to work on, what the athlete's strengths are, whether the athlete is achieving their goals for training, and it provides feedback about the effectiveness of the strength and conditioning program.

The following are qualities that are typically assessed:

- strength;
- power;
- speed;
- agility;
- conditioning.

OUTLINE

Strength

- Bench press
- Back squat
- Power clean
- Power snatch

Power

- Counter-movement jump
- Standing long jump
- Standing triple jump
- Medicine ball, behind
- Medicine ball, front

Speed

- Acceleration
- Maximal velocity

Agility

- The L run
- The 505 test
- The T test
- The pro-agility test

Conditioning

- Suicides
- 300-meter shuttle run

Examples

- Baseball
- Basketball
- Football (American)
- Rugby
- Soccer

How to use this information

Key readings

STRENGTH

The most common tests of strength include the bench press, the back squat, the power clean, and the power snatch. Typically, these tests are performed as *one repetition-maximum* tests (1-RM); in other words, the amount of weight the athlete can lift one time. With some populations, a 1-RM test may not be advisable due to the nature of the sport or the population to be tested. In those circumstances, 3-RM, 5-RM, and even 10-RM tests may be used instead. The strength tests will be described for the 1-RM test; the procedures will need to be modified if more repetitions are being tested.

To prepare for a 1-RM test, the athlete needs to strike a balance between being warmed up enough to prevent injury and doing so much work that it interferes with the results of the testing. To warm-up for a 1-RM test:

1   perform a general warm-up;
2   perform ten repetitions with the barbell;
3   perform ten repetitions with the estimated 50 percent of 1-RM;
4   perform six repetitions with the estimated 75 percent of 1-RM;
5   perform three repetitions with the estimated 85 percent of 1-RM;
6   perform one repetition with the estimated 95 percent of 1-RM;
7   continue increasing the weight gradually after each successful lift until failure.

For the power clean and the power snatch, modify the steps as follows:

1 perform a general warm-up;
2 perform five repetitions with the barbell;
3 perform five repetitions with the estimated 50 percent of 1-RM;
4 perform three repetitions with the estimated 75 percent of 1-RM;
5 perform one repetition with the estimated 85 percent of 1-RM;
6 perform one repetition with the estimated 95 percent of 1-RM;
7 continue increasing the weight gradually after each successful lift until failure.

The bench press

- Lie on the bench.
- A spotter may assist with lifting the barbell off the support racks. Once the barbell has been lifted off, the spotter must release the bar.
- The barbell is held over the chest on extended arms.
- Lower the bar until it touches the chest.
- Press the bar up until the arms are fully extended.
- The following things should disqualify a bench press attempt:
    - bouncing the barbell off the chest;
    - lifting the hips off the bench anytime during the movement;
    - the spotter helping with the lift;
    - failure to extend both arms.

The back squat

- Stand with the barbell on the back of the shoulders.
- Squat down until the upper thigh is at least parallel to the floor.
- Stand up until the knees and hips are fully extended.
- The following things should disqualify a back squat attempt:
    - losing balance during the lift;
    - failure to descend deeply enough;
    - the spotter helping with the lift;
    - failure to stand up completely.

The power clean

- The barbell is lying on the ground.
- Approach the bar, squat down, and grip the bar as described in Chapter Two.

- In one movement, clean the bar to the shoulders and then stand up with the barbell.
- The following things should disqualify a power clean attempt:
  - stopping during the lift (i.e. making it more than one movement);
  - cleaning the bar to a location other than the shoulders (e.g., to the lower chest or stomach);
  - inability to hold on to the barbell while attempting to stand up;
  - loss of balance during the lift.

The power snatch

- The barbell is lying on the ground.
- Approach the bar, squat down, and grip the bar as described in Chapter Two.
- In one movement, snatch the barbell overhead and then stand up.
- The following things should disqualify a power snatch attempt:
  - stopping during the lift;
  - failure to keep both arms extended;
  - loss of balance during the lift.

POWER

The most common field tests of power are the counter-movement jump, standing long jump, standing triple jump, medicine ball toss (behind) and medicine ball toss (front). These tests have the benefit of being very simple to administer. It is possible to use force platforms and cameras to develop more information, but the tests listed are tests that anyone can perform in almost any environment. These tests are typically performed for three to five attempts. Either the best of the attempts is recorded or the attempts are averaged together.

Counter-movement jump

- Stand next to a measuring surface (such as a wall with a ruler or a commercial device that measures jump height).
- Reach up and touch the ruler, this point should be marked.
- Feet will be hip-width apart.
- Quickly squat into a quarter-squat.
- Without pausing, jump up as high as possible.
- While jumping, attempt to reach as high as possible, touching the ruler.
- The height jumped is the difference between the initial reach and where the final mark is.

Standing long jump

- Face the course. Some type of measuring tape or ruler extends on the ground in front.
- Feet will be hip-width apart.
- Quickly squat into a quarter-squat.
- Without pausing, try to jump as far forward as possible.
- The measure will be taken from the start line to where the back heel lands.

Standing triple jump

- Face the course. Some type of measuring tape or ruler extends on the ground in front.
- Feet will be hip-width apart.
- Quickly squat into a quarter-squat.
- Without pausing, try to jump as far forward as possible.
- Land on one leg. Without pausing, push off that leg.
- Land on the other leg. Without pausing, push off that leg.
- Land on both feet.
- The measure will be taken from the start line to where the back heel lands.

Medicine ball, behind

- This is performed with a two- to five-kilogram medicine ball.
- Face away from the course.
- Stand with the feet hip-width apart.
- Holding a medicine ball, quickly descend into a quarter-squat.
- Without pausing, explode upward and hurl the medicine ball as far behind as possible.
- The distance from the start line to where the medicine ball first touches the ground is measured.

Medicine ball, front

- This is performed with a two- to five-kilogram medicine ball.
- Face the course.
- Stand with the feet hip-width apart.
- Holding a medicine ball, quickly descend into a quarter-squat.
- Without pausing, explode upwards and hurl the medicine ball as far forward as possible.
- The distance from the start line to where the medicine ball first touches the ground is measured.

SPEED

Tests of speed are sprints focused on measuring acceleration or maximum velocity. These tests can be timed via stopwatch or technology (such as cameras, infrared beams, etc.). The stopwatch approach is portable and inexpensive, but there can be an error by the person holding the watch. The technology approach reduces user error (i.e. it is more accurate) but it can be expensive and difficult to set up.

Acceleration

Tests for acceleration are designed to measure an athlete's ability to increase velocity. The length of the sprint is determined by the demands of the sport and position. Acceleration is typically evaluated over 5-, 10-, 20-, and 36.6-meter sprints. The athlete should assume a sport-specific starting position. When ready, the athlete should explode out of the starting position and run through the finish line. Timing should begin when the athlete begins moving and end when the athlete crosses the finish line.

Maximal Velocity

Maximal-velocity tests seek to evaluate how fast an athlete can run. These either involve flying sprints or longer sprints from various starting positions depending upon the sport.

The flying sprint involves a 20–40-meter run-up that is not timed. Once the run-up is ended, the timing begins for 20 meters (i.e. the test is a "flying 20-meter sprint").

Longer sprints are performed from sport-specific starting positions. To evaluate maximal velocity, these sprints are performed for 60–100 meters. When ready, the athlete should explode out of the starting position and run through the finish line. Timing should begin when the athlete begins moving and end when the athlete crosses the finish line.

AGILITY

Agility is meant to test the athlete's ability to change directions. Four of the most common agility tests are the L run, the 505 test, the T test, and the pro-agility test. Agility tests involve the athlete assuming a starting position at the beginning of the course, starting explosively, and running the desired drill until they run through the finish line. Timing should begin when the athlete moves and end as the athlete crosses the finish line.

The L run

- Refer to Figure 3.1.
- Stand next to cone 1 (at the start line).
- On command, run as fast as possible to cone 2.
- Run around cone 2 and diagonally to cone 3.
- Run around cone 3 and straight to cone 2.
- Run around cone 2 and run to cone 1 (the finish line).

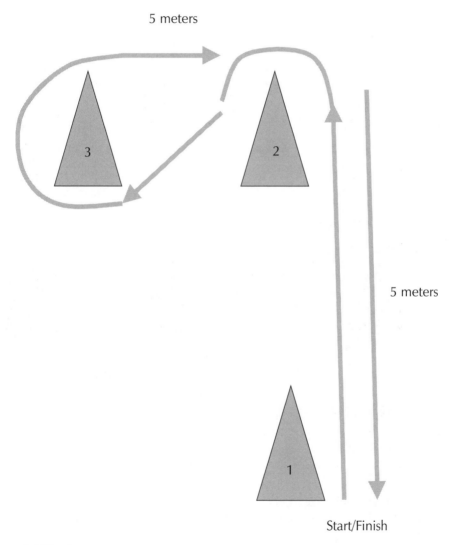

Figure 3.1 The L run.

The 505 test

- Refer to Figure 3.2.
- Cones 1 are placed 10 meters from cones 2.
- Cones 2 are placed 5 meters from cones 3.
- Stand at the start line, in between cones 1.
- On command, run as fast as possible to cones 3.
- When arriving at cones 2, the coach should begin timing.
- At cones 3, turn around and run back to cones 2, which is the finish line.

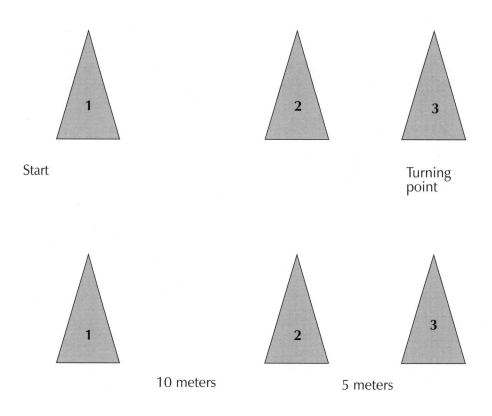

Figure 3.2 The 505 test.

The T test

- Refer to Figure 3.3.
- Cones 1 and 2 are nine meters apart. Cones 3 and 4 are 4.5 meters to the left and right of cone 2.
- Stand next to cone 1 (the start).

- Run as fast as possible to cone 2 and touch the cone.
- Shuffle to the left to cone 3 and touch the cone.
- Shuffle to the right to cone 4 and touch the cone.
- Shuffle to the left to cone 2 and touch the cone.
- Back-pedal past cone 1 (the finish).

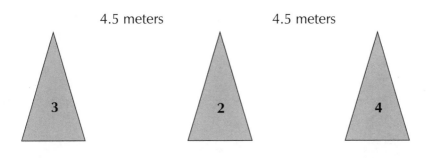

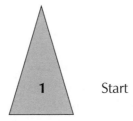

Figure 3.3 The T test.

The pro-agility test

- Refer to Figure 3.4.
- Begin at cone 1.
- Sprint to cone 2 and touch the cone.
- Sprint to cone 3 and touch the cone.
- Sprint back to cone 1, which is the finish line.

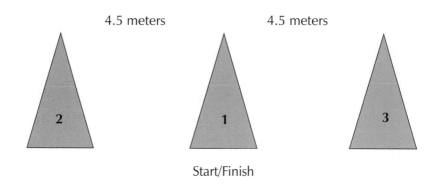

Start/Finish

Figure 3.4 The pro-agility test.

CONDITIONING

Conditioning tests look at the athlete's metabolic fitness. This is primarily done by looking at the athlete's ability to perform in the presence of exhaustion in a sport-specific manner. This is not the same thing as running long sprints. The two primary types of conditioning tests are suicides and the 300-meter shuttle run.

Suicides

Suicides, regardless of the sport, share several common features. First, a number of cones or lines are set up, each one further than the previous one. Second, the athlete will run to the first cone or line, touch it, then run back to the start line and touch it. Then the athlete will run to the second line/cone, touch it, and run back to the start line and touch it. This will be repeated for each subsequent line/cone until the test is completed. It is normal to have the athlete perform this test two to three times after an adequate rest. The athlete's time, ideally, should not vary much between the tests. Each sport will do a different number of runs to different distances based upon the needs of the sport.

300-meter shuttle run

- A cone or line is set up 25 meters away from the start line.
- Run to the 25-meter mark and touch the cone/line.
- Run back to the start line and touch it.
- Repeat until the this has been done six times (i.e. 6 × 50 = 300 meters).
- After adequate rest, run the test a second time. The times are compared.

While the tests described in this section are used frequently and have application to a great deal of sports, norms for the tests do not exist in a comprehensive-enough fashion to make them usable to coaches and athletes. Every sport, position, age group, and ability level will perform differently on these tests. Test results should be used to measure improvement (i.e. Is the training plan working?), identify deficiencies, and help with athlete selection by comparing to other athletes on the team.

EXAMPLES

While the tests described in this section are used frequently and have application to a great deal of sports, norms for the tests do not exist in a comprehensive-enough fashion to make them usable to coaches and athletes. Every sport, position, age group, and ability level will perform differently on these tests. Test results should be used to measure improvement (i.e. Is the training plan working?), identify deficiencies, and help with athlete selection by comparing to other athletes on the team.

This section is going to present some results for several sports from the literature. When possible these results are broken down by position and level of ability.

Baseball

Table 3.1 shows results for male professional baseball players. The table shows the results based upon playing level (A, AA, AAA, or Major League Baseball). In this example, and the ones for each sport that follow:

- sprints are in seconds;
- all jump results are in centimeters.

The results of Table 3.1 are interesting because there is not much difference in terms of performance between the playing levels. This suggests that athletes that make it to the minor and major leagues are fast and explosive, but other factors determine their ability to advance in the sport.

Table 3.1 Male baseball players

	A	AA	AAA	MLB
Vertical jump (cm)	70	69	71	72
Ten-yard sprint (s)	1.6	1.6	1.6	1.5
Pro-agility (s)	4.5	4.4	4.5	4.4

Source: Adapted from Hoffman *et al.* 2009.

Basketball

Tables 3.2 and 3.3 show samples of results for male and female basketball players. Please note that in these tables strength testing is expressed as a percentage of the athlete's body weight (so 1.21 means the athlete lifted 121 percent of body weight).

Table 3.2 Male basketball players

	D1 G	D1 F	D1 C	NT G	NT F	NT C
Vertical jump (cm)	73	71	67	49	47	42
Bench press (% of BW)	1.2	1.1	1.05	.9	.9	.9
Power clean (% of BW)	1.1	1.1	1			
Back squat (% of BW)	1.8	1.7	1.4	2.2	2.1	2
5-meter sprint (s)				1	1.1	1.2
10-meter sprint (s)				1.9	2	2
27.45-meter sprint (s)	3.7	3.8	4			
30-meter sprint (s)				4.1	4.2	
36.6-meter sprint (s)	4.7	4.8	4.9			4.3
T test (s)	8.7	8.9	9.3	9.9	10	10

Source: Adapted from Abdelkrim *et al.* 2010b, Berg and Latin 1995, and Latin *et al.* 1994.
G refers to guards, F to forwards, C to centers. Compares Division I (D1) to National team (NT) members.

Table 3.3 Female basketball players

	Guards	Forwards	Centers
Vertical jump (cm)	44	43	41
20-meter sprint (s)	3.4	3.5	3.6
T test (s)	10	10.5	10.7

Source: Adapted from Delextrat and Cohen, 2009.

assessments

Table 3.2 compares American male collegiate (division I) basketball players and European national team players. They are broken down by guards, forwards, and centers. The American collegiate athletes have greater vertical jumps, stronger upper bodies, and are more agile than their European counterparts. The European athletes have stronger lower bodies than their American counterparts. Regardless of population, Table 3.2 shows that the guard position tends to be stronger in terms of lifting body weight, faster, more explosive, and more agile than the other positions. The center tends to be the slowest, least explosive, and heaviest of the positions covered.

Table 3.3 shows results for female American collegiate (division II) basketball players. The trends concerning the positions holds in Table 3.3 for female athletes, with the guards being slightly faster and more explosive and the centers being the slowest and least explosive athletes.

Football (American)

Table 3.4 shows results for male American football players. The table shows high-school, collegiate division I, and professional football players. At each level, the positions are

Table 3.4 American football players

	HS S	D1 S	NFL S	HS BS	D1 BS	NFL BS	HS L	D1 L	NFL L	HS QB	D1 QB	D1 K
36.6-meter sprint (s)	5.5	4.6	4.5	5	4.7	4.7	4.8	5.1	5.2	4.9	4.7	
Vertical jump (cm)	57	82		67	81		72	70		72	75	71
Standling long jump (cm)		301	305		288	294		262	262			
Pro-agility (s)	5.2	4.2	4.1	4.8	4.3	4.2	4.7	4.7	4.6	4.7		
L drill (s)		7.2	7		7.4	7.3		7.9	7.8			
Bench press (% BW)		1.6			1.5			1.5			1.4	1.2
Back squat (% BW)		2.1			2.1			1.8			1.9	1.6
Power clean (% BW)		1.2			1.2			1			1.2	1
225 bench press (# reps)		17	17		22	23		23	26			

Source: Adapted from Berg and Latin 1995, Black and Roundy 1994, Carbuhn *et al.* 2008, Dupler *et al.* 2010, Secora *et al.* 2004, Sierer *et al.* 2008. Compares high school (HS), Division I (D1), and National Football League (NFL). Skill (S), big skill (BS), line (L), quarterback (QB), and kickers (K).

broken down by skill (wide receivers, cornerbacks, running backs, and safeties), big skill (fullbacks, linebackers, tight ends, and defensive ends), line (offensive and defensive line), quarterbacks, and kickers. As one would expect, collegiate athletes are stronger, faster, and more explosive than high-school athletes. Professional athletes are stronger, faster, and more explosive than high-school and collegiate athletes. The linemen, being the heaviest American football players, tend to be slower, jump for less distance/height, and lift a lower percentage of their body weight.

Rugby

Tables 3.5, 3.6, and 3.7 show results for male and female athletes. Table 3.5 shows results for male professional rugby players broken down by forwards and backs. Note that in the population studied there is not much difference between the positions. Table 3.6 shows results for male club rugby players broken down by level of ability (1st vs. 2nd grade). The first-grade athletes are noticeably faster on the ten-meter sprint, but not on any other measure. Table 3.7 shows results for elite female rugby players broken down by forwards and backs. In this population there are small differences with the backs being a little faster and more explosive than the forwards.

Table 3.5 Male professional rugby players

	Forwards	Backs
Bench press (% of BW)	1.3	1.2
15-meter sprint (s)	2.3	2.3
40-meter sprint (s)	5.2	5.1

Source: Adapted from Meir *et al.* 2001.

Table 3.6 Male club rugby players

	1st grade	2nd grade
5-meter sprint (s)	1.1	1.2
10-meter sprint (s)	1.2	2
20-meter sprint (s)	3.3	3.4
505 agility (s)	2.3	2.4
L run (s)	6.4	6.5

Source: Adapted from Gabett *et al.* 2008a.

assessments

Table 3.7 Elite female rugby players

	Forwards	Backs
10-meter sprint (s)	2.1	2
20-meter sprint (s)	3.6	3.4
505 agility (s)	2.7	2.6
Vertical jump (cm)	35	36

Source: Adapted from Gabbett 2007.

Soccer

Tables 3.8 and 3.9 show results for male and female athletes. Table 3.8 shows results for male American collegiate (division I) soccer players and European national team players. They are broken down by goalkeeper (G), defenders (D), midfielders, and forwards. With the exception of vertical jump, it is impossible to compare the American collegiate soccer players with their European counterparts. The American athletes have greater vertical jumps, but it is possible that there is greater emphasis placed on this measure in American universities than in European soccer. In Table 3.8 the goalkeepers, regardless of the population, tend to be slower and less explosive than the other positions with the defenders and forwards being the fastest and most explosive athletes.

Table 3.9 shows performance testing for female professional athletes.

Table 3.8 Male soccer players

	D1 G	N G	D1 D	N D	D1 MF	N MF	D1 F	N F
Vertical jump (cm)	54	49	64	44	61	44	64	45
5-meter sprint (s)		1.5		1.4		1.5		1.4
9.1-meter sprint (s)	1.8		1.7		1.7		1.7	
10-meter sprint (s)		2.4		2.1		2.2		2
20-meter sprint (s)		3.5		3.4		3.4		3.3
36.5-meter sprint (s)	5.3		4.9		5		4.9	

Source: Adapted from Silvestre *et al.* 2006, Sporis *et al.* 2009. Examining division I (D1) vs. national-caliber goalkeepers (G), defenders (D), midfielders (MF), and forwards (F).

Table 3.9 Female professional soccer players

Female	Professional
Vertical jump (cm)	34
Standing broad jump (cm)	192

Source: Adapted from Can *et al.* 2004.

HOW TO USE THIS INFORMATION

The reader will note that nowhere in this chapter are norms provided. For example, how should an 18–year-old female basketball player be performing on each of the assessments covered in this chapter? This information is not provided because the information does not exist.

The best that can be done is to provide the results extant in the literature, which has been done. The challenge is that this information is not going to be very helpful to most coaches and athletes. While we can find information on how American collegiate basketball guards (for example) perform on various assessments, we don't know if the sample athletes are talented, on good teams, etc. In other words, there are a lot of limitations to the information that has been presented.

Coaches should take a close look at the needs of the sport, the position, and the athlete (see Chapter Six) and select assessments based upon those needs. Once that has been done, over time, the coach should collect the results of those assessments and build up their own database and norms. This is the only way to develop meaningful data that can be used to make decisions.

KEY READINGS

Barnes, M. and Cissik, J. (2008) *Training for the 40–Yard Dash*, Coaches Choice, Monterrey Bay, CA.

Michael Barnes and John Cissik devote an entire book to the 40-yard dash, which is a speed test frequently employed with athletes. The book includes information on how to train for the test. For the athlete, it also includes pointers on how to take the test (starting position, taking the first few steps explosively, and how to run the sprint). For the coach, the book has information on how to train for the 40 as well as the advantages and disadvantages of different ways to measure results.

Berg, K. and Latin, R.W. (1995) Comparison of physical and performance characteristics of NCAA Division I basketball and football players, *Journal of Strength and Conditioning Research*, 9(1): 22–26.

Latin, R.W., Berg, K. and Baechle, T. (1994) Physical and performance characteristics of NCAA Division I male basketball players, *Journal of Strength and Conditioning Research*, 8(4): 214–18.

Berg and Latin (1995) and Latin *et al.* (1994) are important publications because they use large subject pools to provide information on how collegiate basketball and football players perform on selected assessments. It is important to note that the authors did not administer these tests themselves, so they are reporting on information that others administered. This means that when viewing the results one has to keep in mind that there may be variation in assessment protocols, which may impact the validity and reliability of the results.

CHAPTER FOUR

COMPONENTS OF A TRAINING SESSION

A thorough strength and conditioning program involves many different modes of exercise working together. This chapter will describe different components of a typical training session, helping the reader to make decisions about how and why to use each of them.

OUTLINE

The warm-up

- General warm-up
- Specific warm-up

Strength training

Speed training

- Technique drills
- Stride-length drills
- Stride-frequency drills
- Sprints of varying distances
- Assisted sprinting
- Resisted sprinting
- Varied-pace sprinting

Agility training

- Fundamental skills
- Combination skills
- Advanced skills

Plyometrics

- Single-effort jumps
- Multiple-response jumps

Conditioning

■ Sprint-based conditioning
■ Circuit-based conditioning
■ Strongman-based conditioning

The cool-down

Recovery

■ Active recovery
■ Massage
■ Cold/contrast baths

Key readings

THE WARM-UP

The warm-up prevents injuries and prepares the body for work. It prevents injuries by:

1 elevating the heart rate gradually;
2 distributing blood to the muscles and joints that will be trained;
3 increasing temperature through the redistribution of blood flow, use of energy stores, and friction caused by the actions of actin and myosin;
4 increasing the deformability of muscles and connective tissue.

It prepares the body for work by:

1 allowing for practice of the components of the main activity. Athletic skills tend to be complicated movements that can be broken down into components. By practicing the components in isolation during the warm-up, the athlete will be more ready to perform the entire skill during the training session;
2 allowing for the intensity, speed, and complexity to be gradually increased. Most athletes are not ready to jump into complicated, explosive exercises and require time to gradually transition into those qualities;
3 cueing of the nervous system for events requiring strength, speed, or power.

There are two types of warm-up: the general warm-up and the specific warm-up. The general warm-up is meant to elevate the heart rate, distribute blood to the muscles and joints that will be trained, increase temperature, and increase tissue deformability. The specific warm-up prepares the muscles and joints in a manner similar to how they will be trained, allows the athlete to practice skills, and to gradually increase in terms of speed, intensity, and complexity.

General warm-up

The general warm-up consists of a combination of low-intensity cardiovascular exercise and dynamic flexibility exercises. The low-intensity cardiovascular exercise should be performed for five to ten minutes and should be followed by the dynamic flexibility exercises. These exercises are grouped together by joint and/or muscle group. Table 4.1 provides an overview of dynamic flexibility exercises that are appropriate for a general warm-up. The exercises are placed into one of two classes depending upon whether they are joint-specific or movement-specific. A general warm-up should employ exercises from both classes.

Depending on the upcoming workout, two to three exercises should be performed for

Table 4.1 Sample dynamic flexibility exercises, general warm-up

Class of exercises	Joint	Exercise
Joint mobility exercises	Ankle	Ankle circles
	Knee	Knee circles
	Hip	Forward/backward leg swings
	Hip	Lateral leg swings
	Hip	Hip circles
	Hip	Eagles
	Hip/knee	Stomach eagles
	Hip/knee	Kick the fence
	Shoulders	Inchworm
	Shoulders	Windmills
	Shoulders	Wheelbarrows
General movement preparation exercises	Ankle	Walk on toes
	Ankle	Walk on toes, arm circles
	Ankle	Toe taps
	Hip/knee	Walk forward, bend and touch toes
	Hip/knee	March
	Hip/knee	March, touch opposite foot
	Knee	Knee-down butt kicks
	Hip/knee	Forward lunges
	Hip/knee	Posterior lunges
	Hip/knee	Angle lunges
	Hip/knee	Side lunges
	Hip/knee/trunk	Lunges with upper-body rotation
	Hip	Walk forwards, abduct hip
	Shoulder	Prone hold, reach up right/left
	Shoulder	Prone hold, stability ball, walk out
	Shoulder	Prone hold, stability ball, shuffle right/left
	Shoulder	Prone hold, walk up/down

90

each joint, performed for one to three sets each for 10–20 meters each set (or 10–20 repetitions per set, depending upon the exercise). This is dependent upon the environment (colder environments require more extensive warm-ups) and the nature and difficulty of the upcoming training session (more difficult training sessions also require more extensive warm-ups).

Table 4.2 illustrates two sample general warm-ups. The first example involves preparing for a field sport that requires sprinting, sudden starts and stops, and sudden changes of direction. This may include soccer, American football, lacrosse, field hockey, baseball, softball, volleyball, or basketball. The second example involves preparing for a strength-training workout, primarily emphasizing the upper body.

As Table 4.2 illustrates, for the field event sport, the athlete begins with a slow 800-meter jog that should take five to seven minutes. The dynamic flexibility exercises focus on the joints and muscles of the lower body, starting at the ankle and working up from the ground. The volume is one to two sets on each exercise. If these exercises are performed continuously and rhythmically, the athlete should complete the dynamic flexibility exercises in five to ten minutes.

Table 4.2 Sample general warm-up programs

Activity	Joint	Exercise	Sets × Reps
Field sport	Cardiovascular	Slow jog	800 meters
	Ankle	Ankle circles	1 × 20
	Ankle	Walk on toes	1 × 20 meters
	Ankle	Walk on toes, arm circles	1 × 20 meters
	Hip	Leg swings	1 × 20
	Hip	Lateral leg swings	1 × 20
	Hip	Eagles	1 × 20
	Hip	Stomach eagles	1 × 20
	Hip/knee	Walk forward, bend, Touch toes	2 × 20 meters
	Hip/knee	March, opposite hand/ opposite foot	2 × 20 meters
	Hip/knee	Knee-down butt kicks	2 × 20 meters
	Hip/knee	Angle lunges	2 × 20 meters
	Hip/knee	Side lunges	2 × 20 meters
Upper-body workout	Cardiovascular	Upper-body ergometer	5 minutes
	Shoulder	Arm circles	20 each direction
	Shoulder	Inchworms	1 × 20 meters
	Shoulder	Wheelbarrows	1 × 20 meters
	Shoulder	Prone hold, reach up, right/left	1 × 20
	Shoulder	Prone hold, walk up/down	2 × 30 seconds
	Shoulder	Internal/external rotation	2 × 20

With regards to the upper-body strength-training workout, Table 4.2 shows that it begins with five minutes on the upper-body ergometer, which is training the muscles that will be used in the strength-training session. This is followed by dynamic flexibility exercises focusing on the joints and muscles of the upper body. The exercises begin simply (i.e. arm circles), then increase in difficulty (prone holds stepping up/down), then culminate in rotator cuff work, which is a good transition into the specific warm-up.

Specific warm-up

The specific warm-up consists of more advanced dynamic flexibility exercises and progressions for the first exercise in the training session. These advanced exercises could include speed/agility technique drills and other bodyweight exercises, gradually segueing into progression for the first exercise of the training session. Table 4.3 provides an example of dynamic flexibility exercises that are appropriate for a specific warm-up. Notice that these exercises train more than one joint and that some are even performed explosively.

Table 4.3 Sample dynamic flexibility exercises, specific warm-up

Class of exercises	Joint	Exercise
General movement preparation exercises	Shoulder/elbow	Between bench dips
	Shoulder/elbow	Dips
	Shoulder/elbow	Push-ups
	Shoulder/elbow	Incline pull-ups
	Shoulder/elbow	Pull-ups
	Hip/knee/ankle	Bodyweight squats
	Hip/knee/ankle	Squat jumps
	Hip/knee/ankle	Counter-movement jumps
General linear preparation exercises	Hip/ankle	Ankling
	Hip/knee/ankle	Butt kicks
	Hip/knee/ankle	High knees
	Hip/knee/ankle	Walking high-knee pulls
	Hip/knee/ankle	High knee pull-lunge
	Hip/knee/ankle	High knee skips
	Hip/knee/ankle	A walks
	Hip/knee/ankle	A skips
	Hip/knee/ankle	B walks
	Hip/knee/ankle	B skips
General multidirectional exercises	Hip/knee/ankle	Side shuffle
	Hip/knee/ankle	Step-backs
	Hip/knee/ankle	Back-pedal
	Hip/knee/ankle	Carioca

As with the general warm-up, depending on the nature of the upcoming training session, two to three of these exercises should be done per joint for one to three sets each of 10–20 meters (or repetitions).

Training sessions may be classified according to their emphasis. Some focus on strength training, some on speed training, some on agility training, some on plyometrics. The focus of the training session will dictate the rest of the specific warm-up. The last half of the specific warm-up should consist of transition exercises into the main training session. Table 4.4 provides examples of how this can be accomplished using the various foci mentioned above.

In the first example, the athlete is preparing for a strength-training session that begins with the clean or the snatch. The warm-up begins with dynamic flexibility exercises focused on the entire body. Next the athlete performs exercises that break the clean or the snatch into its components. First, the parts are performed at slow speeds (shrug, upright row, squat), then they are integrated at slow speed (muscle clean/snatch). After that, the athlete is ready to perform the first set of the clean or the snatch.

In the second example, the athlete is preparing for a maximal-velocity training session that focuses on 60-meter sprints. The general warm-up focuses on dynamic flexibility exercises geared primarily toward the lower body. Next, exercises are performed to cue the nervous system to help with explosivity, first with fast leg drills, then with falling and standing starts to help reinforce the need to start explosively. Finally, drills are performed to help increase stride length. After this, the athlete is ready to perform the first set of 60-meter sprints.

Table 4.4 Sample specific warm-up exercises

Training session focus	First exercise in training session	Specific warm-up
Strength training	Clean or snatch	Dynamic flexibility exercises Clean/snatch shrug, 10× Clean/snatch upright row, 10× Front/overhead squat, 10× Muscle clean/snatch, 10×
Speed training	60-meter sprints, standing starts	Dynamic flexibility exercises Fast leg drills, 2 × 10 meters Falling starts, 2 × 10 meters Standing starts, 2 × 10 meters Stride-length drills, 2 × 20 meters
Agility training	Reactive, multi-directional training	Dynamic flexibility exercises Start + stop + start, 2× Shuffle + turn + sprint, 2× Back-pedal + turn + sprint, 2×

In the final example the preparation is for an advanced-agility training session. Again, the dynamic flexibility exercises in the general warm-up primarily focus on the muscles of the lower body. Next, agility skills are performed in increasingly faster and more complicated sequences. First, the athlete practices starting and stopping. Next is shuffling, turning, and sprinting; finally, back-pedaling, turning, then sprinting. Once this warm-up has been completed, the athlete has practiced many of the core skills that will be found in the advanced-agility drills and will be ready to begin the training session.

What if athletes do more than one thing? For example, what if an athlete performs a sprinting workout and then goes into the weightroom to lift? In that case, should the athlete warm up for both sessions? The answer is yes and no. The first session (the sprinting) addressed the needs for a general warm-up, but there will still be a need for a specific warm-up of some sort (though it may be abbreviated) prior to the strength-training session.

The reader will note that the section on the warm-up never mentioned static stretching. Had this book been written 30 years ago, the warm-up would have been described as: Perform five to ten minutes of cardiovascular exercise and then stretch the muscles to be trained for another five to ten minutes, holding each stretch for 20–30 seconds.

Today, the thinking is that static stretching as warm-up has a negative impact on performance. Over the last five years, a number of studies have examined the impact of static stretching on isokinetic strength, counter-movement jumps, depth jumps, sprinting, agility, penalty kicks, and five-step jumps. Overwhelmingly, each of these studies finds that static stretching as warm-up has a negative impact on the performance measures described above (see Faigenbaum et al., 2010; Fletcher, 2010; Fletcher and Monte-Colombo, 2010; Gelen, 2010; Manoel et al., 2008; McMillian et al., 2006; Samuel et al., 2008).

What should be done instead of static stretching in the warm-up? As described in the beginning of this chapter, dynamic flexibility exercises should be performed instead. Every study listed above has found that dynamic flexibility exercises result in improved performance in each of the performance measures described. Dynamic flexibility exercises incorporate continuous and rhythmic movements (Manoel et al., 2008). At least when examining their impact on counter-movement jumps and depth jumps, they have been found to increase knee range of motion, heart rate, core temperature, and knee torque (Fletcher and Monte-Colombo, 2010). Recall that the purpose of the warm-up is to achieve all these things to help make the muscles more plastic.

STRENGTH TRAINING

As was covered in more detail in Chapter One, strength training is meant to increase hypertrophy, increase strength, develop power, condition the joints, rehabilitate injured areas, condition specific metabolic pathways, and improve bone strength. This is done through employing a number of different exercise modes including barbells, bands/chains, dumbbells, kettlebells, body weight, and selectorized equipment. Chapter Two detailed how to perform a number of exercises with this equipment.

Much of the equipment listed above has been around for a while with the exception of bands, chains, and kettlebells. Bands and chains are designed to take advantage of the strength curves of free weight exercises.

Bands refer to, essentially, giant rubber bands that are secured to the ends of barbells and either the floor or ceiling. Bands are designed to make it more difficult to raise and lower the weights. This is meant to take advantage of two interesting features of a free weight exercise. First, one can lower a great deal more weight than one can lift. The bands require the lifter to control the barbell during the descent as the bands will try to shorten as the lifter descends with the bar. Second, as the barbell approaches the end of its range of motion during the concentric part of the lift, the lifter is often stronger than at the beginning of the lift. Since the bands are lengthening as the lifter is completing the lift, they will provide increasing resistance as the barbell is lifted up. The use of bands is not well researched, but they do seem promising. Anderson et al. (2008) investigated the effects of bands on seven weeks of training and found that they resulted in significantly better strength gains on both the bench press and the squat than not using bands. This has also been found by Bellar et al. (2010) who found that using bands increased bench-press strength over 13 weeks of training significantly more than not using bands.

Chains refer to chain links that are attached to the ends of barbells. As the barbell is lowered, chain links accumulate on the floor, reducing the load on the barbell. As the barbell is lifted higher, the chains are lifted from the floor, gradually increasing the weight on the bar (McCurdy et al., 2009). The idea being that, normally, lifts become easier the closer to the top of the lift they reach, chain loading counteracts this and increases the load the further the bar is lifted (Neelly et al., 2010).

While a great deal of empirical and coaching literature on the use of chains exists, research on using chains in conjunction with strength training is in its early stages and the results are mixed. McCurdy et al. (2009) examined the impact of chains on the bench-press training of collegiate baseball players. Their subjects were divided into a chain group and a traditional group. After nine weeks of training, both groups significantly increased their strength, but there was no difference between the groups in terms of strength increases.

Another theoretical reason for using chains is that because the resistance is not constant throughout, it may improve an athlete's power more effectively than a traditional plate-only form of strength training. Baker and Newton (2009), when examining the impact of chains on the bench press of professional rugby players, found that the chains increased the barbell's velocity by almost 10 percent when compared to the no-chain condition (both conditions had an equivalent load on the barbell). Berning *et al.* (2008), however, did not find any kinetic or kinematic differences between using chains and not using chains on the performance of the clean. The contradictions in the results underscore the need for more research on the effectiveness of these tools.

Kettlebells are another new tool that can be found in strength and conditioning. Kettlebells are, essentially, metal balls with a handle on top. They have become popular because they allow a wider variety of positions to be achieved than a standard barbell or dumbbell exercise. Despite their popularity, there is almost no research on kettlebells. Farrar *et al.* (2010) represents one of the few studies on kettlebells. In their study, they had subjects perform two-handed swings with a 16-kilogram kettlebell for 12 minutes and determined that the subjects were exercising at 87 percent of their maximum heart rate throughout the 12 minutes. While the study does indicate that swinging a kettlebell for 12 minutes can be an intense cardiovascular workout, it does not address whether this strength or conditioning tool is more or less effective than others.

Barbells, dumbbells, bands/chains, kettlebells, and bodyweight exercises can be classified as *free weights*. They have a number of benefits:

- They require balance: More muscles must be recruited to perform the exercises. Not only must one balance between the right and left sides of the body, but one must also learn to maintain balance while performing many of these exercises.
- They require coordination: Free weights are performed in multiple planes of movement and can be very complex in terms of movement patterns. This requires the involvement of more muscles (stabilizing and antagonist muscles) to perform the exercises. It also means that there is a skill component to performing these exercises.
- A wider variety of exercises is possible: Selectorized equipment allows for one or two exercises to be performed with the equipment. This is not the case with free weights.
- They are less expensive than machines: A barbell with weight plates costs a few hundred dollars. A complete set of dumbbells cost $2,000–3,000. A single piece of selectorized strength-training equipment will cost between $3,500 and $10,000.

When compared to selectorized equipment, free weights have been found to result in greater strength gains (Spennewyn, 2008), greater electrical activity to the muscles (Schwanbeck *et al.*, 2009), and greater electrical activity to synergistic muscles (McCaw and Friday, 1994).

Free weights also have a number of drawbacks:

- They can be dangerous. Athletes can eventually handle a lot of weight with free weights, which can set them up for injuries or put them in dangerous positions. Because of this, considerable time must be spent with technique instruction, providing feedback, monitoring fatigue and its effects on technique, and spotters must be present. All of this may or may not be considered to be a good use of time and resources.

- Supervision. Due to the complexity of the exercises and the inherent dangers, considerable supervision must be present when athletes are using free weights. Anyone supervising athletes using free weights has to be qualified. They must understand the techniques, risk management, and injury prevention, and this usually means possessing both education and certification in the field.
- Free weights require proper technique. Good technique ensures safety and it ensures that the exercises train what they are supposed to. Some exercises are uncomplicated, others (such as the clean and the snatch) are not learnable without proper coaching. There is a learning curve for athletes and free weight exercises that may or may not be a good use of the athlete's time.

Selectorized strength-training equipment can be found in most fitness centers and even athletic facilities. It has a number of benefits when compared to free weights:

- Easy to learn. Selectorized equipment is limited by the design of the machine. This means that it is very easy to master the exercise. Little time is necessary for instruction, little feedback is needed on technique, and more time is spent training, with less on skill development.
- Minimal supervision. Selectorized equipment tends to be easier to learn and it is safer. This means that less supervision is required and the individuals doing the supervision do not have to be as skilled as with free weights.

Selectorized equipment has drawbacks when compared to free weights:

- Equipment is expensive. A piece of selectorized equipment costs considerably more than free weights.
- Equipment has a large footprint. Selectorized equipment takes up a lot of space in a weight room. When combined with the next bullet, it may not add up to an efficient use of space.
- Little variety is possible with each piece of equipment. In general, only one or two exercises are possible on a piece of selectorized equipment.
- The exerciser is limited by the design of the equipment. This equipment is made for the dimensions of the average person. If the exerciser isn't average, the equipment will not work as well for them or could even be dangerous.

Strength-training sessions use free weights and selectorized equipment to focus on one of the following:

- *maximal strength*: the amount of force that can be exerted;
- *power*: the ability to exert force quickly;
- hypertrophy: increasing the size of the muscles. Hypertrophy training isn't always focused on larger muscles, it also includes adaptations to bone and connective tissue.

Chapter Seven will cover how to design strength and conditioning programs for each of these areas of emphasis.

SPEED TRAINING

Speed training is focused on improving straight-ahead speed. It uses a number of tools to do this including technique drills, stride length drills, stride frequency drills, sprints of varying distances, assisted training, resisted training, and varied-pace speed training.

Technique drills

Technique drills break down the sprinting motion into its parts. This allows for those parts to be mastered during slower, less complex situations. Eventually, the athlete can transfer the techniques of the drills to the whole motion. According to Cissik (2004), there is a progression of technique drills:

1   arm-swing drills;
2   ankling;
3   heel kicks;
4   high-knee drills;
5   A drills.

Arm-swing drills

Arm-swing drills teach the motion of the arms during sprinting. During these drills, the focus should be on keeping the arms against the body (i.e. avoid letting the arms cross the midline of the body), having the hands travel from the hip to the height of the shoulder, and driving the arm back forcefully to use the stretch reflex to push the arm forward.

Initially, these drills are performed in a seated position. The athlete sits up tall, and on the "start" command the athlete alternates the swinging of the arms until the drill is completed. Once the athlete has mastered the seated drill, it can be performed standing, then walking, and then jogging.

Arm-swing drills are appropriate for beginners, but they do not require a great deal of time. In general, the drills can be done for five or ten minutes during the first training session and this is usually all the emphasis that the arm swing needs.

Ankling

Ankling teaches how to pick the foot up off the ground and how to set it back down again during sprinting. In ankling, the legs are straight and the motion is from the hips.

Ankling drills begin by focusing on one leg at a time to keep the skill simpler. Begin the drill with the right foot behind the body (right leg is straight). The right ankle should be plantarflexed while it is in contact with the ground. Dorsiflex the right ankle and, using the hip, swing the right leg forward keeping the right ankle dorsiflexed. This dorsiflexion is called *casting* the foot. As the right leg is swung forward, the right foot should remain cast and make contact with the ground just in front of the athlete. The outside of the right forefoot should contact the ground. When the right foot contacts the ground, the athlete should pull themselves forward. As the athlete's hips pass over the foot, the right ankle should go back into plantarflexion and the entire process should repeat. This should be repeated until the desired distance is covered, then the athlete should switch legs.

After there is comfort focusing on one leg at a time, this drill can be performed by alternating legs. Finally, progress into making this an explosive drill by performing straight-leg bounds.

Heel kicks

Heel kicks build on the ankling drill and teach how to bring the heel to the hip immediately following plantarflexion. This is an important skill because it allows the athlete to "shorten the lever" by moving the mass of the leg closer to the axis of rotation, meaning that the leg can be cycled forward faster during sprinting (Cissik, 2004).

Much like ankling, heel-kick drills begin with having the athlete walk, focusing on only one leg at a time. Keep the left leg stiff and step forward with the left foot. As the hips pass over the right foot, the right foot should be plantarflexed. When the right foot leaves the ground, it should immediately be cast. Once the foot is cast, it should be lifted up to the right buttock, touching if possible. If this is done properly, the right hip will flex to approximately 45 degrees (ibid.). Repeat for the desired distance and then switch legs.

Once there is proficiency at the above drill, progress to alternating between the right and left sides. Then progress to performing the drill at a jogging pace (initially focusing on one side and then progressing to alternating legs).

When performing this drill, there are three important points to remember. First, the foot must remain in the cast position throughout. Second, avoid pointing the knee straight down during the performance of this drill. The hip should flex while the heel is being lifted up. Third, if there is a lack of flexibility it will be difficult to bring the heel all the way to the hip. This will improve over time.

High-knee drills

High-knee drills reinforce casting the foot while teaching frontside mechanics (or what is happening in front of the body during sprinting). As with ankling and heel kicks, these drills are initially taught at walking speeds focusing on one leg at a time.

To perform this drill, step forward with the left leg. As the hips move over the right foot, the right ankle should plantarflex. When the right foot breaks contact with the ground, it should immediately be cast. Once the foot is cast, the right knee should be lifted high (parallel to the ground). Keeping the foot cast, the foot should be placed on the ground slightly in front of the hips so that the forefoot should contact the ground. The foot should be driven to the ground from the hips.

As with the other drills, this one begins at a walking pace just focusing on one leg at a time. As the drill is mastered, it progresses to alternating between the right and left legs. Once there is comfort with alternating, progress to a skipping drill.

Initially, do not focus on the arm swing as part of this drill. Over time, this can be included.

There are two important points to remember with high-knee drills. First, the foot should remain cast throughout. Second, remain tall. Allowing the trunk to flex is a bad habit; if this translates to sprinting it will limit the amount of hip extension during sprinting, which will limit the ability to exert force against the ground.

A drills

A drills combine high-knee drills with heel kicks and, basically, put everything together. Some authors feel that these drills are very similar to sprinting and should be employed extensively in training.

Like ankling, heel kicks, and high-knee drills, this one begins at a walking pace focusing on one leg at a time. Keep the left leg stiff and step forward with the left foot. As the hips pass over the right foot, the right foot should be plantarflexed as it leaves the ground. When the right foot leaves the ground, it should immediately be cast. As the foot is cast, it should be lifted up to the right buttock, touching if possible. Keeping the heel in contact with the hip, swing the right leg forward (the coaching cue is to focus on "stepping over the opposite knee"). As the leg is swung forward, the right knee will be lifted high and the leg will begin to unfold. When the leg unfolds, the foot should be driven to the ground using the hip. Repeat until the desired distance has been covered and then switch legs.

As the A drill is mastered, progress to alternating legs. Then progress from a walk to a skip. Like the high-knee drill, initially avoid focusing on the arm swing but integrate it as more experience is gained with the drill.

100

components of a training session

There are a number of important cautions with technique drills. First, they must be kept in perspective. While they are useful for teaching aspects of the sprinting motion, they do not substitute for sprinting. This is because the drills do not resemble the sprinting motion in terms of kinematics (Kivi and Alexander, 2000). Ultimately, to become faster at sprinting one needs to sprint. Second, if the drills are not performed perfectly they reinforce bad technique (West and Robson, 2000). Third, if they are not learned in the proper sequence the athlete will not get the full benefits from the drills (ibid.).

Not all coaches agree on the value of these drills. Jakalski (2002) feels sprinting speed is not enhanced through an ideal technique, rather it is enhanced by exerting more force against the ground. His recommendation is to focus on plyometrics, skipping, bounding, and even strength training rather than technique drills to improve speed.

Stride-length drills

Speed is often considered to be the product of stride length and stride frequency. In theory, this means that improving the length of the strides will allow one to arrive at some place faster. Stride-length drills involve having the athlete run so that longer-than-normal strides are taken. This usually involves some sort of a visual cue that tells the athlete how far apart to place their strides (hurdles, cones, tennis balls, etc.).

Stride-length drills are performed in one of two ways. First, they may be done in an escalating manner. This means that the length of the strides gradually increases as velocity is increased. For example, after the start line, the first hurdle may be placed 30 centimeters in front of the start, the second hurdle 45 centimeters after the first, the third hurdle 60 centimeters after the third, etc. Second, they may be done after there has been a chance to transition into maximal velocity running. In practice, this means setting up the drill so that it begins after 20–40 meters of running. This also means that the strides will be much longer than in an escalating fashion.

With track and field athletes, these distances for these drills are determined very precisely (see Cissik, 2005; Coaching Education Committee, 2001; McFarlane, 1993, for examples). This does not need to be the case with other types of athletes. The best strategy with other types of athletes is to set up courses based upon the athlete's height.

One caution with stride-length drills is that coaches and athletes should be cautious of overstriding. If the strides are set too far apart, more time will be spent braking due to the overstriding, which is ultimately counterproductive.

Stride-frequency drills

Stride-frequency drills are meant to help move the legs faster. According to Cissik (2005), fast leg drills, assisted sprinting, and resisted sprinting are all used to improve stride frequency. Assisted and resisted sprinting will both be covered later in this chapter.

Fast leg drills train one to move the legs faster than normal during the drill. The thinking is that over time this will carry over to sprinting, allowing one to be faster. Fast leg drills are begun with ankling. Begin by ankling with the right foot, then the left, then the right again. On the fourth step (the left foot), perform a fast A drill with the left leg. Then resume ankling for three more steps, and perform another A drill with the fourth step. After the desired distance has been covered, switch legs.

Once the fast leg drill has been mastered, perform it every third step (so that the legs must be alternated). Eventually, combine with straight-leg bounding to speed up the drill.

It should be noted that not all coaches feel that stride frequency is a trainable quality. Some coaches feel that the focus should be on stride length rather than stride frequency.

Sprints of varying distances

Technique drills, stride-length drills, and stride-frequency drills are not substitutes for sprinting. Athletes must sprint using maximal speed if they want to improve their ability to run fast. This is because running (or performing drills) at submaximal speeds will alter running mechanics, stride frequency, and stride length. In other words, failing to train with sprints will teach the athlete to run slowly and with bad form, which is counterproductive.

Some authors are concerned about the existence of a "speed barrier" when it comes to training with sprints. According to Ozolin (1978), athletes learn to run at certain speeds. This speed barrier is extremely difficult for the athlete to overcome. In order to do this, assisted sprints, resisted sprints, and varied-pace sprinting are used.

While these are fine training tools, which will be covered below, sprinting needs to be kept in perspective. If an athlete is not an elite track and field athlete, it's unlikely that they will reach this barrier as part of normal training. This means that the rest of the tools that will be described in this section may be unnecessary for the majority of athletes.

Assisted sprinting

Assisted sprinting allows the athlete to run faster than he or she is capable of. This allows for the body to learn how to run at greater stride frequencies, which will transfer over to non-assisted sprints. Assisted sprinting methods include being towed, downhill sprinting, and using a high-speed treadmill. Assisted sprinting has been linked to improvements in sprint times, stride frequency, and elastic energy production (Jakalski, 2000).

There are several cautions with assisted sprinting. First, athletes can become lazy and allow themselves to be pulled along. This is counterproductive as it means that the athlete is running at submaximal speeds, which defeats the purpose of the exercise. Second, athletes should not be achieving speeds greater than 106 to 110 percent of their maximum speed (Cissik and Barnes, 2010; Jakalski, 2000). This is because when their speed increases too much, athletes have a tendency to overstride, which results in them increasing their braking during sprinting. Third, good technique must be emphasized with assisted sprinting. Failing to do so teaches bad habits.

Resisted sprinting

Resisted sprinting applies a load to make the sprinting motion more difficult. This results in more motor units and muscle fibers being recruited, which could eventually carry over to non-resisted sprinting, resulting in a faster athlete. Resistance includes weighted sleds, tires, parachutes, running uphill, running in sand, etc.

Too much resistance alters running mechanics. If the resistance is too great, athletes have a tendency to do a number of things. First, they begin to lean forward. This means that they are unable to extend their hip completely, which limits the amount of force they can exert against the ground. Second, their stride length decreases. Third, the amount of time spent on the ground increases (Letzelter *et al.*, 1995; Lockie *et al.*, 2003).

With the above in mind, there are guidelines for resisted sprinting. First, the resistance should not slow the athlete down by more than 10 percent (Cissik, 2005; Jakalski, 2000; Lockie *et al.*, 2003). Second, resisted sprints should only be conducted over 15–20 meters (Coaching Education Committee, 2001). Too great a distance results in fatigue, which leads to a slow athlete with bad technique. Finally, proper technique must be emphasized to prevent bad habits.

Varied-pace sprinting

Varied-pace sprints have several changes in velocity during the sprint (Cissik, 2005). This type of training may be more sport-specific than other sprinting tools (ibid.). The most common form of varied-pace sprinting involves alternating between maximum-intensity runs and recharging phases. For example, after a 5–10-meter acceleration zone, the athlete may run at maximum intensity for ten meters, then coast for ten meters, then run at maximum intensity for ten meters, etc.

Chapter Seven will cover how to use all the above tools to enhance an athlete's running speed.

AGILITY TRAINING

Agility training is the closest that many strength and conditioning specialists come to movements that resemble those seen in many sports. It is an extremely challenging area for a strength and conditioning specialist because there is little research on agility training; it requires extensive knowledge of the sport and it relies on some neural factors that may not be trainable.

Training agility can be viewed as a progression of skills mastery. The three levels of skills in agility training are:

1   fundamental skills;
2   combination skills;
3   advanced skills.

Fundamental skills

Every sport has a list of fundamental movement skills that are specific to that sport. While each sport may have slightly different ones, the following is a list of movement skills that can be found in almost every sport:

■   starting;
■   stopping;
■   shuffling;
■   back-pedaling;
■   cutting;
■   running curves.

These skills were covered in detail in Chapter Two. Before beginning any agility-training program, it is important for the strength and conditioning professional to identify the fundamental skills and to begin developing those.

Combination skills

Once the fundamental skills have been mastered, it is time to make them faster and more complex. This is because movement skills do not exist in isolation in athletics' fast-paced and dynamic environment.

components of a training session

Increasing the speed and complexity of agility training is done gradually. First, this is done by having the athletes perform carefully choreographed drills that combine the fundamental skills. Gradually these drills become more complicated, begin to integrate the ball, and require the athlete to respond to a coach or opponent. Table 4.5 provides examples of beginning versions of drills that combine fundamental skills. Figure 4.1 provides an example of how to make these drills complicated. In this example, several skills are combined (starting, sprinting, shuffling, and turning).

Table 4.5 Sample beginning agility drills that combine skills

Drill	Set-up	Purpose	Execution	Coaching points
1	Set up three cones: one at the start, one at 5 meters, one at 15 meters.	Teach starting and stopping.	On command, sprint 5 meters. Stop. Immediately sprint to the 15-meter cone.	Explosive start. Drop the hips to stop. Explosive start. Run through the last cone.
2	Set up six cones: one at the start, one every 5 meters.	Teach sudden changes in direction.	On command, sprint forward two cones. Back-pedal 5 meters. Sprint forward two cones. Back-pedal 5 meters. Etc.	Explosive start. Drop the hips to stop. Keep the hips low during back-pedaling. Get close to the ground before sprinting forward. Run through the last cone.
3	Set up three cones: one at the start, one every 5 meters.	Teach back-pedaling and turning.	Back-pedal 5 meters. Turn around and sprint forward through the cone at 10 meters.	Keep the hips low during back-pedaling. Avoid crossing the feet when turning around. Start explosively.
4	Set up three cones: one at the start, one every 5 meters.	Teach shuffling and turning.	Shuffle to the right or to the left. At the 5-meter mark, turn and run to the right or left through the last cone.	Keep the hips low when shuffling. Keep the weight on the balls of the feet. When turning, pivot on the foot opposite the direction of the turn. Avoid crossing the feet. Start explosively.
5	Set up three cones in the shape of an upside-down "L": one at the start, one 5 meters away, one 5 meters to the right or left.	Teach running curves and sprinting.	Sprint to the first cone. Turn around the first cone and run to the right or the left.	Start explosively. Drop the inside shoulder when turning around the cone. Start explosively in the new direction. Run through the last cone.

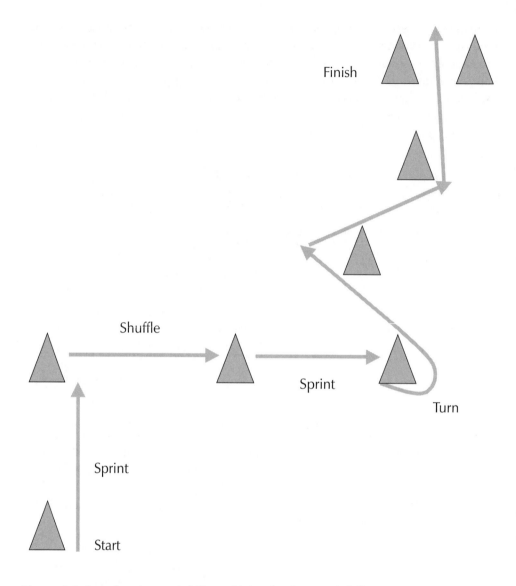

Figure 4.1 Sample advanced drill combining fundamental skills.

Advanced skills

Fundamental and combination skills have the advantage of breaking down movements into manageable segments. The challenge with these approaches is that the athletes tend to become good at the drills, but this may not translate to athletics. Once the skills have been mastered, it is time to progress to advanced drills that force the athlete to react to a stimulus in unplanned ways. This could include the ball, an opponent, or the coach. Table 4.6 provides some example of advanced drills that require the athlete to react in unplanned ways.

Table 4.6 Sample advanced-agility drills that are reactive in nature

Drill	Set-up	Execution
6	Two cones are set up 5 meters apart. An imaginary line is drawn between the cones. Two athletes line up, facing each other on opposite sides of the imaginary line.	One athlete is the offense, one is the defense. When the drill begins, the offense shuffles to the right or left. The defense attempts to stay in front of the offense at all times. The athletes must stay on their side of the line. The athletes must stay in between the cones.
7	The athletes line up facing the coach. The coach is 20 meters away from the athletes.	The athletes must respond immediately to the coach's commands. If the coach commands "Run," the athletes sprint towards the coach. If the coach commands "Go Back," the athletes back-pedal. If the coach waves the athletes to the sides, they shuffle. Etc.
8	Two 5 × 5 meter boxes are set up with cones. Two athletes will each line up in their box as shown in Figure 4.2.	Each athlete will remain in their box throughout the drill. Athlete A is the leader. When the drill begins, Athlete A will move within his/her box. Athlete B will attempt to mimic Athlete A's movements and will remain in front of Athlete A at all times.

PLYOMETRICS

Plyometrics are characterized by a rapid stretch followed by an immediate explosive contraction. This contraction (following the rapid stretch) generates more force than if the stretch had not been there (Makaruk and Sacewicz, 2010). This is thought to be from the storage of *elastic energy* in the tendon and elastic components of the muscle.

Plyometrics are used to improve jumping ability, explosive power, and to help prevent injuries. Female athletes, especially in basketball and volleyball, are many times more

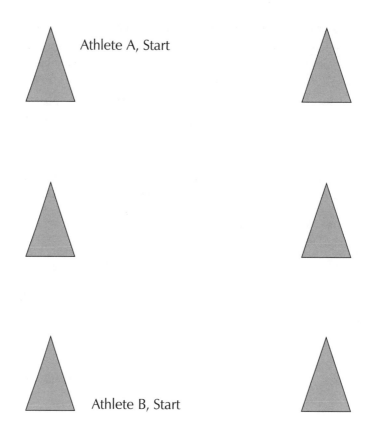

Figure 4.2 Set-up for drill #8.

likely to suffer ACL injuries. Landing mechanics and hamstring strength are thought to be causes of this phenomenon. Done properly, plyometrics can help address those issues (Chapell and Limpisvasti, 2008).

A great deal of research shows that plyometrics are effective at improving jumping, rate of force development, and power. However, the information on how best to design plyometrics programming is non-existent (Ebben et al., 2008). A meta-analysis by De Villarreal et al. (2009) showed that there is a positive correlation between frequency of training, length of a training program, the number of repetitions performed, and the gains in vertical jump. Research seems to indicate that plyometrics are more effective for advanced athletes (ibid.). This should make sense as more advanced athletes will be closer to their genetic limits in terms of strength and muscle size and will require more specialized methods to make gains from training.

Coaches and athletes should take care with plyometrics. First, they require a technique base. It is important to go through the progressions covered in this section. Second, their gains are specific to how they are performed. Third, plyometrics have an effect similar to intense eccentric exercise. This means that performance is reduced for 24–72 hours post-training, delayed onset muscle soreness is present for 24–72 hours post-training, cortisol is elevated post-training, and there is an immune system response after training (Chatzinikolaou et al., 2010).

There are two broad categories of plyometrics exercises. Within each category are a series of progressive steps. Note that all exercises may not be applicable to all sports and all positions. The categories are: single-effort jumps and multiple-response jumps.

Single-effort jumps

Single-effort jumps involve a single, maximal effort to execute the jump. They may be done vertically, in which case the athlete focuses on the height of the jump and lands where they began. They may be done horizontally, in which case the athlete focuses on the length of the jump and lands a distance away from where they began. Single-effort jumps have several progressions:

- double-leg;
- single-leg;
- with resistance;
- depth jumps.

Double-leg jumps

These jumps are performed off two feet and involve landing on two feet. Table 4.7 provides descriptions of vertical double-leg jumps, Table 4.8 provides descriptions of horizontal double-leg jumps. These jumps are designed around the idea of a gradual escalation in terms of complexity. First, athletes learn how to perform the basic jump (squat jump or standing long jump) and how to land safely. Then the exercises become more complicated and more difficult. As the athletes master each exercise they are able to move to the next progression if the sport and their position warrants.

Single-leg jumps

After the athlete has mastered the double-leg jumps, if appropriate the athlete can progress to single-leg jumps. There are two progressions for performing jumps with one leg at a time:

Table 4.7 Sample vertical double-leg single-effort jumps

Exercise	Description	Level
Squat jump	Feet hip-width apart. Hands behind head. Squat into a quarter-squat. Pause. Without a counter-movement, jump as high as possible.	Beginner
Counter-movement jump	Feet hip-width apart. Arms at side. Quick quarter-squat. As you squat, swing the arms back hard. Without pausing, jump as high as possible.	Intermediate
Tuck jump	Feet hip-width apart. Arms at side. Quick quarter-squat. As you squat, swing the arms back hard. Without pausing, jump as high as possible As you leave the ground, bring the knees to the chest and grab them.	Intermediate
Pike jump	Feet hip-width apart. Arms at side. Quick quarter-squat. As you squat, swing the arms back hard. Without pausing, jump as high as possible As you leave the ground, keep your legs straight and bring them up in front of you.	Advanced
Depth jump	Stand on top of box. Feet hip-width apart. Arms at side. Step off box. Land in a quarter-squat. Upon landing, immediately reverse directions and jump as high as possible.	Advanced

■ Jump off one leg, land on both. Performing single-leg jumps takes a great deal of strength. Initially, athletes may not have the lower-body strength to land safely on one leg. As a result, the initial progression is to jump off one leg and land on both.
■ Jump off one leg, land on one leg.

Add resistance

Especially with squat jumps and counter-movement jumps, external resistance can be added to increase the training effect. This can take the form of barbells, dumbbells, or

110

Table 4.8 Sample horizontal double-leg, single-effort jumps

Exercise	Description	Level
Standing long jump	Feet are hip-width apart. Perform a fast quarter-squat. As the squat is performed, drive the arms back hard. Without pausing, launch self forward attempting to jump as far forward as possible.	Beginner
Cone jump	Performed like the standing long jump, only it is done over a cone. The cone can be adjusted to get the athlete to jump further. Adds a vertical element to the horizontal.	Intermediate
Box jump (1)	Performed like the standing long jump, only it is done over a box. The box height can be adjusted and the box can be positioned further away.	Intermediate
Hurdle jump	Performed like the standing long jump, only it is done over a hurdle. The hurdle height can be adjusted and can be positioned further.	Advanced
Box jump (2)	Performed by jumping onto a box. The box height can be adjusted and the box can be positioned further away.	Advanced

other forms of resistance. The theory is that having to overcome external resistance explosively will make the athlete more explosive on the field.

Extreme caution needs to be used if this is selected. Several things should be considered carefully. First, the athlete needs a solid technique base before adding resistance. Second, the athlete needs an adequate strength base before adding resistance. Third, too much resistance will be counterproductive. It will teach the athlete to move slowly and to use bad technique. Finally, with all the cautions that have been mentioned, this training tool should only be implemented if the athlete is no longer responding to other approaches.

Depth jumps

Depth jumps are described in Table 4.6 and are the most advanced version of plyometrics and should only be attempted by athletes with consistent, reliable technique. In addition, athletes need to be strong enough to perform depth jumps. A common recommendation is that athletes should be able to squat 1.5 to 2 times body weight prior to engaging in depth jumps, but this recommendation has no research to support it.

Multiple-response jumps

Multiple-response jumps involve jumping horizontally and vertically, just like single-response jumps. The difference is that the jump is repetitive in nature (i.e. each jump is not an all-out effort) and the athlete is meant to get off the ground as quickly and explosively as possible. Depending upon the event and the position, the progression for multiple-response jumps is:

- double-leg;
- single-leg;
- bounds;
- box jumps.

Double-leg jumps

These jumps are performed off two feet and involve landing on two feet. Table 4.9 provides descriptions of vertical double-leg jumps, Table 4.10 provides descriptions of horizontal double-leg jumps. As with the jumps described for single-effort jumps, the jumps progress in terms of difficulty. Keep in mind that not all jumps are important for all sports or positions.

Single-leg jumps

After the athlete has mastered the double-leg jumps, if appropriate the athlete can progress to single-leg jumps.

Bounds

Bounds involve jumping off one leg and landing on the other. They are meant to help train the sprinting motion, which means that, ideally, the bounds need to resemble sprinting technique in terms of leg mechanics and arm swing. They are normally done for distances of 30–100 meters. Prior to performing bounds, athletes need to have mastered sprinting technique.

Good technique must be reinforced with this exercise or the drill will only serve to develop and reinforce bad habits.

Table 4.9 Sample vertical double-leg, multiple-effort jumps

Exercise	Description	Level
Jump and reach	Feet hip-width apart. Arms at side. Quick quarter-squat. As you squat, swing the arms back hard. Without pausing, jump as high as possible reaching up with the right hand. Land, immediately jump again and reach up with the left hand. Repeat for the desired number of repetitions.	Intermediate
Tuck jump	Feet hip-width apart. Arms at side. Quick quarter-squat. As you squat, swing the arms back hard. Without pausing, jump as high as possible As you leave the ground, bring the knees to the chest and grab them. Land, immediately repeat for the desired number of repetitions.	Intermediate
Medicine ball jump and throw	Feet hip-width apart. Hold a medicine ball overhead. Quick quarter-squat. Without pausing, jump as high as possible. As you jump, throw the medicine ball straight up overhead. Catch the medicine ball as you land. Without pausing, repeat for the desired number of repetitions.	Advanced

Box jumps

Box jumps involve jumping onto or over a box. A number of things can be done to make this a multiple-response drill:

- Line up multiple boxes. Jump onto or over the boxes.
- Jump onto a box. Without pausing, jump backwards off the box. Repeat until the desired number of repetitions have been performed.
- Perform the above drills but jump sideways to the right or left.

Box heights can be changed to modify the level of difficulty. Several boxes can be lined up and these distances can be changed to make the exercises more challenging.

Athletes need a solid technique base before attempting multiple-response box jumps. These exercises will not be forgiving of technique mistakes.

Table 4.10 Sample horizontal double-leg, multiple-effort jumps

Exercise	Description	Level
Ankle hops	Feet are hip-width apart and plantarflexed. Hands are on hips or behind the head. Primarily from the ankles, with minimal knee and hip movement, hop forward for the desired distance.	Intermediate
Hops	Feet are hip-width apart. Hands are at the sides. Without pausing, launch self forward attempting to jump as far forward as possible. Upon landing, immediately repeat for the desired number of repetitions.	
Hops over obstacles	Hops can be performed over cones or hurdles of different heights. This can increase the difficulty of the vertical component. By placing the obstacles further apart this can increase the difficulty of the horizontal component.	Advanced
Standing triple jump	Feet are hip-width apart. Perform a fast quarter-squat. As the squat is performed, drive the arms back hard. Without pausing, launch self forward attempting to jump as far forward as possible. Land on the right leg. Immediately jump off the right leg, attempting to launch self as far forward as possible. Land on the left leg. Immediately jump off the left leg, attempting to launch self as far forward as possible. Land on both feet.	Advanced

CONDITIONING

Conditioning refers to *metabolic conditioning*. It involves getting athletes into shape for the specific energy system demands of their sport and position. While strength training, plyometrics, sprinting, and agility training all help, they do not adequately duplicate the volume, work-to-rest intervals, and intensity of game situations.

Before designing a conditioning program, one must analyze the sport to get a sense of its specific demands. After that has been done, individual positions in the sport (if applicable) should be examined to determine if their demands are different.

For example, by analyzing a sport we may determine that the average play lasts eight seconds and has 30 seconds before the next play commences. We may find that there

components of a training session

is a range of four to 16 seconds that plays last, with a range of 14 to 34 seconds' recovery before the next play commences. There may be, on average, eight plays in a series with a range of one to 12 plays. This information begins to give us some direction in terms of the program-design variables for a conditioning program.

Analyzing specific positions on a team may reveal that they are only active for a small part of the play, or it may reveal that they are active longer than the average play. This also needs to be factored in.

There are several approaches to conditioning programs:

- sprint-based conditioning;
- circuit-based conditioning;
- strongman-based conditioning.

Sprint-based conditioning

This is one of the easiest approaches to take for conditioning. Distances to be run, recovery intervals, and the number of sprints can be determined by the needs of the sport and the position. Common approaches to sprint-based conditioning include:

- sprints for a given distance;
- sprints with a stepwise approach.

Sprints for a given distance

The idea here is to have athletes perform x number of sprints at y distance. This will often be based upon the average length of a play and the average recovery period. For example, using the above example the average length of the play is eight seconds with an average of 30 seconds before the next play. There are, on average, eight plays in a series. This would equate to the following sprint workout: 8 × 60 meters, 30 seconds recovery between each sprint

As laid out, this would take a little over five minutes to complete. This workout could then be repeated several times to stress the athlete. For example, have the athlete perform four to five sets of 8 × 60 meters, with 30 seconds recovery between each sprint and two to three minutes recovery between each set.

This approach to conditioning is easy to administer and the athletes understand what is expected of them. The drawbacks are that it does nor prepare athletes for extremes (for example, what if the play lasts longer than eight seconds?), it is monotonous, and many athletes will save their energy for the end of the workout.

Sprints with a stepwise approach

The stepwise approach prepares for the range of what occurs in game situations. It differs from the given-distance approach in several ways:

- there is a variety of distances and recovery intervals;
- the athlete is not told what these ranges will be;
- athletes will be motivated to run the sprints quickly.

How is this accomplished? Based upon the game variables, the coach lays out a series of sprints that gradually escalate or de-escalate in terms of distance (i.e. length of the sprints either increases as the workout progresses or decreases as the workout progresses). The coach then decides on an optimal time that the sprints should be run in and develops a recovery period based upon that. None of this information is communicated to the athlete; in that sense this resembles real life where athletes don't know when the play will end. If the sprint is run in the optimal time, the athlete will have the recovery time to rest. If the athlete runs the sprint in a faster time than the optimal time, they have more recovery time. Running the sprint in a slower time than the optimal time will result in less recovery time. In other words, they have incentive to run the sprints quickly.

Using the example game variables (average play eight seconds, range of four to 16 seconds; average recovery of 30 seconds, range of 14 to 34 seconds; average number of plays/series of eight, with a range of one to 12), a conditioning program using this method might look like the workout outline below. A note about notation, 2 × 10 meter (5″, 15″) refers to two sprints of ten meters in length, with a five-second optimal sprint time and a 15-second recovery. In other words, 20 seconds after the sprint command is given, the athlete will be running the next sprint:

2 × 10-meter sprints (5″, 15″);
2 × 20-meter sprints (10″, 15″);
2 × 40-meter sprints (15″, 20″);
2 × 80-meter sprints (20″, 30″);
2 × 100-meter sprints (25″, 30″);
2 × 200-meter sprints (30″, 40″).

As written, the above workout would take 8.5 minutes. This could then be repeated as many times as necessary with several minutes of rest between sets.

Circuit-based conditioning

Sprinting doesn't have to be the only tool used for metabolic conditioning. It can be integrated with other exercise modes. Circuit-based conditioning can be designed to stress the appropriate work and rest intervals, but can be used to take a more total-body approach to conditioning. This serves to make the conditioning more challenging, can be more sport-specific, and can be more interesting for the athletes.

For example, using the same game variables as in the previous examples, a sample circuit-based conditioning program might look like the one that follows:

- sprint 60 meters, perform bodyweight squats for 30 seconds;
- sprint 60 meters, perform lunges for 30 seconds;
- sprint 60 meters, perform inchworms for 30 seconds;
- sprint 60 meters, perform burpees for 30 seconds;
- sprint 60 meters, perform push-ups for 30 seconds;
- sprint 60 meters, perform dips for 30 seconds;
- sprint 60 meters, perform pull-ups for 30 seconds;
- sprint 60 meters, perform crunches for 30 seconds.

As written, this circuit would take approximately five minutes and could be repeated as many times as necessary. The 60-meter sprint would take about eight seconds (which would cover the average time of a play) and the 30 seconds of exercise would cover the average recovery period.

This approach has the advantage of being more challenging for the athlete than a simple sprint followed by a walking or standing recovery. The difficulty with this approach is to be able to program for the possible range of game variables. This could be done by each set of the circuit having a different sprinting distance and exercise time. For example:

- set one, sprint for 60 meters then exercise for 30 seconds on each station;
- set two, sprint for 20 meters then exercise for 40 seconds on each station;
- set three, sprint for 80 meters then exercise for 20 seconds on each station.

Strongman-based conditioning

Strongman training has grown very popular in recent years, not only because of its popularity on television but also because it is applicable to athletics. Basing conditioning around these types of movements can have a great deal of transfer to sports that involve physical contact with large athletes, especially ice hockey, rugby, and American football.

Strongman training does have drawbacks. If it is being done with a team of athletes then it requires a great deal of equipment. If it is done improperly it can result in injury.

Using the game variables from our sample above, a strongman-based conditioning program might appear as follows:

- tire flip for ten meters, sprint 60 meters;
- wheelbarrow for ten meters, sprint 60 meters;
- medicine ball forward toss, sprint to ball, toss again, for 30 seconds, sprint 60 meters;

- farmer's walk for ten meters, sprint 60 meters;
- sandbag clean and press for 30 seconds, sprint 60 meters;
- one-handed kettlebell snatch for 30 seconds, sprint for 60 meters;
- grab sandbag, sprint ten meters, set it down, sprint back, repeat for 30 seconds, sprint 60 meters;
- medicine ball wood-choppers for 30 seconds, sprint 60 meters.

As written, this circuit would take approximately five minutes and could be repeated as many times as necessary. The 60-meter sprint would take about eight seconds (which would cover the average time of a play) and the 30 seconds of exercise would cover the average recovery period.

THE COOL-DOWN

The cool-down provides a transition between the training session and rest. It typically consists of one or more of the following types of activities that were not present in the main workout:

- Injury prevention exercises. The cool-down is a good time to address low-intensity exercises that are meant to help prevent injuries.
- Low-intensity cardiovascular exercise. Several minutes of low-intensity cardiovascular exercise can help to circulate and remove metabolic waste products from exercise and can have a calming effect. For example, Dolgener and Morien (1993) studied the effects of passive recovery, massage recovery, and low-intensity bicycle recovery after a maximal treadmill run. They found that after 20 minutes of recovery the bicycle-recovery group had 55 percent less lactate than three minutes post-exercise (this was compared to 22 percent less for the passive group and 26 percent less for the massage group).
- Static stretching. The cool-down is a good location for the inclusion of static stretching. All the major muscles/joints that have been trained can be addressed via static stretching during the cool-down without interfering with performance.

RECOVERY

A number of classic coaching texts recommend the use of recovery methods for the athlete after training sessions and after competitions (Bompa, 1999, Harre, 1982, Kurz, 1991, Matveyev, 1981). A lack of recovery between sessions and competition results in an athlete being unable to train at the desired level could increase the athlete's risks of injury and could decrease the athlete's performance (Barnett, 2006).

Research on recovery methods is limited and conflicting (Bishop *et al.*, 2008). Few

studies use athletes as subjects (Higgins *et al.*, 2010). This is problematic because athletes may have a different genetic makeup, a different training history, and may respond to training and recovery differently than non-athletes (Barnett, 2006). Research has largely focused on the following recovery methods: active recovery, massage, and cold/contrast baths.

Active recovery

Active recovery involves performing low-intensity aerobic exercise after the training session or competition, the idea being that the active recovery may increase blood flow resulting in enhanced repair of tissues and enhanced clearance of metabolic byproducts. There has been little research support for this recovery mode (Tessitore *et al.*, 2007). In fact, Barnett (2006) suggests that this method might actually be detrimental to recovery glycogen resynthesis.

Massage

In theory, massage reduces soreness, increases blood flow, and increases blood lactate removal (Barnett, 2006; Dolgener and Morien, 1993; Howatson *et al.*, 2005). Research does not support the beneficial effects of massage on recovery (ibid., ibid., ibid.).

Cold/contrast baths

Cold-water immersion is done to reduce inflammation and to reduce soreness. Cold-water immersion by itself has been found to be beneficial to perceived pain levels (Vaile *et al.*, 2007) but it has also been found to be detrimental to performance variables (Higgins *et al.*, 2010; Vaile *et al.*, 2007). Contrast baths involve alternating between cold-water immersion and hot water (either immersion or showers). There is also no research to support this practice.

There is a need for a great deal more research on the use of recovery methods.

KEY READINGS

Cissik, J.M. (2004) Means and methods of speed training, part I, *Strength and Conditioning Journal*, 26(4): 24–29.

Cissik, J.M. (2005) Means and methods of speed training, part II, *Strength and Conditioning Journal*, 27(1): 18–25.

Both of these articles by Cissik review the coaching and scientific literature for speed training. Covered in these articles is the science behind speed training, techniques, drills, progressions, a literature review on training tools, and sample programs.

Chu, D.A. (1998) *Jumping into Plyometrics*, 2nd edn, Human Kinetics, Champaign, IL.

Radcliffe, J.C. and Farentinos, R.C. (1999) *High-powered Plyometrics*, Human Kinetics, Champaign, IL.

These two books are the reference books for plyometrics and helped to popularize this exercise mode. Both have a scientific foundation for plyometrics and both have extensive drills, exercises, and programs. When reading these books, it needs to be kept in mind that the scientific foundation does not extend into the actual exercises, progressions, and volume/intensity recommendations. As this chapter covered, there is no research foundation for things like strength levels and plyometrics, volume, intensity, rest, etc.

CHAPTER FIVE

PRINCIPLES OF TRAINING

There are a number of fundamental principles of exercise that must be applied to ensure that a strength and conditioning program is safe and effective. This chapter will cover four principles and how to apply them: specificity of training, overload, progression, and exercise order.

OUTLINE

Specificity of training

- Muscles and movements
- Energy systems
- Speed of movement

Overload

- Increasing the resistance
- Increasing the volume
- Manipulating the rest/recovery
- Modifying the exercises

Progression

Exercise order

Examples

Key readings

SPECIFICITY OF TRAINING

The principle of specificity states that the body adapts to exercise according to how it is exercised. In other words, one gets what one trains for. Specificity applies to the following:

■ muscles and movements;
■ energy systems;
■ speed of movement.

Muscles and movements

Those muscles and movements that are trained adapt to exercise; those that are not trained will not adapt. For example, performing the leg press does not help to improve one's bench press. In order to apply specificity to muscles and movements, consider the following questions:

1 What muscles are involved in the movement to be trained?
2 Do these muscles have a primary role or a supportive one?
3 Is the activity to be trained performed standing, sitting, or lying down?
4 Is it performed on one leg, on both legs, or does this change throughout the activity?
5 Does the activity involve twisting or rotation?

Based upon the answer to the above questions, one can begin to select exercises to address the muscles and movements that one wants to train. Table 5.1 provides an example of using these questions to analyze the bench press exercise. In this example, an athlete wants to improve how much they can bench press one time. The table shows us that the bench press is performed lying down, it uses the pectoralis major, triceps brachii, and anterior deltoids to press the barbell. However, it also requires the latissimus dorsi and posterior deltoids to lower the barbell under control.

Energy systems

Those energy systems that are trained will adapt as a result of exercise; those that are not trained will not adapt. Exercise needs to be designed to address those energy systems that contribute to the event to be trained. Questions to consider are:

■ How long does the event last?
■ Of that time, how much is spent in activity?
■ What is the work to rest ratio of the activity?

Table 5.1 Sample muscle/movement specificity analysis for the bench press exercise

Question	Analysis
Muscles involved?	Pectoralis major, anterior deltoid, triceps (pressing) Latissimus dorsi, posterior deltoids (descent) Medial deltoids
Primary muscles?	Pectoralis major, anterior deltoid, posterior deltoid, triceps, latissimus dorsi
Stabilizing muscles?	Medial deltoids
Standing, sitting, lying?	Lying
One leg, both?	Not applicable
Twisting, rotation?	Not applicable

Using the answers to the questions above, one can design the program around training the specific energy systems involved. For example, in American football, the game lasts 60 minutes. On the surface this would seem to indicate that the sport requires aerobic fitness. However, when it is broken down, the average play only lasts around five seconds with 30–45 seconds between each play, which means that the primary energy system contributor to success is the phosphagen energy system with some contribution from anaerobic glycolysis.

Speed of movement

The adaptations from exercise are believed to be specific to the velocities at which those exercises are performed. This is known as *velocity specificity*. Velocity specificity is the concept that resistance training performed at a specific speed increases strength at that speed, but not necessarily at other speeds (Behm and Sale, 1993; Morrissey *et al.*, 2000). This concept is the foundation behind exercise selection in many strength and conditioning programs. For example, it is part of the rationale behind the inclusion of plyometrics and variations of the Olympic lifts.

According to Behm and Sale (1993), in their review of the subject, the majority of research has documented the existence of a velocity-specific effect with strength training. This is a controversial statement because there are conflicting results in the research (Cronin *et al.*, 2001; Kanehisa and Miyashita, 1983). According to Young (2006), the transfer of strength training might depend upon the level of the athlete. It is very possible that there is better transfer of strength training for beginners than for elite athletes.

There are concerns that there is a lack of research relating training velocity to the velocity seen in sport-specific tasks and with the fact that many of the studies on this topic use isokinetic modes of strength training, which are not modes of strength training used in most athletic populations.

One of the classic studies that examined this concept was done by Kanehisa and Miyashita (1983). This study had three groups of subjects perform knee extensions at different velocities, six times per week for eight weeks. Each group had a completely different loading scheme:

- Group S (Slow): Three sets of ten repetitions at 1.05 radians/second;
- Group I (Intermediate): Three sets of 30 repetitions at 3.14 radians/second;
- Group F (Fast): Three sets of 50 repetitions at 5.24 radians/second.

The intent was to ensure that each group spent the same amount of time performing the exercise.

At the conclusion of eight weeks of training, subjects were tested on their power production at different testing velocities. Group S experienced the greatest gains at slow speeds, Group F actually lost strength on the slow speeds. The interesting result is that Group F did not make the best gains at fast speeds; it was Group I that did that. In other words, the data in this study would seem to argue against the concept of velocity specificity as it applies to high velocities.

A study published by Cronin et al. (2001) indicates the challenges with strength training and sport-specific velocities. The authors investigated two groups of female netball players. Each group performed a similar four weeks of strength training to get into shape. They were then split into two groups for six weeks of specialized training:

- Strength group: three sets of six repetitions at 80% of 1-RM;
- Power group: three sets of eight repetitions at 60% of 1-RM.

In order to harness transfer to the sport task, the athletes were asked to perform 20 netball passes after each set of strength training.

Athletes were evaluated on the netball chest pass, bench-press throw, and a 25 kg bench press for reps. After the intervention, strength and power increased on everything but there was no difference between the groups. The concern in this study is that even when attempting to move the bar quickly, the bar velocity only ranged from .308 to .398 meters/second, compared to 11.38 meters/second for the netball pass. In other words, even explosive strength training is unable to achieve the velocities seen in the sport that brings the concept of velocity specificity into question.

This is an area that needs more research. Does velocity specificity exist? Is it possible to achieve using general modes of training like strength training? If it is not possible to achieve with strength training, is it more important that the athlete attempt to move as explosively as possible in the weight room? Does velocity specificity only apply to certain populations?

OVERLOAD

The overload principle states that because the body adapts to exercise, one must find a way to make exercise more difficult in order to keep the body adapting. There are a number of ways to apply the overload principle in a strength and conditioning program:

- increase the resistance;
- increase the volume;
- manipulate the rest/recovery;
- modify the exercises.

Increasing the resistance

By increasing the resistance, one stimulates the body to continue adapting to the exercise. There are some cautions with this approach, however. First, it cannot continue indefinitely. Every athlete has a genetic limitation on their strength, which means that the resistance cannot be increased indefinitely over time. Eventually the athlete is going to begin to approach their limits. Second, the risk/reward ratio changes over time. To a certain point, increasing strength is going to increase performance. Beyond that point, the return that additional strength provides is not going to be worth the amount of time, energy, and injury risks associated with gaining that additional strength. Third, specificity has to be observed in terms of speed of movement and energy-system emphasis. If training focuses too much on extremely heavy weights lifted at slow speeds, this may be detrimental to certain athletic events due to the lack of specificity.

Increasing the volume

Performing more work will force the body to continue adapting to the program. This can be done by performing more repetitions, adding more sets, or even adding more exercises. For example, if an athlete performed three sets of eight reps today (i.e. 24 total reps), having them do 25 reps on the next session will increase the difficulty level of the program.

This is a good tool to a point; however, several things should be considered when using this approach. First, the athlete doesn't have unlimited time to train. Increasing the volume increases the amount of time that the workout will take. While this is warranted on occasion, training time needs to be maximized. Second, specificity needs to be observed with regards to energy systems. Increasing the volume will rapidly change the energy systems that contribute to the exercise. For example, there is a big difference between performing sets of two and sets of 20 in terms of the energy system primarily being taxed. Third, volume that is too great is ineffective in training for hypertrophy, strength, and power. Too great a volume on exercises that are supposed to be explosive will fatigue athletes and train them to be sloppy and slow.

Manipulating the rest/recovery

Changing the rest in between each set or the amount of recovery time between training sessions will change the training stimulus. There are several ways that this can be accomplished:

- Change the rest between sets. Changing the amount of rest between each set influences how much weight can be lifted and how many repetitions can be performed. By reducing the rest, less work can be done. By increasing the rest, more work can be done. Either approach can make the exercise more difficult and will cause the body to adapt. Care must be taken with this approach in that specificity with regards to energy systems must be observed.
- Combine exercises. Exercises can be performed in a manner where the athlete alternates between them without resting. In bodybuilding literature this is called a *superset*. This allows for more work to be done in a given period of time.
- Change the recovery between training session. Changing the recovery time between exercise sessions will influence how difficult the sessions are. By speeding up the recovery time between sessions (i.e. performing them more frequently) this means that the body has less time to recover. To an extent, this will cause the body to adapt, but there is a fine line that must be observed when taking this approach as it may lead to overtraining and injury.

Modifying the exercises

There are a number of exercises that, essentially, do the same thing: they have very similar movement patterns, train the same muscle groups, have similar velocities, etc. This means that the exercises that an athlete uses can be changed regularly, which will keep the overall program challenging for the athlete while observing specificity. For example, the following exercises could be performed instead of the back squat: pause back squats, eccentric back squats, front squats, pause front squats, eccentric front squats, split squats, pause split squats, eccentric split squats, any of the already mentioned squat variations with bands or chains. Substituting any of those exercises will keep the muscles of the lower body trained in a manner similar to the back squat.

principles of training

This approach does have disadvantages. First, new exercises have to be learned. Second, if the original exercise is not being performed, the athlete will lose strength on that exercise. Third, athletes are creatures of habit and may not be comfortable with changing exercises on a regular basis.

PROGRESSION

The principle of progression states that exercise needs to be approached as a series of steps, with each step building on the one that came before. This should be observed in terms of exercise techniques and fitness. Following this principle allows the athlete to get the maximum benefit from an exercise and prevents injuries.

For example, athletes need a strength and landing technique base prior to performing depth jumps. This is developed over time through a combination of exercises to increase lower-body strength and progressing through lower-intensity vertical jumps before getting to depth jumps. Figure 5.1 shows a sample progression to get an athlete to the point of being able to perform depth jumps. The athlete begins performing both comprehensive strength training and plyometric training. The strength training is designed to strengthen both the athlete's lower body and their ability to move explosively. Over time, the athlete's strength levels will increase. The plyometrics moves through a progression of exercises designed to teach the athlete how to jump, how to land, and how to react to the ground. Eventually, both these paths culminate in the athlete being ready to perform depth jumps.

EXERCISE ORDER

There are broad guidelines on how to organize strength and conditioning training sessions to allow them to maximize their effectiveness. There are always exceptions, but in general the following guidelines should be observed:

- Exercises requiring speed and power should be performed first. These types of exercises require good technique and fast velocities. Fatigue interferes with both and teaches bad habits. For this reason these exercises should be performed first.
- Complex, multi-joint movements should be performed next. Exercises that require coordination between many muscle groups and precise techniques should be performed towards the beginning of the session before fatigue interferes.
- Larger muscle groups before smaller. The performance of the larger muscle groups (e.g. the pectoralis) is often limited by the strength and endurance of smaller muscle groups (e.g. the triceps). For this reason larger muscle groups should be trained before smaller ones.
- "Isolation" exercises should be performed last. Exercises that seek to isolate a muscle group should generally be performed towards the end of a training session.

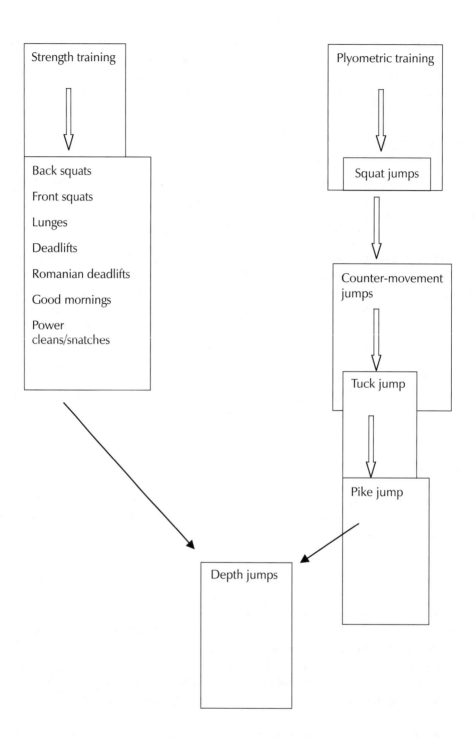

Figure 5.1 Applying progression to the depth jump.

principles of training

For example, an athlete will perform the following exercises in a training session: calf raises, Romanian deadlifts, back squats, and power snatches. Since the power snatch requires speed and technique, it should be done first. The back squat is a multi-joint exercise with technical requirements; it trains the hip/knee flexors and hip/knee extensors, so it should be performed second. The Romanian deadlift is a multi-joint exercise, but it focuses on only the hip extensors so it should be trained third. Calf raises seek to isolate the plantarflexors, which are important for all the above exercises. For this reason they should be performed last.

Figure 5.2 provides a chart for how to apply the exercise order principle to strength training assuming that the entire body is being trained in one session. Total-body exercises would be performed first, followed by the lower body (as those are the largest muscles in the body), followed by multi-joint, upper-body exercises, then "isolation" upper-body exercises.

EXAMPLES

This part of the chapter is going to provide two examples of applying the above principles. The first example will deal with an athlete wanting to improve their functional upper-body strength in terms of pull-ups and dips. The second example will deal with an athlete that wants to improve their vertical jump.

Example 1: Functional upper-body strength

Our sample athlete wants to improve their ability to perform pull-ups and dips. Currently, the athlete is unable to perform either exercise correctly. The principles of specificity, overload, progression, and exercise order can all be applied to this situation.

Specificity

The pull-up involves the muscles of the upper back, posterior deltoid, and biceps and involves lifting the athelte's bodyweight against gravity. The dip involves the muscles of the chest, anterior deltoids, and triceps and also involves lifting the athlete's body weight against gravity. Both are endurance tasks (i.e. perform as many repetitions as possible), which will primarily stress the glycolytic energy system. Speed of movement isn't really a factor with these exercises. Both exercises involve a very specific movement pattern that is very difficult to duplicate without performing the exercises themselves.

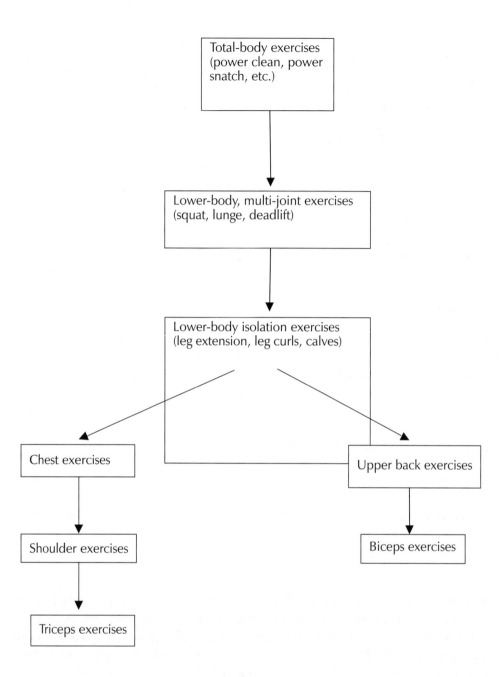

Figure 5.2 Chart for organizing strength-training workouts geared towards hypertrophy.

principles of training

Overload

Because the pull-up and dip are specific movement patterns, a way must be found to allow the athlete to train those movement patterns and make this more challenging over time. In the beginning, the athlete will be performing eccentric versions of both the pull-ups and dips. This will be done by having the athlete get assistance to get into the top position, then taking as long as possible to lower themselves. In this way, the athlete is able to train the movement and train the muscles in a movement-specific way, and this can gradually be made more difficult as the athlete is able to take longer to lower themselves.

At the same time, other strength-training and body-weight exercises will be selected that train the appropriate muscles and energy system. Because the focus is on training the glycolytic energy system, repetitions will be moderate to high with little rest. These exercises will become heavier and more repetitions will be performed as the athlete progresses.

Progression

The ultimate goal is for the athlete to be able to perform pull-ups and dips. Initially, the athlete will be performing eccentric versions of the lifts. As the athlete becomes stronger, they will attempt to perform a pull-up and dip while still training with the eccentric versions and supplemental exercises. Once the athlete can do one pull-up and dip, each training session will begin with the athlete performing as many as they can followed by the eccentric versions and the supplemental exercises. When the athlete can correctly perform ten or more pull-ups and dips, the eccentric versions will be dropped from the routine.

Exercise order

As the focus is on the pull-up and dip, these will be performed first. This will be followed by eccentric versions. The eccentric versions will be followed by multi-joint exercises for the upper body (such as pull-downs, bench presses, etc.). Finally, any isolation work will be done.

Table 5.2 shows a sample 12-week program incorporating the above information. Notice that the workouts address the movement patterns and muscles involved in performing pull-ups and dips. As the weeks progress, the volume of pull-ups/dips increases as the volume of eccentric work decreases. The workouts also gradually become heavier over the 12 weeks.

Table 5.2 Sample 12-week program for pull-ups and dips

	Week 1	Week 4	Week 8	Week 12
Pull-up workout	Eccentric pull-ups, 5 × max Lat pulldowns, 3 × 12–15 Bent-over rows, 3 × 12–15 Rear deltoid raises, 3 × 12–15 Biceps curls, 3 × 12–15	Pull-ups, 1 × max Eccentric pull-ups, 5 × max Lat pulldowns, 3 × 8–12 Bent-over rows, 3 × 8–12 Rear deltoid raises, 3 × 8–12 Biceps curls, 3 × 8–12	Pull-ups, 3 × max Eccentric pull-ups, 5 × max Lat pulldowns, 3 × 6–10 Bent-over rows, 3 × 6–10 Rear deltoid raises, 3 × 8–12 Biceps curls, 3 × 8–12	Pull-ups, 5 × max Eccentric pull-ups, 3 × max Lat pulldowns, 3 × 6–10 Bent-over rows, 3 × 6–10 Rear deltoid raises, 3 × 6–10 Biceps curls, 3 × 6–10
Dip workout	Eccentric dips, 5 × max Bench press, 3 × 12–15 Military press, 3 × 12–15 Between bench dips, 3 × max Triceps push-downs, 3 × 12–15	Dips, 1 × max Eccentric dips, 5 × max Bench press, 3 × 8–12 Military press, 3 × 8–12 Between bench dips with weight, 3 × 8–12 Triceps pushdowns, 3 × 8–12	Dips, 3 × max Eccentric dips, 5 × max Bench press, 3 × 6–10 Military press, 3 × 6–10 Between bench dips with weight, 3 × 6–10 Triceps pushdowns, 3 × 8–12	Dips, 5 × max Eccentric dips, 3 × max Bench press, 3 × 6–10 Military press, 3 × 6–10 Between bench dips with weight, 3 × 6–10 Triceps pushdowns, 3 × 8–12

Example 2: Vertical jump

This sample athlete wants to improve their vertical jump. Again, the principles of specificity, overload, progression, and exercise order can all be applied to this situation.

Specificity

The vertical jump involves the athlete leaping as high as possible. This involves the lower-body muscles as well as the arms (a vigorous arm swing helps performance on the vertical jump). It is performed using a fast squat immediately followed by a fast triple extension of the hips, knees, and ankles.

Overload

A combination of slow strength training (for example, back squats), Olympic lifts, and plyometrics will be used to train the vertical jump. The weights on strength-training exercises will gradually be increased to make the athlete stronger and more explosive while the volume of plyometrics can be increased to directly train the vertical jump.

Progression

Exercises will be used to teach the athlete first how to jump and land without coordinating arm movement. Then arm movement will be incorporated as the athlete becomes more consistent in their technique. At the same time, the Olympic lifts will be introduced and will gradually become more complex as the athlete moves through the program.

Exercise order

In the strength-training sessions, the Olympic lifts will be performed first. These will be followed by multi-joint exercises such as squats. Then any isolation exercises (such as calf raises) will be performed last.

Table 5.3 provides a sample 12-week program for improving the athlete's vertical jump. The strength-training workouts gradually integrate the power clean while the intensity of the workouts increases over the 12-week period (along with a drop in volume). The plyometrics gradually incorporate the counter-movement jump exercise and then carefully increase the volume of the plyometrics across the 12-weeks.

KEY READINGS

Behm, D.G. and Sale, D.G. (1993) Velocity specificity of resistance training, *Sports Medicine*, 15(6): 374–388.

While almost 20 years old, this is an important paper because it reviewed the state of the knowledge regarding strength training and velocity specificity. While work has been done on this subject subsequently, this is still a highly quoted and referenced paper.

Cronin, J., McNair, P.J. and Marshall, R.N. (2001) Velocity specificity, combination training and sport specific tasks, *Journal of Science and Medicine in Sport*, 4(2): 168–178.

This is an important, though little-known, study that reinforces the fact that true velocity specificity can never be achieved through strength training. Even explosive strength training does not approach the velocities seen in athletics.

Table 5.3 Sample 12-week vertical-jump program

	Week 1	*Week 4*	*Week 8*	*Week 12*
Strength training	Clean pulls, h, AK, 3 × 4	Power clean, h, AK, 3 × 4	Power clean, h, AK, 3 × 4 × 60%	Power clean, h, AK, 3 × 4 × 70%
	Back squats, 3 × 12–15	Clean pulls, h, AK, 3 × 4	Clean pulls, h, AK, 3 × 4 × 70%	Clean pulls, h, AK, 3 × 4 × 80%
	Romanian dead-lifts, 3 × 12–15	Back squats, 3 × 8–12 × 80%	Back squats, 3 × 6–10 × 85%	Back squats, 3 × 4–8 × 90%
	Calf raises, 3 × 12–15	Romanian deadlifts, 3 × 8–12	Romanian deadlifts, 3 × 6–10	Romanian deadlifts, 3 × 4–8
		Calf raises, 3 × 8–12	Calf raises, 3 × 6–10	Calf raises, 3 × 4–8
Plyo-metrics	Ankle hops, 3 × 10 meters	Ankle hops, 3 × 10 meters	Ankle hops, 3 × 10 meters	Ankle hops, 3 × 10 meters
	Squat jumps, 3 × 10	Squat jumps, 3 × 10	Squat jumps, 3 × 10	Squat jumps, 3 × 10
		Counter-movement jumps, 3 × 5	Counter-movement jumps, 3 × 10	Counter-movement jumps, 4 × 10

Kanehisa, H. and Miyashita, M. (1983) Specificity of velocity in strength training, *European Journal of Applied Physiology*, 52: 104–106.

Kanehisa and Miyashita's 1983 paper is one of the most quoted studies with regards to velocity specificity and strength training. This is another of the most misinterpreted studies in strength and conditioning and is also a flawed study. Reading this study is important to see what the results actually were as well as to get a sense of the limitations of the methods.

CHAPTER SIX

NEEDS ANALYSIS

The *needs analysis* refers to the process of analyzing the sport and the position that the athlete plays to determine how a strength and conditioning program should be focused to best prepare athletes to be successful. Once that analysis has been done, it is followed by assessing how well the athlete is prepared for the sport. An important process, the needs analysis forms the foundation of a good strength and conditioning program.

OUTLINE

Needs of the sport

- Motions/muscles involved
- Energy systems involved
- Speed of movement
- Injury patterns
- Models of the sport
- Schedule of the sport

Needs of the position

Needs of the athlete

- Status
- Health
- Effectiveness of training programs

Examples

- 100-meter sprinter
- Basketball guard

Key readings

NEEDS OF THE SPORT

Before developing a strength and conditioning program, it is important to consider carefully what is essential to improving performance in the sport. When examining the needs of the sport, it is important to develop a program around the following:

- motions/muscles involved;
- energy systems involved;
- speed of movement;
- injury patterns;
- models of the sport;
- the schedule of the sport.

Motions/muscles involved

The movements involved in playing the sport should be considered to determine if these movements are trainable or if the muscles involved are trainable. To consider this, ask the following questions:

- Is the sport played from trainable positions?
- Is the athlete standing, lying, or sitting in the sport?
- Is the sport performed on one leg or both?
- Does the sport involve twisting, throwing, or kicking across the midline of the body?

Understanding this information allows for exercises to be selected that have the best chance of transferring results to the sport. For example, sports that involve kicking, throwing, and most of the jumping events in track and field require the athlete to lever off one side of the body. This suggests that these sports would benefit from one-legged lifts and split variations of the Olympic lifts. Other sports involve moving out of the athletic stance, such as offensive and defensive line in American football. These would benefit more from exercises like back squats and deadlifts that involve exerting force against the ground from a similar stance.

Energy systems involved

The ability of the body to supply energy can be a limiting factor in performance. To analyze this, ask the following:

- How long does the sport last? For some sports this is a relevant question; for others the answer is deceptive. A 100-meter sprint lasts 10–12 seconds, which helps us to develop energy system-specific conditioning. However, an American football game has four quarters, each lasting 15 minutes. In theory that's 60 minutes of playing time, which is deceptive because of the next question.

- Is the entire team playing the entire time the sport lasts? In some sports, the athletes participate during the entire time that the sport lasts. In others, there are player substitutions, offensive players, defensive players, etc., so that not every player is active during the entire game.
- When the athletes play, how long does a play last?
- What is the nature of the athletes' involvement in each play? Does the athlete walk, jog, sprint, perform a variety of movements?
- How much rest is in between plays?
- What is the nature of the rest in between plays? What is the athlete doing between each play?

Understanding which energy systems are involved in performing the sport will allow for strength training, speed training, agility training, and conditioning to be put together to have the most impact on the athlete's performance. If, for example, the average play in an American football game lasts four to five seconds, with 20–30 seconds recovery, then sprints and conditioning drills can be put together to mimic these work–rest ratios, allowing the athlete to be optimally conditioned to meet the metabolic needs of the sport.

Speed of movement

In theory, the outcome of most athletic contests hinge on a handful of explosive movements. This might be the goal, but it is not always the reality as it is not possible to be explosive throughout an entire athletic event. With this in mind, there are a number of things to evaluate with regards to speed of movement:

- What is the nature of the explosive movement(s) in the sport? Jumping? Vertically or horizontally? Sprinting? Throwing? etc.
- What are the kinematic/kinetic characteristics of the event? In other words, the rate of force development, velocity of movement, power production, etc.
- When there is no explosive movement, what is the athlete doing?

While this seems self-evident, this is something that many overlook when designing strength and conditioning programs. Every sport is going to have different needs with regards to speed of movement. For example, volleyball players are not going to have the same sprinting and agility needs as a basketball player. A 200-meter sprinter has different needs compared to a baseball first baseman, etc.

Injury patterns

Different sports have injuries that are common to the sport. For example, hockey players suffer groin injuries, runners/sprinters suffer hamstring and shin injuries, baseball players suffer shoulder and elbow injuries, etc. Understanding this can allow for a strength and conditioning program to be designed to help prevent these injuries. Questions to consider are:

- Are there injuries common to the sport? If so, what are they?
- Are the injuries a result of contact?
- If the injuries are not a result of contact, what causes them?

Not all injuries can be prevented. Injuries from contact cannot be prevented from a strength and conditioning program. It is not even clear if fitness can minimize the effects of a contact injury. However, a proactive strength and conditioning program could have an impact on non-contact injuries, such as sprains, strains, stress fractures, shin splints, etc. By understanding what injuries are common to a sport, some of these can be prevented or minimized.

Models of the sport

Some sports lend themselves to statistical models. These are largely individual sports that can easily be quantified such as weightlifting, sprinting, jumping, swimming, throwing in athletics, etc. In these cases, a statistical model can be put together that allows a coach to compare the performance of their athletes to it in order to determine if there are areas where the athlete is deficient. Other sports have a great deal of information on how athletes experience the sport. For example, there is great research on how athletes move during the sports of basketball and soccer, how much time and distance is spent on each movement pattern, and the intensity of those movement patterns. Combined with information on the energy-system requirements, this can be a powerful tool in the design of a strength and conditioning program.

Schedule of the sport

A strength and conditioning program should be focused on peaking athletes for competition. This means that the competition schedule must be factored in during the needs analysis. Understanding this information will allow for a program to be designed that maximizes that athlete's success in competition.

Questions to consider are:

- What time of year do the competitions occur?

needs analysis

- How long is the competitive season?
- Are there days of the week when the competitions commonly occur?
- How many competitions are there, typically, in a week?
- Are all of the competitions equally important?

There are sports where an athlete competes infrequently, which makes every competition extremely important. For example, at time of writing, professional American football only has a 16-game season. In contrast, other sports compete several times a week, which makes the importance of each game less important (e.g., professional baseball has a 162 game season).

In some sports, competitions occur, generally, on the same day of the week. When that is the case, the athlete can be conditioned year-round around this schedule. In other sports this is not the case; the schedule is more random and this will need to be factored into a program.

NEEDS OF THE POSITION

With individual sports, the analysis of the sport is sufficient. With team sports, a deeper level of analysis needs to be performed as different positions have different roles and this may influence their strength and conditioning program. For example, in American football the center, kicker, and quarterback all have different functions, and conditioning needs to be adjusted accordingly. In the sport of soccer, the goalkeepers, defenders, midfielders, and forwards all have different roles and this impacts how they experience the game. Midfielders, who link the defense to the offense, tend to cover the greatest distance during the game and cover the greatest distance at high intensities. Forwards, who are responsible for most of the team's scoring, cover greater distances (and greater distances at higher intensities) than defenders but less than midfielders. Defenders, who mainly focus on stopping the opponent's attack, cover the shortest total distances and cover the lowest distances at higher intensities. All of this goes to reinforce the need to recognize that different positions are going to have different strength and conditioning needs.

Many of the same factors need to be considered with regards to the needs of the position:

- motions/muscles involved;
- energy systems involved;
- speed of movement;
- injury patterns;
- is a model available?

NEEDS OF THE ATHLETE

Once we have analyzed the sport and (if applicable) the position, it's time to apply this knowledge to the athlete. The information that we have learned about the sport and position determine what qualities we want the athlete to develop as a result of the strength and conditioning program. This can be divided into the following areas:

- status;
- health;
- effectiveness.

Status

Status refers to where the athlete is, relative to those qualities that are important for successful performance. This is evaluated in terms of:

- Fitness. Athletic fitness is evaluated in terms of speed, agility, power, strength, and conditioning. Where is the athlete compared to where he/she *should* be for optimal performance? The analysis that has been performed on the sport and the position dictates what specific assessments will be used for each fitness quality.
- Technique. Technique is evaluated in terms of how the athlete's sport-/position-specific technique compares to the ideal.
- Performance. This refers to the athlete's current status. Is the athlete performing at a high level? Is the athlete meeting expectations? If not, why?

Health

Health refers to the health of the athlete. Questions to consider include:

- Is the athlete injured?
- If so, what is injured?
- Can this be trained around?
- Can training be modified around the injury?
- Can the cause of the injury be addressed?

Effectiveness of training programs

Until now, the needs analysis has focused on what qualities are necessary for success in a sport/position and determining where the athlete is, relative to those qualities. One thing that needs to be factored in is that every athlete is a unique individual and will respond to training differently. With this in mind, the effectiveness of the training program should be evaluated on an ongoing basis. Questions to consider are:

- Is the athlete's performance improving as it should?
- Is this performance improvement carrying over to the event? Is the athlete playing better? If not, is this a result of the strength and conditioning program or due to another reason?
- Is the athlete staying healthy? If the athlete is injured, is this related to the strength and conditioning program?
- Is the athlete motivated to train? If the athlete is not motivated to train, he or she may be experiencing overtraining and burnout.
- Is the athlete peaking when he/she is supposed to? If not, what needs to be adjusted?

EXAMPLES

Example 1: 100-meter sprinter

In the 100-meter sprint, the athlete must react to the starting gun, get out of the starting blocks quickly, accelerate maximally, attain a high maximal velocity, and maintain it for as long as possible. The muscles of the lower body are heavily involved in performance of the sprint.

In terms of motion, there are instances where one side of the body exerts more force than the other. For example, when leaving the starting blocks, the rear leg exerts 61 percent of the force that the front leg does (Coh et al., 2009). This, combined with the sprinting motion described in Chapter Two, indicates that in a great part of the race, one leg at a time is exerting force.

The event lasts 10–13 seconds depending upon the level of competition, which suggests that it will be fueled primarily by the phosphagen and glycolytic energy systems.

Speed of movement is very fast, with the entire race lasting 10–12 seconds. Athletes may attain velocities of over 11 meters/second (Mackala, 2007).

The 100-meter sprint can be divided into the following phases (Letzelter, 2006):

- Reaction to the starting gun. The period from when the gun is fired until the rear foot is lifted off the blocks. This should range from 0.12–0.18 seconds (Schmolinsky, 1996).
- Block clearance. The period from when the rear leg is lifted until the front leg leaves the blocks.
- Acceleration. The time from when the front leg leaves the blocks until maximal velocity is achieved. Faster sprinters have a longer acceleration phase (Letzelter, 2006; Mackala, 2007). Elite sprinters may not reach maximal velocity until the 80-meter mark (Coh et al., 2007; Mackala, 2007).

- Maximal velocity. This period refers to the time that the athlete can maintain his or her maximal velocity. This phase tends to be shorter for faster sprinters because they spend a longer time accelerating.
- Deceleration. This is the period of time where velocity decreases during the end of the sprint.

Hamstring and shin injuries are common for sprinters. These are due to a combination of faulty running mechanics, a lack of conditioning, and increasing the volume at a rate faster than the athlete can tolerate.

In U.S. collegiate track and field, there are two competition seasons, one indoor and one outdoor. The indoor season begins in January and runs into March; the outdoor season picks up in March and can run into July, depending upon the level of ability of the athlete. Competitions occur primarily on the weekend and the athlete will run multiple sprints throughout a competition.

Our hypothetical athlete is a male collegiate sprinter who has entered college running the 100-meter sprint in the 11-second range. Figure 6.1 shows the splits of the athlete's best 100-meter sprint, where he finished in 11.18 seconds. The athlete's time is compared against the model of a sprinter completing the race in ten seconds. We can see that the sample athlete starts the sprint very strong, getting out of the starting blocks ahead of the model and staying ahead of the model until the fortieth meter, at which point the athlete falls progressively further behind the model.

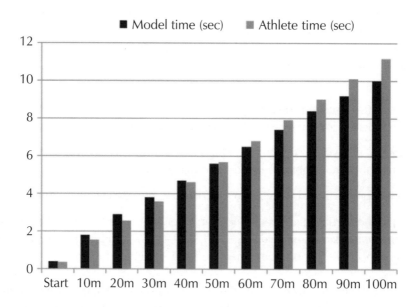

Figure 6.1 Sample time splits for a model ten-second 100-meter sprint (black) compared with a sample athlete (grey). (Model adapted from Kuznyetsov et al. 1983).

needs analysis

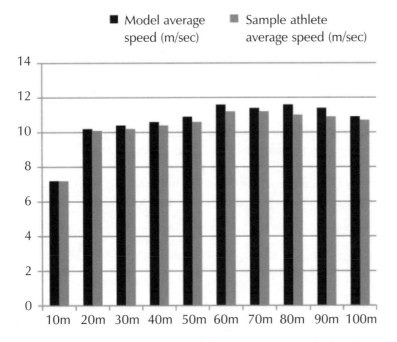

Figure 6.2 Velocities for a ten-second 100-meter sprinter (black) compared to a sample athlete (grey). (Model from Kuznyetsov, *et al.* 1983).

Figure 6.2 shows a breakdown of the athlete's average velocity at each of the ten-meter splits, compared to the model. This figure shows that the athlete falls behind the model due to the fact that he/she is not achieving the running velocities necessary to run a ten-second sprint. The athlete is only achieving a peak velocity of around 11 meters/second, compared to the model's 11.6.

The sample athlete responds well to training. He is currently back-squatting 220 percent of body weight, power cleaning 115 percent of body weight, and has a standing long jump of 300 centimeters. He has a history of hamstring injuries, particularly late in the off-season when more of the maximal velocity work is performed.

From the above information we can determine a number of things about this athlete:

- He has the strength and explosiveness to be successful in the 100-meter sprint.
- He is getting out of the starting blocks very explosively. If he can put together the rest of the race, this will give him a huge advantage.
- He accelerates fine through the first ten meters. Again, if the rest of the race can be put together, this will give him an advantage over his competition.

- He is not achieving a high-enough maximal velocity to run a fast 100-meter sprint.
- The fact that he has the physical qualities to be successful at the sprint indicates that something else is limiting performance. The history of hamstring injuries that appears to be tied with increasing the volume of maximal velocity work seems to indicate that the athlete's running mechanics may be contributing to his injuries and his lack of performance.

From the above, a strength and conditioning program is going to need to support the track program. This means maintaining strength and explosiveness while focusing on hamstring exercises in the off-season to prepare the athlete for maximal-velocity sprinting. This should be done via the warm-up, hip-extension exercises in the strength training, and even eccentric work (eccentric squats, eccentric hip extension exercises, etc.).

Example 2: Basketball guard

Basketball is a total-body sport. It is characterized by running, walking, standing, and shuffling at varied speeds and by jumping (Table 6.1 provides an overview of movement patterns during a series of basketball games for Tunisian national-caliber players). While it may not have been intended to be a contact sport, there is contact between players in basketball and this is a source of injury (Borowski et al., 2008; Deitch et al., 2006; Dick et al., 2007). According to Abdelkrim et al. (2010a), the average sprint/stride in a basketball game covers 12–21 meters and lasts less than two seconds.

Table 6.1 Movement patterns during a basketball game

Activity	Speed of movement	Total distance covered	Percentage of time spent in activity
Standing	0	0	32%
Walking	≤ 6 km/h	1,720 meters	31%
Jogging	6.1–12 km/h	1,870 meters	5.6%
Running	12.1–18 km/h	928 meters	4.5%
Sprinting	>24 km/h	763 meters	2.8%
Striding	18.1–24 km/h	406 meters	2.4%
Low-intensity shuffling	≤ 6 km/h	606 meters	8.5%
Moderate-intensity shuffling	6.1–9 kh/h	691 meters	6.5%
High-intensity shuffling	>9 km/h	169 meters	3.1%
Sideways running	>12 km/h	218 meters	1.9%
Jumping	0	0	1.7%

Source: Adapted from Abdelkrim et al. 2010a

needs analysis

International basketball is played with four ten-minute periods (i.e. 40 minutes of basketball). Not every player is active during the entire game. In addition, the activity level is inconsistent during a game. According to Abdelkrim et al. (2010a), there is a 1:3.6 work–rest ratio for basketball, with each six seconds of high-intensity activity resulting in approximately 22 seconds of low-intensity activity. Table 6.1 shows that the intensity of the activities can be broken down as follows:

- high intensity (>18 km/hour): 10.17 percent of the time;
- moderate intensity (6.1–18 km/hour):18.01 percent of the time;
- low intensity (≤ 6 km/hour): 71.82 percent of the time.

In other words, basketball is characterized by bursts of high intensity interspersed with jogging, walking, or standing. This calls for conditioning both the phosphagen and the glycolytic energy systems.

From the breakdown of movement patterns in Table 6.1, one can see the need for fast sprints (>24 km/hour) and jumping vertically, both of which are fast and explosive movements. With each sprint lasting less than two seconds, there is a need to focus on the skill of acceleration.

Across all playing levels, ankle and knee injuries are the most common injuries in basketball (Borowski et al., 2008; Deitch et al., 2006; Dick et al., 2007). These injuries are largely ligament sprains and muscle/tendon strains.

Euroleague basketball is characterized by a ten-game season from mid-October to mid-December, then playoffs from mid-January until May.

In terms of physical attributes, the guard position is the most athletic of the basketball positions. The guard prepares offensive situations through ball control, assists, turnovers, passing, steals, and three-point field goals (Jelicic et al., 2010; Sampaio et al., 2006).

Table 6.2 shows an ideal model for a guard based upon the amalgamation of a number of research studies. Guards tend to be faster, stronger in terms of lifting their body weight, and jump higher than forwards and centers. Compared with the ideal is a sample athlete playing the guard position for a Euroleague basketball team.

The sample athlete is tall enough to play the guard position, but is heavier and has more body fat than is ideal. He has a high vertical jump and great strength, but is a very slow sprinter and is not very agile. The athlete is having a number of challenges with his basketball performance:

- The athlete is a great three-point field goal shooter, but is not able to contribute to the offense in terms of steals and assists.
- The athlete is getting fatigued after the first period of play and his accuracy in three-point field goals declines after the first period.

Table 6.2 Model basketball guard and sample player

Variable	Model	Sample player
Height (cm)	189.5	189
Weight (kg)	84.5	92.9
Body fat (%)	9	12
Vertical jump (cm)	61	62
5m-sprint (s)	1	1.2
10m-sprint (s)	1.9	2.2
40m-sprint (s)	4.1	5
T test (s)	9.3	11.2
Bench press (% of body weight)	1.1	1.2
Back squat (% of body weight)	2	2.3

Source: Adapted from Abdelkrim *et al.* 2010b, Berg and Latin 1995; Ostojic *et al.* 2006.

▪ The athlete is plagued by non-contact ankle injuries. Over the last three years the athlete has had more than ten days lost to lateral ankle sprains in each of the last three seasons. The injuries occur either in training camp or in the first five games of the season and then plague the athlete throughout the season.

Based upon the knowledge of the guard position and the characteristics of the athlete, it appears that the athlete's weight is an issue. While the athlete is very strong, his size may be contributing to his ankle injuries and to his slow speed. In addition, the athlete lacks metabolic conditioning for the game of basketball. All of this contributes to his challenges with assists and steals. This information would lead to the development of a strength and conditioning program that maintains speed and explosiveness, but that focuses heavily on sprinting and metabolic conditioning.

KEY READINGS

Cissik, J.M. (2001) You need a needs analysis, *Track Coach*, 155: 4952–4.

This is the only article that the author is aware of that details the process of conducting a needs analysis. Geared towards track and field, but can be adapted to other sports.

Kuznyetsov, V.V., Petrovskiy, V. and Schustin, B.N. (1983) The model for sprinters, in Jarver, J. (ed.) *Sprints and Relays*, 2nd edn. Mountain View, CA: TAFNEWS Press: 30–31.

Though dated, this article provides a statistical model for 100-meter sprint performance broken down by ten-meter splits. Included in the article is velocity at each split as well as time. Performances have changed since this was first published, but it still serves as a good reference for an aspiring coach to show trends in sprinting performance during the race.

Abdelkrim, N.B., Castagna, C., Jabri, I., Battikh, T., El Fazaa, S. and El Ati, J. (2010a) Activity profile and physiological requirements of junior elite basketball players in relation to aerobic-anaerobic fitness, *Journal of Strength and Conditioning Research*, 24(9): 2330–42.

An important article for anyone working with basketball players. While the subject pool is limited, it provides a strong analysis of what is going on during a basketball game. The methods outlined in the paper can be adapted to other situations and other sports.

CHAPTER SEVEN

PROGRAM DESIGN

Strength and conditioning programs can have varied goals using many different modes of exercise. These goals may range from simple, using only one mode of exercise, to a desire to develop multiple qualities, which requires the balancing of several modes of exercise. This chapter will cover how to train for various goals and how to integrate all this information into a larger program.

OUTLINE

Training for hypertrophy

- Variables
- Program design

Training for strength

Training for power

- Strength-training exercises
- Plyometrics

Training for speed

- Sprinting program focus
- Program design

Training for agility

Putting it all together

Key readings

TRAINING FOR HYPERTROPHY

Hypertrophy refers to an increase in the size of the muscle fibers. When training begins, hypertrophy seems to be governed by an increase in protein synthesis rates. As it progresses, it is governed by an increase in the RNA content in the muscle fibers mediated by satellite cells. This is an important distinction because many studies examine untrained individuals over the short term (eight to 12 weeks). During this time-frame, almost everything works to increase hypertrophy. Some studies, in fact, report significant hypertrophy after only 20 days of training (Seynnes *et al.*, 2007).

Variables

Several variables impact hypertrophy:

- satellite cells;
- exercises;
- volume, intensity, rest, frequency.

Satellite cells

Satellite cells provide the additional nuclei that generate long-term hypertrophy (Adams, 2006). They seem to be a limiting factor to hypertrophy. Petrella *et al.* (2008) studied the impact of satellite cells on responding to 16 weeks of strength training. They divided their subjects into three groups based upon their response to the training program: non-responders, moderate responders, and extreme responders. After 16 weeks of training, the non-responders had, essentially, no change in satellite cells, the moderate group increased the population of satellite cells by almost 50 percent whereas the extreme group increased the population of satellite cells by almost 200 percent. Accompanying this change, the moderate group increased the number of myonuclei per fiber by almost 9 percent while the extreme increased by 26 percent (no change for non-responders). Mean fiber area increased by almost 75 percent for the extreme responders, 20 percent for the moderate responders, and did not increase at all for the non-responders. All of this goes to suggest that satellite cells are going to be a limiting factor to an athlete's ability to undergo hypertrophy. According to Adams (2006) there is a threshold stimulus for satellite cell activation. This is an important statement because it would explain why many training protocols work with untrained subjects over the first eight to 12 weeks of training but more intensity is going to be needed for working with trained athletes.

Exercises

Exercises involving larger muscle groups produce the greatest hormonal responses to training. Recall from Chapter One that the hormonal response is important for driving hypertrophy. This means that the bulk of the exercises in a hypertrophy training program should be multi-joint exercises.

Volume, intensity, rest, frequency

Volume refers to the quantity of work done, in other words the number of repetitions multiplied by the number of sets. In theory, increasing the volume increases the overload. However, as volume is increased, the amount of resistance that can be lifted decreases, meaning that at a certain point there may not be enough stimulus to elicit a hypertrophy response.

Intensity refers to the quality of the work done and is usually expressed as a percentage of one-repetition maximum. As with volume, there is a fine balance that must be struck with intensity. An intensity that is too high means that very few repetitions can be performed, which may limit the hypertrophic effect. An intensity that is too low allows for many repetitions but may not be stimulating enough to force the muscles to respond.

Rest refers to the amount of rest in-between each set. Longer rest periods allow for a greater intensity.

Frequency refers to how often one trains each week. In theory, training more frequently would provide a stronger stimulus to the muscles, though a balance must be struck so that the muscles are not trained so frequently that they cannot recover.

When it comes to making recommendations about these training variables, a distinction needs to be drawn between untrained individuals and trained athletes. A number of studies look at the various training variables but focus on untrained individuals. These studies recommend training for between three to five sets per exercise, more than three sets per muscle, seven to 15 reps/set, at 60–85 percent of 1-RM, with anywhere between 30 seconds' and five minutes' rest between each set and two to four sessions/week (Ahtianen *et al.*, 2005; Bird *et al.*, 2005; Buresh *et al.*, 2009; de Souza *et al.*, 2010; Goto *et al.*, 2004; Holm *et al.*, 2008; Kreiger, 2010; Wernbom *et al.*, 2007; Wilborn *et al.*, 2009).

The challenge with the above studies is that many use untrained subjects, use strength-training protocols that are not accessible to athletes (e.g., isokinetic equipment), and are for a short duration. Athletes have a longer training background, which means that they are not going to respond the same to a program that an untrained subject uses. In fact, there may be a completely different hypertrophy mechanism for untrained compared to athletic populations, especially given the importance of satellite cells for longer-term adaptations.

With the differences in mind, a number of key coaching publications have recommendations for hypertrophy training and athletes (Matveyev, 1981; Medvedyev, 1989; Plisk, 2001; Zatsiorsky, 1995). These publications recommend three to six sets per exercise, five to 12 repetitions/set, 60–90 percent of 1-RM, and one to four minutes rest between each set.

Program design

When designing training programs geared towards hypertrophy, there are two general approaches to a training program:

- Total-body workouts. Total-body workouts train the entire body in each session. This is a great approach for beginnings or for the early off-season. The challenge is that it can become difficult to train everything with the desired intensity, especially as athletes become stronger. Table 7.1 provides a sample week of this type of training.
- Split-body workouts. With split-body workouts, the body is split into different workouts for training. Examples are to use a push/pull/leg approach (see Table 7.2): pushing muscles – chest, shoulders, triceps become one workout; pulling muscles – back, biceps become another workout, and legs become the third workout; upper-body/lower-body approach; or even to split the workouts even smaller (shoulders, biceps, etc.). When hypertrophy is the goal, one needs to be careful with the splits as everything should be trained twice a week. Making the workouts too restrictive in terms of the muscles to be trained will limit how frequently muscles can be trained each week and the threshold stimulus might not be applied.

Table 7.1 Sample total-body hypertrophy workouts. Notation is # of sets × # of reps/set × intensity (% refers to percentage of 1-RM; 10–12-RM refers to failing at 10–12 repetitions)

	Monday	Wednesday	Friday
Workouts:	Back squats, 5 × 8–12 × 70–80%	Leg press, 5 × 10–12-RM	Front squats, 3 × 5–7 × 70–80%
	Good mornings, 3 × 10–12	Deadlifts, 3 × 5-7 × 70–80%	Romanian deadlifts, 3 × 8–12-RM
	Bench press, 5 × 8–12 × 70–80%	Incline press, 3 × 10–12-RM	Dumbbell bench press, 3 × 10–12-RM
	Bent-over rows, 3 × 10–12-RM	Pull-ups, 3 × 10–12-RM	Dumbbell rows, 3 × 10–12-RM
	Standing military press, 3 × 10–12-RM	Dumbbell shoulder press, 3 × 10–12-RM	Seated military press, 3 × 10–12-RM

Table 7.2 Sample split-body hypertrophy workouts

	Monday (Push)	Tuesday (Pull)	Wednesday (Legs)	Thursday (Push)	Friday (Pull)	Saturday (Legs)
Workouts:	Bench press, 5 × 8–12 × 70–80% Dumbbell incline press, 5 × 10–12-RM Seated military press, 3 × 10–12-RM Lateral raises, 3 × 10–12 Triceps pushdowns, 3 × 10–12-RM	Pull-ups, 5 × 10–12-RM Bent-over rows, 5 × 10–12-RM Barbell curls, 3 × 10–12-RM Dumbbell curls, 3 × 10–12-RM	Back squats, 5 × 8–12 × 70–80% Leg press, 3 × 10–12-RM Leg extensions, 3 × 10–12-RM Romanian deadlifts, 3 × 10–12-RM Calf raises, 5 × 10–12-RM	Incline press, 3 × 10–12-RM Dumbbell bench press, 3 × 10–12-RM Dips, 3 × 10–12-RM 3-in-1 Shoulders, 3 × 10–12-RM each Triceps extensions, 3 × 10–12-RM	Dumbbell rows, 3 × 10–12-RM Pull downs, 3 × 10–12-RM Seated rows, 3 × 10–12-RM Dumbbell curls, 3 × 10–12-RM	Front squats, 3 × 5–7 × 70–80% Lunges, 3 × 10–12-RM Good mornings, 3 × 10–12-RM Back raises, 3 × 10–12-RM Calf raises, 5 × 10–12-RM

TRAINING FOR STRENGTH

Maximal strength is the ability to exert force. It is important for performance in many sports and even influences power output (Cronin *et al.*, 2000). A number of factors influence strength. These include:

- Muscle cross-sectional area. Larger muscles have the ability to exert more force than smaller ones.
- Percentage of fast-twitch muscle fibers. Fast-twitch muscle fibers are larger, generate more force, and do so more rapidly than slow-twitch.
- Muscle-fiber pennation angle. Muscle fibers with a larger angle of pennation can generate more force. This is achieved through hypertrophy-oriented strength training, which reinforces the need for this type of training to develop a foundation for future strength.
- Ability to recruit muscle fibers. The greater the number of muscle fibers that are recruited, the more force the muscle can exert.
- Technique. Good technique on exercises means that an athlete is more efficient at performing the exercise, allowing them to lift more weight.

program design

To train for strength, one needs to lift heavier weights than when training for hypertrophy. This has a number of effects on training variables. Because the weight is heavier, fewer repetitions per set can be performed. Because the weight is heavier, it requires more rest between each set. When training for strength, most authors recommend performing three to eight sets an exercise, for one to six repetitions per set, at a resistance greater than 80 percent of 1-RM, with 1.5 to eight minutes of rest between each set (Bompa, 1999; Dick, 2002; Kurz, 1991; Lawton et al., 2004; Medvedev, 1989; Plisk, 2001; Tan, 1999).

As with hypertrophy training, there are several approaches to organizing training for strength:

- Total-body workouts. This approach is appropriate for beginners, but it is difficult to maintain the desired intensity with more advanced athletes. Table 7.3 provides a sample total-body workout with a strength focus.

Table 7.3 Sample total-body strength workouts

	Day 1	Day 2	Day 3
Workouts:	Back squats, 5 × 6 × 90%	Bench press, 5 × 6 × 90%	Leg press, 3 × 4–8-RM
	Romanian deadlifts, 5 × 4–8-RM	Seated rows, 5 × 4–8-RM	Back raises, 3 × 4–8-RM
	Dumbbell bench press, 3 × 4–8-RM	Standing military press, 5 × 4–8-RM	Incline press, 3 × 2–6-RM
	Bent-over rows, 3 × 4–8-RM	Front squats, 3 × 4–8-RM	Dumbbell rows, 3 × 2–6-RM
	Seated military press, 3 × 4–8-RM	Good mornings, 3 × 4–8-RM	Dumbbell shoulder press, 3 × 4–8-RM

- Split-body workouts. This approach is usually organized around pushing, pulling, and lower-body training. Usually, each type of workout is trained twice per week. This is time-consuming, but it produces better results for advanced athletes than the total-body approach. Table 7.4 provides a sample split-body workout with a strength focus.
- Training a specific lift. It is not unusual to focus a training session around addressing a single lift, for example the back squat. The exercises selected for the workout would address either components of the lift or address its weak points. Table 7.5 provides a sample workout focusing on the back-squat (days 1 and 4), bench press (days 2 and 5), and deadlift (day 3).

Table 7.4 Sample split-body strength workouts

	Day 1 (Push)	Day 2 (Pull)	Day 3 (Lower body)	Day 4 (Push)	Day 5 (Pull)	Day 6 (Lower body)
Workouts:	Bench press, 5 × 6 × 90% Incline press, 3 × 4–8-RM Dips, 3 × 4–8-RM Standing military press, 3 × 4–8-RM	Bent-over rows, 5 × 4–8-RM Pull-ups, 3 × 4–8-RM Seated rows, 3 × 4–8-RM Barbell curls, 3 × 4–8-RM	Back squats, 5 × 6 × 90% Leg press, 3 × 4–8-RM Lunges, 3 × 4–8-RM Lying leg curls, 3 × 4–8-RM Calf raises, 5 × 4–8-RM	Dumbbell bench press, 3 × 2–6-RM Dumbbell incline press, 3 × 4–8-RM Seated military press, 3 × 2–6-RM Close-grip bench press, 3 × 4–8-RM	Lat pull-downs, 5 × 4–8-RM Dumbbell rows, 3 × 2–6-RM Pull-ups, 3 × 2–6-RM Dumbbell curls, 3 × 4–8-RM	Front squats, 3 × 2–6 × 90% Leg press, 5 × 2–6-RM Romanian deadlifts, 3 × 4–8-RM Good mornings, 3 × 4–8-RM Calf raises, 3 × 2–6-RM

Table 7.5 Sample strength workouts focused on specific lifts

	Day 1 (Back squat)	Day 2 (Bench press)	Day 3 (Deadlift)	Day 4 (Back squat)	Day 5 (Bench press)
Workouts:	Back squats, 5 × 2–6 × 85–95% Pause back squats, 3 × 4–8 × 80–85% Walk-outs, 3 × 2–6 × 110–120% Calf raises, 3 × 4–8-RM	Bench press, 5 × 2–6 × 85–90% Close-grip bench press, 3 × 4–8-RM Seated rows, 3 × 4–8-RM Dumbbell shoulder press, 3 × 4–8-RM	Deadlifts, 5 × 1–4 × 85–95% Partial deadlifts, 3 × 2–6 × 95–105% Back raises, 3 × 4–8-RM Deadlift holds, 3 × 1	Pause back squats, 5 × 2–6 × 85–95% Front squats, 3 × 2-6 × 80–90% Split squats, 3 × 8-RM Calf raises, 3 × 4–8-RM	Eccentric bench press, 5 × 2–6 × 85–95% Board bench press, 3 × 4–8 × 80–90% Bent-over Barbell rows, 3 × 4–8-RM Dumbbell front raises, 3 × 8-RM

TRAINING FOR POWER

Power is the ability to exert force quickly. According to Kawamori and Haff (2004), power depends upon a number of factors:

- The ability to recruit motor units. The more motor units that can be recruited, the more force the athlete will be able to generate quickly.

- The ability to synchronize the recruitment of motor units allows the athlete to generate more force quickly.
- Rate coding. The ability to recruit the larger fast-twitch muscle fibers gives an athlete the ability to generate more power.
- Percentage of fast-twitch muscle fibers. Fast-twitch muscle fibers generate more force and contract more quickly than slow-twitch fibers. Possessing a higher percentage of fast-twitch fibers presents an advantage with power.
- Cross-sectional area. Muscles with a larger cross-sectional area have the potential to exert more force.
- Maximal strength. Stronger athletes have greater power outputs and may respond more favorably to power training (Cormie et al., 2010a; Cormie et al., 2010c; Cronin et al., 2000).

Due to the importance of cross-sectional area and maximal strength, and their inter-relatedness, a number of authors recommend a progression in terms of training for power. First, athletes should focus on hypertrophy training to increase their cross-sectional area. Second, athletes develop maximal strength. Third, athletes focus on power training. The first phase develops cross-sectional area, the second phase uses that cross-sectional area and applies it to strength training, the third phase applies the strength to athletics by teaching the athlete how to exert force quickly (Kurz, 1991, Matveyev, 1981).

The primary tools used to train power include:

- Strength-training exercises;
- Plyometrics.

Strength-training exercises

Slow strength-training exercises (like the back squat and the bench press) can be used to improve power. Heavy resistance training on those exercises (80 percent of 1-RM and greater) could, theoretically, recruit fast-twitch motor units, thereby improving power. In fact, according to Kawamori and Haff, the intent to move fast (as opposed to actually moving fast) may be enough to increase the muscle's rate of force development. Several studies on non-athletic college students have found that heavy strength training does improve power (Cormie et al., 2010a; Cormie et al., 2010c).

Another approach with slower strength-training exercises is to lighten the load and perform the exercises more explosively. Kawamori and Haff (2004) recommend using intensities of 60–80 percent of 1-RM. Studies with both college-aged athletes and college student non-athletes confirm that this is an effective approach to improving power (Bauer et al., 1990; Cormie et al., 2007b).

The clean, snatch, jerk, and their variations require the athlete to generate a great deal of power to complete the lift successfully (see Chapter Two) and are also widely used to develop power in athletes. Studies examining the hang power clean and the power clean found that peak power occurred when lifting 80 percent of 1-RM, though there was no statistically significant difference in terms of peak power with 50–90 percent of 1-RM (Cormie et al., 2007b; Kilduff et al., 2007).

Plyometrics

Plyometrics were described in Chapter Four. Plyometrics are effective at improving power and jumping height (Boraczynski and Urniaz, 2008). The effectiveness of a plyometrics program may depend upon training status. Several studies that compare the effects of plyometrics with strength training on untrained college students show that both are equally effective at improving peak power (Bauer et al., 1990; Cormie et al., 2010a; Cormie et al., 2010c; Cormie et al., 2007a). However, when trained athletes are used the results are different, with plyometrics being more effective than strength training (Cormie et al., 2007a).

For athletes, the effectiveness of plyometrics may be increased by adding resistance to the eccentric phase of the exercise. Sheppard et al. (2008) had volleyball players hold weight plates while performing the eccentric part of jumps. The plates were dropped as the athletes switched to the concentric phases of the jumps. While this would take some practice, those athletes that added resistance to the eccentric phase increased their vertical jump height by 11 percent and increased their peak power by 20 percent after five weeks of training.

In addition to the above tools, there are two hybrid approaches that combine power-training tools:

- Contrast training. Contrast training refers to alternating between heavier and lighter loads with regards to strength training (Alves et al., 2010), the idea being that the heavier loads recruit motor units maximally; the lighter loads (which are performed explosively) take advantage of that enhanced recruitment. For example, alternating between sets of 90 percent of 1-RM and 60 percent of 1-RM on the back squat would be an example of contrast training.
- Complex training. Complex training refers to alternating between heavier strength training and similar plyometrics exercises on a set-for-set basis (Alves et al., 2010). For example, performing a set of heavy squats followed by a set of counter-movement jumps. This can be performed in either order (strength then plyos, plyos then strength) (Stone et al., 2008). As with contrast training, the idea is to maximally recruit the nervous system with the heavier training and to use that enhanced recruitment (called post-activiation potentiation) to improve performance on the

plyometrics exercises. Research on complex training is mixed. Studies looking at athletes find that it enhances power output (Baker, 2003; Kilduff et al., 2008), whereas studies looking at untrained college students find that it has no effect (Hrysomallis and Kidgell, 2001). When complex training is used, it is recommended that four to eight minutes of recovery be given between the heavy set and the plyometrics set (Comyns et al., 2006; Kilduff et al., 2008).

When it comes to program design to improve power, several things should be kept in mind:

▪ Beginners respond to almost anything. Almost any training mode will increase a beginner's power. This will not be the case with trained athletes.
▪ Maximal strength is important for power. It is important to possess maximal strength to be explosive, but it is also important to have maximal strength because stronger individuals respond more favorably to power training.
▪ Trained athletes may respond better to plyometrics and complex training.
▪ Power training should not be conducted under fatigued conditions. Fatigue reduces speed of movement, rate of force development, power production, force production, and technique, the combination of which teaches bad habits to athletes. This means that power training should be performed when an athlete is fresh. It also means that the focus of power training needs to be on quality movements as opposed to getting athletes tired. This translates into fewer repetitions per set, longer rests between sets, and fewer exercises in each training session.

TRAINING FOR SPEED

According to Cissik and Barnes (2010), several factors will influence an athlete's ability to run fast:

▪ Fast-twitch muscle fibers. Possessing a greater percentage of fast-twitch muscle fibers would give an athlete an ability to exert more force over a shorter period of time.
▪ Muscle-fiber length. Muscles with longer muscle fibers are able to shorten more quickly (Abe et al., 2000). It is unclear if this is trainable or if it is genetic.
▪ Muscle shape. Muscle cross-sectional area is important for force generation. However, cross-sectional area is not as important as the shape of the muscle. It appears that faster sprinters have greater muscle thickness in the upper portion of their thighs (Abe et al., 1999; Kumagai et al., 2000). It is unclear if this is trainable or if it is genetic.
▪ Pennation angle. Muscle fibers with a smaller pennation angle are able to shorten more quickly (Abe et al., 2000). Strength training can increase the pennation angle of muscle fibers, it's unclear if training can reduce the pennation angle.
▪ Leg length. Athletes with longer legs relative to their heights are, potentially, able to

157

run faster than athletes with shorter legs (Abe *et al.*, 1999; Coh and Tomazin, 2005).

- Fatigue. Fatigue interferes with speed. This means that speed work needs to be performed when the athlete is fresh. It also means that when fatigue sets in, speed work should be stopped.
- Mobility. The greater an athlete's ability to move their joints through an unrestricted range of motion, the faster they will be, potentially.
- Stride length/frequency.
- Technique.

Sprinting program focus

Sprinting program design focuses around improving one of three aspects of a sprint:

- acceleration;
- maximal velocity;
- speed endurance.

Acceleration

Acceleration is the phase of the sprint where the athlete is increasing their velocity. Elite sprinters may accelerate for as long as six to seven seconds before reaching maximum velocity (Cissik and Barnes, 2010), which translates to 40–80 meters for a 100-meter sprinter. In few sports will an athlete be able to run in a straight line for 40–80 meters. Most athletic situations involve short sprints with sudden starts, stops, and changes of direction. As a result, the ability to accelerate is going to be extremely important for most athletes.

Acceleration is trained using several tools:

- Short sprints. Chapter Four covered the importance of performing sprints in training to get better at sprinting. Acceleration is generally trained with sprints under 80 meters in distance. These sprints should be performed at maximum velocity, allowing for full recovery between each sprint, while emphasizing good technique. As a general guideline, collegiate sprinters should not be running more than 300–500 meters of these short sprints in a training session (Coaching Education Committee, 2001).
- Stride-length drills. These drills were described in Chapter Four. When training acceleration, these drills typically cover five to ten meters in length and are repeated three to five times, emphasizing an explosive start and good technique.
- Resisted sprints. Adding resistance in the form of a weighted sled or weighted vests will make accelerating more difficult. This should increase the number of motor units

recruited and increase strength in an acceleration-specific manner, which should both translate into greater velocities during acceleration. Research looking at the impact of resisted sprints on the performance of athletes shows that it does improve performance on short sprints but not in a manner that is more significant than unresisted sprinting (Spinks et al., 2007). A coach must be cautious with resisted sprinting because even adding 10 percent to the athletes' bodyweight will change kinematic variables, which could teach the athlete bad habits (Alcaraz et al., 2009; Lockie et al., 2003; Maulder et al., 2008).

■ Strength training. A stronger athlete should be able to have a greater acceleration than a weaker one. Baker and Nance (1999) with professional rugby players and Nimphius et al. (2010) with national-caliber softball players report a relationship between strength and acceleration. However, other authors do not find a relationship between strength and acceleration (Cronin and Hansen, 2005; Moir et al., 2007). The conflict in the research reinforces the need to train acceleration specifically and not rely on strength training alone.

Maximal velocity

Maximal velocity is the fastest that the athlete can run. Maximal velocity is trained using several tools:

■ Sprints at maximal velocity. Sprinting at maximum velocity is a specific skill and must be practiced to be perfected. These sprints cover distances of 20–80 meters, with a total volume of 300–800 meters per training session (for collegiate sprinters), with full recovery in between each sprint.
■ Technique drills. Technique drills were described in Chapter Four. These are done for 10–20 meters and are best performed as part of the warm-up. While important for developing aspects of the sprinting technique, they are not a substitute for sprinting.
■ Stride-length drills. To a point, increasing the length of the strides will increase running velocity. When trying to improve maximal velocity, these have a 20–40-meter run-up before the drill begins (i.e. the athlete has a chance to reach maximal velocity before beginning the drill), at that point the drill is conducted for 10–20 meters and repeated three to five times.
■ Stride-frequency drills. Stride-frequency drills are performed for distances of 10–20 meters and repeated three to five times. These are performed as part of the warm-up and serve as a great bridge between the specific warm-up and the workout proper.
■ Resisted sprints: To improve maximal velocity, weighted vests/belts, parachutes, and weighted sleds are the options most studied. Weighted sleds and weighted vests have been found to be effective at increasing velocity, but resisted sprints are not

more effective than unresisted sprints (Clark *et al.*, 2010). All have a significant impact on the kinematics of running at maximal velocity by decreasing velocity, increasing sprinting time, decreasing stride frequency/length, and in the case of weighted sleds, increasing the angle of the trunk lean (which reduces hip extension during the sprint) (Alcaraz *et al.*, 2008; Alcaraz *et al.*, 2009). This impact on kinematics means that these tools must be used with care to prevent the athlete from being taught bad habits. Resisted sprints generally involve an acceleration phase of 20 meters followed by 20–40-meter sprints with the resistance, performed three to five times, allowing for complete recovery between each sprint.

■ Assisted sprints. For reasons outlined in Chapter Four, assisted sprints should be performed in a manner that ensures that the athlete's speed is not more than 106 percent of maximum. It is important that the athlete is an active participant in the sprint (as opposed to allowing themselves to be pulled along) and that good technique is employed. These are typically performed three to five times, with complete recovery between each set, for 20–40 meters.

Speed endurance

Speed endurance is the ability to maintain maximal velocity. This is not the same as metabolic conditioning. Speed-endurance training involves longer sprints (80–300 meters), with volumes of 300–900 meters in a training session, allowing for complete recovery between each sprint (for longer distances up to 15 minutes between each sprint). The focus is on quality sprinting and reaching maximal velocity, this means that the recovery time between each sprint is critical as fatigue needs to be avoided. This quality is not going to be needed for the majority of sports.

Program design

When it comes to designing speed-training programs, several principles should be kept in mind:

■ Sprinting should not be performed under fatigued conditions. Performing sprints while fatigued means that the athlete is learning how to run slowly with bad technique. As a result, sprints should be done at the beginning of the workout. The volume should be kept low, and the athlete should have the chance to recover fully between each sprint.
■ To be better at sprinting, athletes have to practice. Drills and tools are not a substitute for sprinting at high velocities; athletes must practice this skill to become better at it. Running at submaximal velocities teaches an athlete different running kinematics and should be avoided.

- Train one aspect in a training session. Each training session should focus around acceleration, maximal velocity, or speed endurance. Training more than one aspect (e.g., acceleration and speed endurance) can reduce the overall effectiveness of the training session.

TRAINING FOR AGILITY

Agility can be viewed as the ability to change direction suddenly. It involves possessing the motor skills to perform the change in direction as well as the perceptual and cognitive skills to recognize the need to change direction and to react to the stimulus. It is the most challenging of all the aspects of strength and conditioning to train and it comes the closest to linking strength and conditioning to the athlete's sport. It is also one of those qualities that distinguishes elite athletes from non-elite ones (Kaplan et al., 2009).

There is a paucity of literature on training agility. A study by Young et al. (2001) reflects the state of the literature. Relatively untrained individuals were divided into a speed-training group and an agility training group. The speed-training group trained straight-ahead sprints, the agility group trained with various changes of direction. After six weeks, the speed-training group made the most improvement on the speed tests and the agility group made the most improvement on the agility tests, with little crossover between the two.

Due to the shortage of literature on how to train agility, most training recommendations focus on training those factors that influence agility, the thinking being that if those factors are trained, then agility will improve. These factors are:

- Mobility. Being able to move a joint through its full range of motion without restriction would improve an athlete's ability to quickly react and adjust to a stimulus.
- Strength and power. Being able to exert force quickly would, theoretically, benefit agility, which involves exerting force against the ground. The literature is conflicted on this. Using athletes as subjects, studies have found both significant relationships between strength/power and agility (Nimphius et al., 2010) as well as only moderate relationships between strength/power and agility (Markovic, 2007). It appears that strength/power is a factor in agility performance, but there are other factors as well.
- Acceleration and maximal velocity. Logically, acceleration and maximal velocity would have an impact on agility. Research on this is conflicted, reporting both weak relationships (Little and Williams, 2005; Sassi et al., 2009; Vescovi and McGuigan, 2008) and strong relationships (Gabbett et al., 2008a; Nimphius et al., 2010). It appears that acceleration and maximum velocity may be factors in agility performance, but there are other factors as well.
- Fundamental skills. The performance of most sports can be broken down into fundamental skills. If these skills can be mastered, they provide a foundation for advanced training.

- Cognitive/perceptual skills. Improving an athlete's ability to perceive the need for a change of direction and speeding up their decision-making process could improve agility, especially if done in conjunction with training the above factors.

With the above in mind, several principles should be kept in mind when it comes to agility-program design:

- The athlete needs a base in terms of strength, power, acceleration, and maximum velocity.
- Fundamental skills should be analyzed and mastered.
- Once the fundamental skills are mastered, they should be made more challenging by being combined (see Chapter Four).
- As the athlete is mastering combined skills, the athlete should be trained to react to stimulus and to make decisions based upon those stimuli through the types of advanced skills covered in Chapter Four.
- Agility training can be performed daily.
- Because agility training has a technique base, the athlete should not be fatigued. This means low volume, quality execution, and full recovery.

PUTTING IT ALL TOGETHER

Between hypertrophy, maximal strength, power, plyometrics, acceleration, maximum velocity, speed endurance, agility, metabolic conditioning, dynamic flexibility, and core training there are a lot of potential tools and approaches to training that can be included in a strength and conditioning program. It is easy to design a training program for any one of them, but incorporating most of them into a program and doing so in a way that accounts for how they interact with one another is extremely challenging. This section will cover how to put all these aspects of a training program together over the short term. Table 7.6 provides a summary of the volume, intensity, and rest recommendations that have been covered thus far.

Principles for putting together programs:

- Perform the needs analysis. Chapter Six covered the needs analysis. This is important prior to designing a strength and conditioning program as it identifies what abilities are important. For purposes of this section, these will include hypertrophy, maximal strength, power, acceleration, maximal velocity, speed endurance, and metabolic conditioning.
- Link abilities/energy systems. When putting programs together, each day should attempt to link the abilities. This can be done by abilities or by energy systems. For example, if the focus is on power training on one day, it would make sense to perform plyometrics and the Olympic lifts that day. If the focus is on the glycolytic energy system, that would be a good day for hypertrophy training and metabolic conditioning.

Table 7.6 Summary of training variable recommendations

Focus	Volume (sets × repetitions or total meters)	Distance of repetitions (speed training only)	Intensity (% of 1-RM or % of best speed)	Rest (rest between sets; for sprints written as rest between sprints/ rest between sets)
Hypertrophy	3–5 × 7–15 (untrained) 3–6 × 5–12 (trained)		60–85% (untrained) 60–90% (trained)	30"–5' (untrained) 1'–4' (trained)
Strength	3–8 × 1–6		80–100%	1.5'–8'
Power	3–5 × 1–6		50–90%	1.5'–8'
Acceleration	300–500	<80 meters	90–100%	1–2'/5–7'
Maximal velocity	300–800	20–80 meters	90–100%	3–5'/6–8'
Speed endurance	300–900	80–300 meters	90–100%	5–15'

■ Allow sufficient recovery. Once abilities have been linked, the athlete should be given sufficient recovery time prior to training those abilities again. There are always exceptions, but 48 hours is standard practice.

■ If possible, link to sport practice. Some sports lend themselves to linking the training of abilities to what is being done in practice. For example, Cissik (2007) and Cissik and Barnes (2010) describe how to do this with track and field athletes. This works well with sports like track and field, weightlifting, and swimming but it could be a great deal more challenging with the majority of team sports.

Steps for incorporating multiple modes of exercise:

■ Determine the exercise modes to be used. This is an important first step and limits what will be included in the program.

■ Determine the abilities that those modes will train. For the purposes of this section, these could include mobility, power, maximal strength, hypertrophy, metabolic conditioning, acceleration, maximal speed, speed endurance, and cardiovascular endurance.

■ Determine the most important ability/mode for the current cycle. Each cycle of training should have a focus or several foci that the entire program is built around. For this example, we are going to build our program around prioritizing power and maximal strength training.

Table 7.7 Planning the most important ability, strength training, first

	Day 1	Day 2	Day 3	Day 4	Day 5
Ability focus	Power	Maximum strength	Recovery	Power	Maximum strength
Energy system focus	Phosphagen	Phosphagen/ glycolytic	Glycolytic	Phosphagen	Phosphagen/ glycolytic
Strength-training workout	Power clean, 3 × 3 × 60% Clean pulls, 3 × 4 × 65% Push jerk, 3 × 3 × 60%	Back squats, 3 × 4–6 × 85% Romanian deadlifts, 3 × 4–6-RM Bench press, 3 × 4–6 × 85% Bent-over rows, 3 × 4–6-RM Military press, 3 × 4–6-RM	Off	Power snatch, 3 × 3 × 60% Snatch pulls, 3 × 4 × 65% Speed squats, 3 × 10" × 60%	Front squats, 3 × 2–4 × 80% Good mornings, 3 × 4–6-RM Incline press, 3 × 4–6-RM Pull-ups, 3 × 4–6-RM Dumbbell shoulder press, 3 × 4–6-RM

- Plan the training of that ability/mode. Table 7.7 shows the planning of power and maximal strength training for this example. Strength training to develop these qualities will be performed four times a week, alternating between using strength training for power and for maximal strength. Note that in the middle of the week is a day off.
- Determine the second most important ability/mode. Once the first ability/mode has been planned, the second most important one should be planned in a way that it supports the first. Table 7.8 shows this being done using plyometrics. With a primary focus of the phase being power training, plyometrics should be pretty important.
- Plan the training for that ability/mode, linking it to the first. The second ability/mode to be planned needs to be done in a way that supports and complements the first. Since plyometrics enhances power, it is performed on the same days that the power strength training is performed.
- Tables 7.9, 7.10, and 7.11, show the integration of speed training, agility training, and metabolic conditioning with strength and plyometrics training. The speed and agility work are of short-enough distances that they link up well with the maximal strength training. Metabolic conditioning is being performed on the day off as it focuses on a radically different energy system than the other training modes.
- The program should be progressive. Any program that is designed must become more challenging over time while balancing the need to keep athletes from becoming injured. This progression is usually expressed in terms of an equation, something like 3 + 1, where the first number represents the number of weeks where

Table 7.8 Linking the second most important ability, plyometrics, to the first

	Day 1	Day 2	Day 3	Day 4	Day 5
Ability focus	Power	Maximum strength	Recovery	Power	Maximum strength
Energy system focus	Phosphagen	Phosphagen/ glycolytic	Glycolytic	Phosphagen	Phosphagen/ glycolytic
Strength training workout	Power clean, 3 × 3 × 60% Clean pulls, 3 × 4 × 65% Push jerk, 3 × 3 × 60%	Back squats, 3 × 4–6 × 85% Romanian deadlifts, 3 × 4–6-RM Bench press, 3 × 4–6 × 85% Bent-over rows, 3 × 4–6-RM Military press, 3 × 4–6-RM	Off	Power snatch, 3 × 3 × 60% Snatch pulls, 3 × 4 × 65% Speed squats, 3 × 10" × 60%	Front squats, 3 × 2–4 × 80% Good mornings, 3 × 4–6-RM Incline press, 3 × 4–6-RM Pull-ups, 3 × 4–6-RM Dumbbell shoulder press, 3 × 4–6-RM
Plyometric workout	Counter-movement jumps, 3 × 10 Jump and tuck, 3 × 10			Squat jumps, 3 × 10 Jump and tuck, 3 × 10	

the training will be made more difficult (in this case three) and the last number the number of weeks of reduced training that follow the weeks of increases. In other words, the first three weeks will see an increase in terms of volume, intensity, or both, followed by a week of reduced loading.

KEY READINGS

Petrella, J.K., Kim, J-S., Mayhew, D.L., Cross, J.M. and Bamman, M.M. (2008) Potent myofiber hypertrophy during resistance training in humans is associated with satellite cell-mediated myonuclear addition: a cluster analysis, *Journal of Applied Physiology*, 104: 1736–42.

An important study for helping to document the role of satellite cells in muscle hypertrophy. This study related the hypertrophic responses of the subjects to the presence of satellite cells and found a relationship.

Table 7.9 Linking the third most important ability, speed training, to the first two

	Day 1	Day 2	Day 3	Day 4	Day 5
Ability focus	Power	Maximum strength	Recovery	Power	Maximum strength
Energy system focus	Phosphagen	Phosphagen/ glycolytic	Glycolytic	Phosphagen	Phosphagen/ glycolytic
Strength training workout	Power clean, 3 × 3 × 60% Clean pulls, 3 × 4 × 65% Push jerk, 3 × 3 × 60%	Back squats, 3 × 4–6 × 85% Romanian deadlifts, 3 × 4–6-RM Bench press, 3 × 4–6 × 85% Bent-over rows, 3 × 4–6-RM Military press, 3 × 4–6-RM	Off	Power snatch, 3 × 3 × 60% Snatch pulls, 3 × 4 × 65% Speed squats, 3 × 10" × 60%	Front squats, 3 × 2–4 × 80% Good mornings, 3 × 4–6-RM Incline press, 3 × 4–6-RM Pull-ups, 3 × 4–6-RM Dumbbell shoulder press, 3 × 4–6-RM
Plyometric workout	Counter-movement jumps, 3 × 10 Jump and tuck, 3 × 10			Squat jumps, 3 × 10 Jump and tuck, 3 × 10	
Speed workout		Acceleration: 3 × 5 × 20 meters, standing starts			

Clark, K.P., Stearne, D.J., Walts, C.T. and Miller, A.D. (2010) The longitudinal effects of resisted sprint training using weighted sleds vs. weighted vests, *Journal of Strength and Conditioning Research*, 24(12): 3287–95.

Spinks, C.D., Murphy, A.J., Spinks, W.L. and Lockie, R.G. (2007) The effects of resisted sprint training on acceleration performance and kinematics in soccer, rugby union, and Australian football players, *Journal of Strength and Conditioning Research*, 21(1): 77–85.

Clark et al. (2010) and Spinks et al. (2007) are important studies because both challenge long-held beliefs about the effectiveness of resisted sprinting on athletic populations that are not sprinters. By failing to find an advantage in using resisted sprinting with these populations, they suggest that an athlete's training time may be better used on other approaches to training.

Table 7.10 Linking the fourth most important ability, agility, to the first three

	Day 1	Day 2	Day 3	Day 4	Day 5
Ability focus	Power	Maximum strength	Recovery	Power	Maximum strength
Energy system focus	Phosphagen	Phosphagen/ glycolytic	Glycolytic	Phosphagen	Phosphagen/ glycolytic
Strength training workout	Power clean, 3 × 3 × 60% Clean pulls, 3 × 4 × 65% Push jerk, 3 × 3 × 60%	Back squats, 3 × 4–6 × 85% Romanian deadlifts, 3 × 4–6-RM Bench press, 3 × 4–6 × 85% Bent-over rows, 3 × 4–6-RM Military press, 3 × 4–6-RM	Off	Power snatch, 3 × 3 × 60% Snatch pulls, 3 × 4 × 65% Speed squats, 3 × 10" × 60%	Front squats, 3 × 2–4 × 80% Good mornings, 3 × 4–6-RM Incline press, 3 × 4–6-RM Pull-ups, 3 × 4–6-RM Dumbbell shoulder press, 3 × 4–6-RM
Plyometric workout	Counter-movement jumps, 3 × 10 Jump and tuck, 3 × 10			Squat jumps, 3 × 10 Jump and tuck, 3 × 10	
Speed workout		Acceleration: 3 × 5 × 20 meters, standing starts			
Agility workout				Start/stop/start (5m/10m) × 3 Shuffle right/left, 3 × 5m each T test, 5 ×	

Little, T. and Williams, A.G. (2005) Specificity of acceleration, maximum speed, and agility in professional soccer players, *Journal of Strength and Conditioning Research*, 19(1): 76–8.

This study establishes that in professional soccer players, acceleration, maximum velocity, and agility are all different skills. This is a profound statement because it means that each skill has to be trained separately. In other words performing the 60-meter sprint is not going to improve agility.

Table 7.11 Linking the fifth most important ability, metabolic conditioning, to the first four

	Day 1	Day 2	Day 3	Day 4	Day 5
Ability focus	Power	Maximum strength	Recovery	Power maximum	Strength
Energy system focus	Phosphagen	Phosphagen/ glycolytic	Glycolytic	Phosphagen	Phosphagen/ glycolytic
Strength training workout	Power clean, 3 × 3 × 60% Clean pulls, 3 × 4 × 65% Push jerk, 3 × 3 × 60%	Back squats, 3 × 4–6 × 85% Romanian deadlifts, 3 × 4–6-RM Bench press, 3 × 4–6 × 85% Bent-over rows, 3 × 4–6-RM Military press, 3 × 4–6-RM	Off	Power snatch, 3 × 3 × 60% Snatch pulls, 3 × 4 × 65% Speed squats, 3 × 10″ × 60%	Front squats, 3 × 2–4 × 80% Good mornings, 3 × 4–6-RM Incline press, 3 × 4–6-RM Pull-ups, 3 × 4–6-RM Dumbbell shoulder press, 3 × 4–6-RM
Plyometric workout	Counter-movement jumps, 3 × 10 Jump and tuck, 3 × 10			Squat jumps, 3 × 10 Jump and tuck, 3 × 10	
Speed workout		Acceleration: 3 × 5 × 20 meters, standing starts			
Agility workout				Start/stop/start (5m/10m) × 3 Shuffle right/left, 3 × 5m each T test, 5 ×	
Metabolic conditioning workout			2 × 100m (1′), 2 × 50m (1′), 2 × 25m (30″), 2 × 10m (15″)		

CHAPTER EIGHT

PERIODIZATION OF TRAINING

Periodization is an approach to the long-term organization and planning of training. Periodization is an attempt to make training more measurable and more objectively planned. It involves carefully planning out an athlete's training so that they peak at the right time while avoiding overtraining. It also seeks to incorporate all of the training modes that the athlete engages in.

OUTLINE

Objectives of periodization

Principles of periodization

- Peak the athlete
- Structure training
- Develop a fitness base
- Gradually make training more specific
- Make training progressive and continuous
- Prevent injuries

Structure of training

- Identify the peak(s)
- Organize the year
- Plan the focus for each period of training
- Plan the first phase of training in concept
- Plan the first mesocycle in detail
- Competition and testing

Challenges with periodization

- Periodization is from a closed system
- The research on periodization is limited
- The effectiveness of periodization is a matter of debate

Key readings

OBJECTIVES OF PERIODIZATION

With periodization, training is structured into blocks. Each succeeding block is meant to build on the one that came before it until the athlete reaches their peak during the most important competition(s) of the training year. Each year is supposed to build upon the one that came before. In theory, as a result of proper planning, periodization will allow an athlete to improve from year to year.

Periodization has a number of advantages:

- It provides a structure to training that allows for it to be organized in a logical, systematic, sequential fashion.
- It helps the coach to organize all of the modes of exercise in a progressive fashion.
- It allows training to be balanced to prevent injuries and overtraining.
- It focuses training on peaking the athlete to perform at their best when it is needed.

Periodization also has a number of drawbacks:

- It may be best for beginning and intermediate-level athletes.
- It doesn't work for long seasons.
- Athletes are not mathematical equations or spreadsheets; often when real athletes meet the plan the plan must be modified.
- Planning is extremely time-consuming.
- The language can be confusing, with different authors using different terminology for essentially the same thing.
- It is often arbitrary and based upon the calendar, not necessarily on biology.

PRINCIPLES OF PERIODIZATION

This section is going to cover several principles that can be followed when using periodization. Following these principles will make the planning process easier:

- Peak the athlete.
- Structure training.
- Develop a fitness base.
- Gradually make training more specific.
- Make training progressive and continuous.
- Prevent injuries.

Peak the athlete

When beginning the planning process, the first step is to determine when the athlete has to be at their best. This may be during a single event, like the world championships, or it may be during an entire season. Once that has been determined, training is going to be organized around working backwards so that everything leads to that peak.

To complicate matters, there may be more than one peak in a year. For example, to go to the world championships, an athlete may still need to qualify at a national championship. There also may be more than one season. For example, in American collegiate track and field there is an indoor season and an outdoor season, both with national championships.

This section is going to use two hypothetical athletes as examples to develop these concepts. The first, athlete A, is an athlete participating in an individual sport. This athlete is striving for two peaks: national championships on May 1 and world championships on July 15. The second, athlete B, is participating in a team sport and is striving for a peak during the sport's competitive season from September through November.

Structure training

Once the peak has been determined, it's time to structure training around achieving that peak. Every training-theory author uses different terminology, but, essentially, the structural units for periodization are:

- Macrocycles. A macrocycle can be viewed as the entire training year or it can represent the period of time from the last peak through the next peak.
- Periods. There are three periods, which are subdivisions of the macrocycle. The periods are the preparatory period (this is when the athlete gets in shape for the sport), the competition period (this is when the athlete is peaking), and the recovery period (the time between the competition period and the start of the next macrocycle, a time for rest and recovery). Note that not all macrocycles will have each period; very short ones (for example, one from May 2 to July 15, in the case of athlete A) may skip periods.
- Phases. Phases are subdivisions of periods. The preparatory period is divided into the general preparation phase (this is the period where the athlete trains to train) and the special preparation phase (fitness developed in the general preparation phase is applied to the event). The competition period is divided into a pre-competition phase (usually a sharp increase in intensity and a focus on tools with a direct transfer to the sport) and the competition phase (normally a time of maintaining physical qualities).

- Mesocycles. Mesocycles are subdivisions of the phase. These last four weeks, but may last longer or shorter depending upon circumstances. Dividing the phase into smaller mesocycles makes planning more manageable and flexible.
- Microcycles. Microcycles are subdivisions of the mesocycle. Each microcycle lasts a week. It is the most basic unit of a periodization plan and includes the integration of all of the modes of exercise, recovery, and competitions that will be used.

Develop a fitness base

Periodization is meant to be organized in a sequence with the preparatory period beginning the training year, followed by the competition period, and ending with the recovery period.

Within the preparatory period, the general preparation phase begins training and is then followed by the specific preparation phase. The purpose of the general preparation phase is to develop the athlete's fitness base. This is done in different ways depending upon the mode of exercise:

1 Strength training. Most authors see this as the time of year spent largely with hypertrophy training, or at least training meant to develop tendons and ligaments. Traditionally, the volume of training is moderate to high with a moderate to low intensity. This is also when the techniques on the fundamental exercises (squats, cleans, presses, etc.) are emphasized the most.
2 Plyometrics training. Foundational techniques are emphasized during this phase with a low volume of training and low intensity. Volume, intensity, and complexity increase as the phase progresses.
3 Speed training. Technique, speed endurance, and acceleration work from various starting positions are emphasized during the general preparation phase of training. The volume of work and complexity gradually increases as the phase progresses.
4 Agility training. Fundamental techniques are emphasized during this phase of training. Volume, intensity, and complexity are low and gradually increase as the phase progresses.
5 Metabolic conditioning. This phase of training often sees the greatest emphasis on metabolic conditioning as the athletes are getting into shape.

The general preparation phase of training will be longer or shorter depending upon the level of the athlete and their needs. Advanced athletes will spend less time in this phase of training; beginning athletes will spend a great deal more time in it.

Gradually make training more specific

After the general preparatory phase of training, the athlete progresses to the specific preparatory phase. In this phase of training, the athlete seeks to use the fitness base that was developed in the previous phase and begins to develop those physical qualities specifically needed for performance. How this is done will depend upon the mode of exercise used:

1   Strength training. This phase uses the hypertrophy that was developed in the general preparatory phase and applies it to strength and power training. The volume of training is moderate to low with the intensity moderate to high. Technique on fundamental exercises is reinforced but the exercises become more complex.
2   Plyometrics training. Foundational techniques are still emphasized during this phase with a low volume of training. However, the intensity will be higher than in the general preparation phase. More complex exercises will be introduced as the athlete is ready for them.
3   Speed training. Technique, speed endurance, and acceleration work from various starting positions are still emphasized during the special preparation phase of training. Maximum-velocity work will be introduced and gradually the starts will be from a sport-specific position. The volume of work and complexity gradually increases as the phase progresses.
4   Agility training. Fundamental techniques are still emphasized but intermediate drills will be introduced beginning with this phase. Volume, intensity, and complexity are gradually increasing as the phase progresses.
5   Metabolic conditioning: This phase of training still has a great emphasis on metabolic conditioning as the athletes are getting into shape.

The special preparatory phase is generally shorter than the general preparatory phase, though the length will depend upon the level of the athlete and their specific needs.

After the preparatory period of training, the athlete moves into the competitive period of training, which is split up into two phases, a pre-competition phase and a competition phase.

As a transition between the preparatory period and competition, the pre-competition phase is focused on laying the foundation to peak the athlete in the next phase of training. This is done in different ways depending upon the mode of exercise:

1   Strength training. This phase uses the hypertrophy and strength that was developed in the preparatory period. The volume of training is moderate to low with the intensity moderate to high. Exercises are more complex and a great focus is on maximal strength and power training.
2   Plyometrics training. The volume and intensity will be higher than in the preparatory period. More complex exercises will be introduced as the athlete is ready for them.

3   Speed training. Maximal velocity and acceleration work is the emphasis during the pre-competition phase. Sprints are performed from sport-specific starting positions. If necessary, this is the phase where special speed-training tools, such as resisted sprinting, assisted sprinting, etc., will be introduced.
4   Agility training. As the athlete is prepared for them, intermediate and advanced drills are used during this phase. Volume, intensity, and complexity are gradually increasing as the phase progresses.
5   Metabolic conditioning. This period of training begins to de-emphasize metabolic conditioning unless it is a weakness of the athlete. Essentially, this quality is maintained from this point onwards.

Four weeks is a standard length for the pre-competition phase, though the length is going to depend upon the sport and the level of the athlete.

The competition phase seeks to peak the athlete so that they perform at their best during competition. This is complicated by the fact that athletes will be competing and traveling, so training must be balanced around this. It is normal for the number of days spent training to be reduced, so the emphasis is often on maintaining the physical qualities that have been developed. The manner in which this is done depends upon the mode of exercise to be used:

1   Strength training. This phase reduces strength training to two to three sessions per week. The focus is on maintaining strength and power. This sees some of the most intense training and it also sees the incorporation of advanced training tools such as complex and contrast training so that the athlete is able to perform more work in a short amount of time.
2   Plyometrics training. More plyometrics work will be performed in the competition phase than in any other. It may be combined with strength training, used in separate workouts, or both.
3   Speed training. Unless the athlete is in a track and field event or is deficient in sprinting speed, this is often reduced or dropped during this phase and combined with agility training.
4   Agility training. For athletes where this quality is important, this will be heavily emphasized during the competition phase. This phase will see the most advanced drills.
5   Metabolic conditioning. This quality will be maintained during the competition phase unless it is a weakness.

The competition phase lasts the length of the competitive season. It may be four to six weeks around one competition (e.g., the Olympic Games), or it may last six months (e.g., a professional baseball season).

Make training progressive and continuous

As it has been described so far, training is a logical, systematic, and progressive process where each period flows into the next period. It is important to view the athlete's training from a multi-year standpoint in these terms as well, where each year builds on the previous one. This way the athlete is in a process of continual progression.

Prevent injuries

When training is performed in a logical, systematic, and progressive manner, it helps to prevent injuries associated with training. Another aspect of training that helps to prevent injuries and overtraining is including a recovery period of training. This is a period of training with a great reduction in volume and intensity and, typically, has the athlete perform activities that are not normally part of their strength and conditioning, so that they stay in shape. This period normally lasts for two to four weeks after the competition period of training.

STRUCTURE OF TRAINING

To keep the process of planning a periodized strength and conditioning program from being overwhelming, the following are steps that should be followed:

- Identify the peak(s).
- Organize the year.
- Plan the focus for each period of training.
- Plan the first phase of training in concept.
- Plan the first mesocycle in detail.
- Halfway through the first mesocycle, plan the second.
- Etc.

Identify the peak(s)

This was covered above, but it is the most important step because everything works backwards from this point. Recall that athlete A is looking to peak at the national championships on May 1 and at the world championships on July 15. To accomplish this, a competition period will be set up running from April 1 (four weeks prior to competition) through May 1, and another from June 1 to July 15.

Athlete B will be competing from September through November. To peak this athlete, the competition period will be set up running from August 1 through November.

Organize the year

This is done by first deciding when the three periods will occur and how long they will last. After the periods have been organized, they will be divided up into phases.

The competition period runs from April through May 1 and June 1 through July 15 for athlete A. This will mean that the recovery period will follow July 15 and will run for four weeks (i.e., mid-August). The time from mid-August until April will be a preparatory period (i.e., seven months). In addition there will be a preparatory phase between May 1 and June 1.

The competition period runs from August through November for athlete B. This means that the recovery period will follow and will make up the month of December. The time from January through July will be a preparatory period (i.e., seven months).

In the case of athlete A, there will be four general preparation phases, four special preparation phases, one pre-competition phase, one recovery phase, and two competition phases. In the case of athlete B, there will be four general preparation phases, three special preparation phases, one pre-competition phase, one recovery phase, and three competition phases. Tables 8.1 and 8.2 illustrate the phases of training for athletes A and B.

Table 8.1 Dividing the year into phases for athlete A (GP: general preparatory, SP: special preparatory, PC: pre-competition, C: competition, R: recovery)

Month	Jan	Feb	Mar	Apr	May	June	July	Aug	Sep	Oct	Nov	Dec
Period	P	P	P	C	P	C	C	R	P	P	P	P
Phase	SP	SP	SP	PC	SP	C	C	R	GP	GP	GP	GP

Table 8.2 Dividing the year into phases for athlete B (GP: general preparatory, SP: special preparatory, PC: pre-competition, C: competition, R: recovery)

Month	Jan	Feb	Mar	Apr	May	June	July	Aug	Sep	Oct	Nov	Dec
Period	P	P	P	P	P	P	P	C	C	C	C	R
Phase	GP	GP	GP	GP	SP	SP	SP	PC	C	C	C	R

Plan the focus for each period of training

The next step is to plan the focus for each period of training. This involves deciding what areas will be emphasized and developing general trends about volume, intensity, and modes of exercise. It does not involve writing workouts and is kept vague because planning too far out will be an exercise in futility.

Table 8.3 breaks down the focus for each period of training for athlete A:

■ Preparatory period. This athlete has all the hypertrophy that is needed but needs to learn how to use that and become stronger and more explosive. Further, this explosiveness needs to be applied in a horizontal direction. While the athlete will be improving acceleration, they will also be focusing on maximal-velocity sprinting techniques. Agility training is not a primary need, but will be used in a limited

Table 8.3 Planning the focus of each period of training for athlete A

Period	Mode of exercise	Focus
Preparatory	Strength	Maintain existing hypertrophy. Increase maximal strength. Increase power.
	Plyometrics	Increase horizontal jumping ability.
	Speed	Improve acceleration. Improve maximal-velocity technique.
	Agility	Fundamental exercises as cross-training.
	Metabolic conditioning	Maintain metabolic conditioning.
Competition	Strength	Maintain hypertrophy and maximal strength. Increase power.
	Plyometrics	Increase horizontal jumping ability.
	Speed	Improve acceleration. Improve maximal velocity.
	Agility	N/A
	Metabolic conditioning	Maintain metabolic conditioning.
Recovery	Strength	Maintain hypertrophy, strength, and power through circuit training.
	Plyometrics	Maintain jumping ability through circuit training.
	Speed	Maintain speed and acceleration through games.
	Agility	Maintain agility through games.
	Metabolic conditioning	Maintain metabolic conditioning through games.

fashion for cross-training. Metabolic conditioning is not a weakness, so it will be maintained during this period.

■ Competition period. Hypertrophy and strength are maintained while power is a primary focus, particularly in the horizontal direction. The athlete will be emphasizing both acceleration and maximal-velocity sprinting and will be maintaining metabolic conditioning. Agility training will not be present. In between the competition phases, there will be a special preparation phase to give athlete A time to develop and address any deficiencies prior to getting ready for the world championships.

■ Recovery period. The athlete's fitness level will be maintained through the use of total-body circuit training and participation in games such as soccer and basketball.

Table 8.4 breaks down the focus of each period of training for athlete B:

■ Preparatory period. This athlete seeks to develop more hypertrophy and to improve maximal strength. Plyometrics will be used to improve vertical jumping. Acceleration, agility training, and metabolic conditioning will also be emphasized in this period of training.

■ Competition period. Maximal strength and power will be developed in this period and they will be applied in a vertical direction. Speed training will not be performed except as part of agility training. Metabolic conditioning will be maintained.

■ Recovery period. Athlete B will maintain hypertrophy, strength, and power by performing strongman circuit workouts. The other physical qualities will be maintained through participating in games like lacrosse and soccer.

Plan the first phase of training in concept

The first phase of training is the first phase that follows the recovery period; i.e., it is usually a general preparation phase. To plan for this phase in concept, a number of things must be determined:

■ goals for the phase;
■ what types of exercise will be used in each mode of exercise;
■ trends in training variables.

Goals for the phase

Determining the goals for the phase is based upon a combination of the focus for the period and the needs analysis. This important first step drives the rest of the steps in planning for the phase.

For athlete A, the focus of the preparatory period is to maintain hypertrophy, increase maximal strength, increase power, improve horizontal-jumping ability, improve

Table 8.4 Planning the focus of each period of training for athlete B

Period	Mode of exercise	Focus
Preparatory	Strength	Increase hypertrophy. Increase maximal strength.
	Plyometrics	Improve vertical-jumping ability.
	Speed	Improve acceleration.
	Agility	Develop fundamental and intermediate agility skills.
	Metabolic conditioning	Improve metabolic conditioning.
Competition	Strength	Maintain hypertrophy. Increase maximal strength. Increase power.
	Plyometrics	Improve vertical-jumping ability.
	Speed	Use agility training to improve acceleration.
	Agility	Develop intermediate and advanced agility skills.
	Metabolic conditioning	Maintain metabolic conditioning.
Recovery	Strength	Maintain strength, power, and hypertrophy through strongman circuits.
	Plyometrics	Maintain vertical jumping, acceleration, agility, and metabolic conditioning through participation in games.
	Speed	
	Agility	
	Metabolic conditioning	

acceleration, improve maximal-velocity technique, and to maintain metabolic conditioning. Based upon that, the general preparation phase will have the following goals: maintain hypertrophy, increase maximal strength, increase power, improve acceleration, and maintain metabolic conditioning. Since horizontal-jumping ability and maximal-velocity techniques will depend upon the strength, power, and acceleration developed in this period, they will be goals in the special preparation phase.

For athlete B, the focus of the preparatory period is to increase hypertrophy, increase maximal strength, improve vertical-jumping ability, improve acceleration, improve fundamental agility skill performance, and improve metabolic conditioning. Based upon that, the general preparation phase will have the following goals: improve hypertrophy, improve acceleration, improve fundamental agility skill performance, and improve metabolic conditioning. Since strength and vertical-jumping ability will depend upon the hypertrophy that is created in the general preparation phase, they will be goals in the special preparation phase.

Determine what types of exercise will be used

The goals for the phase will determine how the various modes of exercise will be used. Recall that there are many choices for each mode of exercise based upon an athlete's goals:

- strength training: Olympic lifts and their variations, squats, presses, hip-extension exercises, rows/pulls, core training, upper- and lower-body assistance exercises;
- plyometrics: single-effort jumps (horizontal and vertical), multiple-effort jumps (horizontal and vertical);
- speed training: sprints of varying distances, technique drills, stride-length drills, stride-frequency drills, assisted sprints, resisted sprints, varied-pace sprinting;
- agility training: fundamental skills, intermediate skills, advanced skills;
- metabolic conditioning: sprints, circuit training, strongman training.

Determine trends in training variables

This is the time where the coach should begin to think through the trends for the various training variables. To determine this, consider for each mode of exercise how volume and intensity will progress throughout the phase. It is not unusual to gradually increase the intensity of training as a phase progresses.

Tables 8.5 and 8.6 provide an overview of this process for athletes A and B. Athlete A has three general preparation phases, athlete B has four. There is a steady increase in the overload as the phases progress. Some training variables (such as sprints and plyometrics) are always performed at high intensity, which means that volume increases over time. In both athletes there is an adjustment phase to give the athletes a chance to get adjusted to sprinting, agility work, conditioning work, etc.

Plan the first mesocycle in detail

Now that a broad outline exists, it is time to plan the first mesocycle in detail. This is done by using the planning steps outlined in Chapter Seven. To review, these are:

periodization of training

Table 8.5 Volume and intensity trends for athlete A, general preparation phases (H: high, M: moderate, L: low)

Exercise category	GPP 1 (intensity/volume)	GPP 2 (intensity/volume)	GPP 3 (intensity/volume)
Strength	M/M	M/M	H/L
Plyometrics	N/A	N/A	N/A
Speed	H/L	H/L	H/M
Agility	L/L	L/L	L/L
Metabolic conditioning	H/M	H/M	H/M

Table 8.6 Volume and intensity trends for athlete B, general preparation phases

Exercise category	GPP 1 (intensity/volume)	GPP 2 (intensity/volume)	GPP 3 (intensity/volume)	GPP 4 (intensity/volume)
Strength	L/M	M/M	M/M	H/M
Plyometrics	N/A	N/A	N/A	N/A
Speed	H/L	H/L	H/M	H/M
Agility	H/L	H/M	H/M	H/M
Metabolic conditioning	M/M	H/M	H/M	H/H

■ Determine the most important ability for this mesocycle.
■ Plan the training for that ability.
■ Determine the second most important ability.
■ Plan that ability, linking it to the first.
■ Etc.

For athlete A, the following is the order of importance for the abilities to be trained:

1 maximal strength/power;
2 acceleration;
3 metabolic conditioning;
4 agility cross-training.

Using that order, Table 8.7 shows how each week (or microcycle) will be organized to accommodate all the modes of exercise. Given the training volumes and recovery periods, acceleration and power training link up with each other. Metabolic conditioning and agility training will be performed on the same day as they are not a strong emphasis.

Table 8.7 Microcycle organization for athlete A, mesocycle 1

	Day 1	Day 2	Day 3	Day 4	Day 5	Day 6	Day 7
Power	X			X			
Maximal strength		X			X		
Acceleration	X			X			
Metabolic conditioning			X				
Agility			X				

For athlete B, the following is the order of importance for the abilities to be trained:

1 hypertrophy;
2 metabolic conditioning;
3 agility;
4 acceleration.

Using those priorities, Table 8.8 shows how each microcycle will be organized to accommodate all the modes of exercise. Hypertrophy training and metabolic conditioning will be performed on the same days as both essentially develop the same energy systems. Given the short-distance nature of each, acceleration and agility work will be performed on day 2.

Table 8.8 Microcycle organization for athlete B, mesocycle 1

	Day 1	Day 2	Day 3	Day 4	Day 5	Day 6	Day 7
Hypertrophy	X		X		X		
Metabolic conditioning	X		X		X		
Agility		X		X			
Acceleration		X					

After all of this has been done, the coach is ready to write the actual workouts. As the athlete is performing the workouts, the coach should begin planning the next mesocycle in concept. Once the athlete is halfway through the current mesocycle, the following one should be planned in detail. Tables 8.9 and 8.10 show the training variables for athletes A and B. There is a gradual increase in training volume and intensity for the first three weeks of the mesocycle, with the last week being an unloading week.

Table 8.9 Overview of training variables for Mesocycle 1, athlete A

Exercise category	Week 1	Week 2	Week 3	Week 4
Squats, hip extensions, presses, rows/pulls	3–5 × 4–8 × 80% 2×/week	3–5 × 4–8 × 82.5% 2×/week	3–5 × 4–8 × 85% 2×/week	3–5 × 2–6 × 80% 2×/week
Power cleans, power snatches, jerks, pulls	3 × 4–6 × 60% 2×/week	3 × 4-6 × 62.5% 2×/week	3 × 4-6 × 65% 2×/week	3 × 3 × 60% 2×/week
Short sprints from varied starting positions	3 × 5 × 5–10m 2×/week	3 × 5 × 5–15m 2×/week	3 × 5 × 10–20m 2×/week	3 × 5 × 5–10m 2×/week
Shuffles, back-pedals, running curves	1–3 × 5m 1×/week	1–3 × 5m 1×/week	1–3 × 5m 1×/week	1–3 × 5m 1×/week
Metabolic conditioning	3–5 × 100m 1×/week	3–5 × 110m 1×/week	3–5 × 120m 1×/week	3–5 × 130m 1×/week

Table 8.10 Overview of training variables for Mesocycle 1, athlete B

Exercise category	Week 1	Week 2	Week 3	Week 4
Squats, hip extensions, presses, rows/pulls, assistance	3 × 10–15 × 60% 3×/week	3 × 10–15 × 65% 3×/week	3 × 10–15 × 70% 3×/week	3 × 12–15 × 60% 3×/week
Short sprints from varied starting positions	3–5 × 10m 1×/week	3–5 × 15m 1×/week	3–5 × 20m 1×/week	3–5 × 5m 1×/week
Starts, stops, shuffles, back-pedals, running curves, cutting	3–5 × 5m each 2×/week	3–5 × 5m each 2×/week	3–5 × 5m each 2×/week	3–5 × 5m each 2×/week
Sprints, circuit training, strongman training	400 meters, 20 minutes, 20 minutes 3×/week	440 meters, 22 minutes, 22 minutes 3×/week	480 meters, 24 minutes, 24 minutes 3×/week	400 meters, 20 minutes, 20 minutes 3×/week

Competition and testing

Competition and testing present challenges for planning. Athletes still need to train around competitions. Competitions should be viewed as high-intensity training days, which means that they should be followed by a training session of either low-intensity or of rest. Training that precedes competition is going to depend upon the athlete. Some athletes perform better after a moderate- to high-intensity training session, others do not.

Testing is another matter entirely. It does not make sense to completely shut down training for a week or more for testing of the athlete. It's best to incorporate that testing into the athlete's training when it is desired.

CHALLENGES WITH PERIODIZATION

Periodization is widely accepted in practice by strength and conditioning professionals. Despite this acceptance, there are significant challenges with this concept. These include:

- it comes from a system many cannot access;
- there are limitations on the research;
- there is debate about its universal effectiveness.

Periodization is from a closed system

As Gambetta (1991) articulated, the concept of periodization comes from eastern European countries that had carefully controlled societies that were unable to provide many of the services and goods that many western societies take for granted. Sporting success could mean access to goods, services, food, housing, status, etc. The challenge that this presents is that those situations and motivations cannot be duplicated by most sporting situations outside of those societies, which makes it difficult to achieve success using the exact same training methods.

The second challenge is that many of the translated articles and training-theory books may be out of context. With the advent of strength and conditioning as a field, there has been an interest in eastern European training-theory books and articles. The difficulty with many of these articles and books is that without living in those societies we may not be able to put the material in perspective. For example, it may have been fringe material, part of a larger debate, controversial, only meant to be used in certain settings, etc.

Finally, it is worth noting that the popularity of periodization is linked to the emigration of many eastern European training theorists to the west and the associated marketing of their products and services. There is nothing wrong with this, but sometimes marketing is accepted over substance.

The research on periodization is limited

Periodization is accepted in strength and conditioning research and in practice. Despite this, there are limitations to the research on this topic. Cissik *et al.* (2008) highlight a number of challenges with the state of the research on periodization. These include:

- Research is primarily on strength/power. Periodization research does not examine the effect of periodization outside of the weight room. Since periodization is meant to incorporate all the modes of exercise, this is a large gap.
- Research doesn't use athletes as subjects. For understandable reasons, athletes and their coaches are reluctant to have their training programs modified just to determine what will happen. This means that the majority of training-intervention studies are going to uses non-athletes (primarily college students) as subjects. The difficulty is that untrained individuals respond well to just about anything. This is not the case with athletes that have long training histories. It also makes it impossible to apply the results of research on the untrained to athletes.
- Research has challenges with using volume and intensity. Many periodization studies that compare a periodized program to a non-periodized one are fundamentally flawed in the sense that the periodized subjects have a higher training volume, higher training intensities, or both. Therefore it may be the greater volume/intensity that results in the gains from training as opposed to the special nature of a periodized program.
- Research is not long enough. Most research lasts four to 16 weeks (i.e. no longer than a college semester). Gains from training level off over time; periodization is meant to help avoid that leveling off. If a study only looks at the short term, it is unable to draw conclusions about training's long-term effectiveness.

The effectiveness of periodization is a matter of debate

Not all training theorists agree about the primacy of periodization. Verchoshanskij (1999) expressed a number of concerns about this:

- Periodization has not changed since it was introduced. First introduced in 1965, periodization's model has not changed. This means that it may not be incorporating advancements being made in sports science.
- It is contrived. Vercoshanskij (1999) goes as far as to call it arbitrary. According to him, it is based on sports pedagogy, as opposed to hard science. The pedagological nature means that things that merely sound logical can be presented as fact.
- It may restrict gains from training. Vercoshanskij (1999) notes that the artificial structure of the various periods and phases ignores the variability of how each athlete adapts to training. As a result, it is very likely to slow down their gains from training.

Periodization is used extensively in strength and conditioning. Many models and approaches exist. Despite this, it is not perfect, and a great deal of research using athletes over a long period of time needs to be done.

KEY READINGS

Matveyev, L. (1981) *Fundamentals of Sports Training*, Moscow, Progress Publishers: 6–85, 166–85.

Matveyev's book is a must read for the strength and conditioning professional. This is the book that established periodization and many of its terms and approaches. It is largely a pedagological text; in other words it takes the training process and treats it as if it were a curriculum to achieve a learning outcome rather than a scientifically based approach to training. Nevertheless, it is important to read for the background that it provides to this subject.

Verchoshanskij, J.V. (1999) The end of "periodization" of training in top-class sport, *New Studies in Athletics*, 14(1): 47–55.

This article is a strong criticism of Matveyev's work and covers a number of shortcomings to Matveyev's approach to periodization. It should be pointed out that Verchoshanskij had his own approach to the subject that he was marketing, so this is hardly unbiased. Nevertheless, the author raises a number of interesting points in this article.

Cissik, J., Hedrick, A. and Barnes, M. (2008) Challenges applying the research on periodization, *Strength and Conditioning Journal*, 30(1): 45–51.

Cissik *et al.* (2008) point out a number of important flaws to the research foundation of periodization in this article. Essentially, they point out that periodization research rarely uses athletes as subjects, rarely lasts longer than 12 to 16 weeks, and only uses strength training. These are important shortcomings because periodization is about the totality of the athlete's training experience; research that does not examine that is limited in its applicability.

CHAPTER NINE

INJURIES

Injuries are a fact of life in athletics. Athletes may not be able to take time off from training and competition as a result of injury. This chapter is going to examine some of the more common injuries in athletics, discuss what is occurring as a result of these injuries and how they are treated, and cover how they can be trained around and rehabbed.

OUTLINE

Shoulder injuries

Lower back injuries

- Sprains/strains
- Spondylolysis/spondylolisthesis
- Lumbar disc injury

Hamstring injuries

Knee injuries

- Tendinitis
- Ligament injuries
- Meniscus injuries

Groin injuries

Shin splints

Ankle injuries

Key readings

SHOULDER INJURIES

The shoulder is probably the most complicated joint in the human body. There are four joints associated with the shoulder:

■ Scapulothroacic. Interaction between the fascia of the muscle and the thorax helps to provide for stability and shock absorption when the arm is outstretched or overhead.
■ Sternoclavicular. This connects the clavicle to the sternum and prevents the upward displacement of the middle clavicle.
■ Acromioclavicular. This connects the scapula to the clavicle. The ligaments involved here form the roof of the rotator cuff.
■ Glenohumeral. The humerus connecting to the scapula. It has very little bony stability; all the stability is provided by ligaments and the rotator-cuff muscles.

This chapter will deal with rotator-cuff injuries, which are primarily related to the glenohumeral and acromoclavicular joints. In the shoulder-joint complex, the rotator cuff is one of the injuries most frequently seen by strength and conditioning professionals. The rotator cuff involves the subscapularis, supraspinatus, infraspinatus, and teres minor muscles. All of these muscles attach the humerus to the scapula and pass below the acromiclavicular joint. The tendon for the biceps brachii also passes through this region. The result is an extremely crowded place just under the acromioclavicular joint (see Figure 9.1), which means that if there is any inflammation in this region it will result in the supraspinatus being pushed up against bone or ligaments, causing pain. This inflammation could be from weak rotator cuff muscles suffering strains, from an overhead motion (such as a baseball pitch) that results in the supraspinatus tendon being "caught" between the humerus and the glenoid fossa, from an inflamed biceps tendon that pushes the supraspinatus up, from a weak trapezius that misaligns the scapula, or from the shape of the acromion.

Rehabilitation is designed to address weak rotator-cuff and trapezius muscles. Rotator-cuff exercises are meant to be done with very light resistance and are focused on endurance. This should make sense as there is not enough room under the acromioclavicular joint for large, hypertrophied rotator-cuff muscles. Scapular-stabilization exercises begin with isometric holds (shrug, protract, retract, etc.), progress to performing those holds on all fours, to progressive weight-training exercises.

Depending upon the severity of the injury, strength training can be modified to allow the athlete to continue training with rotator-cuff injuries. There are several ways that this is done:

■ Limited range of motion. By limiting the range of motion of many exercises, the stress to the rotator cuff can be reduced or eliminated. With pressing exercises, this is done by ensuring that the bar is only lowered to a 90-degree angle at the elbows

188

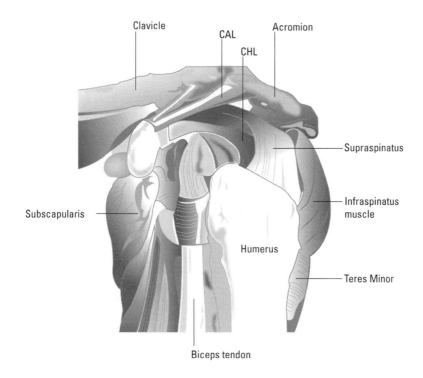

Figure 9.1 The rotator cuff.

and shoulders. This can be done by performing the bench press while lying on the floor, with boards on the chest, or with a large bath towel on the chest.

- Neutral grip/elbows in. Performing presses, rows, and pull-downs with a neutral grip (i.e., with both palms facing in towards each other) helps to reduce the stress on the rotator cuff. In terms of presses, this requires that they be performed with dumbbells. As the exercises are being performed with a neutral grip, the arms should be kept tight against the sides.

Table 9.1 summarizes modifications that can be made to popular upper-body exercises to account for a rotator-cuff injury. Table 9.2 provides a number of exercises that are used to help rehabilitate rotator-cuff injuries.

LOWER BACK INJURIES

The lower back is an area that is often injured in sports. It consists of five lumbar verte-brae that are separated by pads of tissue called discs. The discs are made of two parts:

189

Table 9.1 Exercise modifications to account for a rotator-cuff injury

Exercise	Modifications
Bench press	Towel bench press Floor bench press Close-grip bench press
Incline press	Towel-incline press Close-grip incline press
Decline press	Towel-decline press Close-grip decline press
Dumbbell bench/incline/decline press	Neutral grip dumbbell bench/incline/decline press
Pull-ups/lat pull-downs	Neutral grip pull-ups/pull-downs
Rows	Neutral grip rows, elbows against the body
Military press	Neutral grip dumbbell shoulder press

Table 9.2 Rehabilitation exercises for rotator-cuff injuries

Exercise	Description
Lying internal rotation	Lie on left side. Hold dumbbell in left hand. Flex left elbow to 90 degrees and hold upper arm against the body. Keeping the upper arm against the body, lift the dumbbell towards the body. Lower and repeat; switch sides.
Lying external rotation	Lie on left side. Hold dumbbell in right hand. Flex right elbow to 90 degrees and hold arm against the body. Keeping the upper arm against the body, lift the dumbbell upward until the back of the hand faces away from the body. Lower and repeat; switch sides.
Front raises	Stand with a dumbbell in each hand. Arms should be at the sides, with the thumbs pointing up (i.e., neutral grip). Keeping the arm straight, raise the right arm until it is parallel to the floor. Lower and repeat; switch sides.
Shrugs	Stand with a dumbbell in each hand. Arms should be at the sides, with the hands neutral. Without flexing the elbows, lift the shoulders straight up. Lower and repeat.

the *annulus*, which is the rough outer ring, and the *nucleus*, which is the inner core. Intervertebral discs act as shock absorbers and keep the spine flexible.

Sprains/strains

Sprains (tearing of ligaments) and strains (overstretching or tearing of muscles) are common lower-back injuries and result in pain, muscle spasms, and debilitation. The lower back must support body weight, generate force to overcome external resistance, maintain posture, protect the spine, and allow for movement in multiple planes. At times, the combination of these can result in a strain or sprain.

Sprains and strains are treated with rest and anti-inflammatories. They can be trained around once it is determined what activities result in pain and those activities are avoided or modified.

Spondylolysis/spondylolisthesis

Spondylolysis refers to a stress fracture in one of the vertebrae that make up the spinal column. If the stress fracture weakens the vertebrae to the point that it is unable to maintain its proper position, it can shift out of place, eventually causing it to press on nerves. This is referred to as *spondylolisthesis*.

These injuries are normally caused by overuse, particularly in sports like gymnastics, weightlifting, and American football, which put a great deal of stress on the lumbar vertebrae. Spondylolysis may feel like a muscle strain and can cause muscle spasms, tight hamstring muscles, and pain that radiates down the legs as the nerves are compressed.

These injuries are treated with a combination of rest, anti-inflammatories, and abdominal/lower-back exercises designed to strengthen the supporting structures of the lower back. If safe, exercises that do not load the vertebrae of the lower back could be continued, though weight-bearing exercises should be discontinued until the athlete is medically cleared to resume them.

Lumbar disc injuries

Intervertebral discs can lose their integrity as a result of injury. When this happens, the nucleus begins to push out (called a *bulging disc*). The bulge of the nucleus begins to rub against the spinal cord and nerves, resulting in pain that refers to different parts of the body and muscle spasms. If the injury is severe enough, the annulus will rupture and the nucleus will push out of the disc (called a *herniated disc*) (see Figure 9.2).

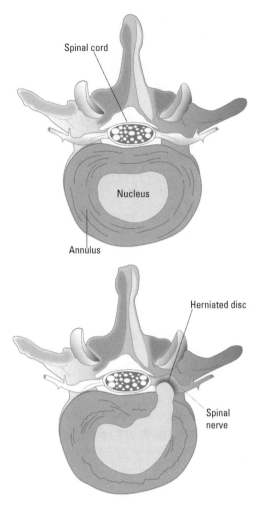

Figure 9.2 Herniated disc.

These types of lumbar disc injuries are incapacitating while in the acute stage. They are treated with rest, anti-inflammatories, rehabilitation, modalities to address the muscle spasms, and, in some circumstances, surgery. Rehabilitation is designed to strengthen the muscles of the lower back and abdomen, restore range of motion, and teach the patient how to quiet the muscle spasms.

Once the acute phase of the injury has subsided, it is possible to train around these injuries provided that this is done in a way that does not load the lumbar spine. For example, an individual with a herniated disc at the lumbar spine will not be able to back squat but they may be able to perform leg extensions and leg presses.

HAMSTRING INJURIES

Many athletes suffer hamstring injuries during the sprinting motion. During the sprinting motion, the athlete's heel is lifted up to their hip, then the leg cycles forward. As the leg cycles forward the heel uncouples from the hip, at which point the foot is driven down to the ground. It is this uncoupling motion that is often the cause of hamstring injuries, this is because the hamstring serves as a brake on the lower leg so that the knee is not hyperextended. The hamstring must have a strong eccentric contraction during this part of the sprinting motion.

Hamstring injuries are extremely limiting to athletes. They interfere with sprinting, jumping, changing directions, and starting explosively. For the most part, these injuries will be treated with a combination of rest, ice, and anti-inflammatory medications. With extreme injuries, they may require surgery. Progressively, hamstring injuries are rehabbed using static stretching and exercises like Romanian deadlifts to restore range of motion, followed by low-velocity eccentric strengthening, then gradually performing plyometrics and speed/agility training (Brughelli and Cronin, 2008; Comfort et al., 2009).

Hamstring injuries, depending upon severity, can be trained around. A number of cardiovascular exercises, such as stationary bicycles and elliptical cross-trainers, can be used instead of running or sprinting. The range of motion on most lower-body exercises can be reduced to limit hamstring strain (for example, a quarter-squat instead of a half-squat). Even with these modifications, for most athletes, sprinting and agility work will be impossible with a hamstring injury. Table 9.3 provides a summary of modifications to exercises that can be done to account for hamstring exercises. Table 9.4 provides exercises that can be used to rehabilitate or help prevent hamstring injuries.

Table 9.3 Exercise modifications to account for a hamstring injury

Exercise	Modification
Sprinting, jogging	Stationary bicycle or elliptical cross-trainer
Squats (back, front, pause, eccentric)	Only descend to 50–60 degrees of knee flexion
Leg press	Only descent to 50–60 degrees of knee flexion
Lunges, split squats	Avoid
Leg curls	Avoid

KNEE INJURIES

The knee is another complicated joint that is frequently injured in sports. Some of these injuries are a result of overuse, others as a result of an accident or incident. This chapter will cover tendinitis, ligament injuries, and meniscus injuries.

Table 9.4 Exercises for hamstring injury rehabilitation

Exercise	Description
Walk, touch toes	Face the course. Keeping the left knee straight, swing the left leg forward from the hip. Take the right hand, lean forward, and touch the left foot. Alternate sides until the desired distance has been covered.
March, touch toes	Face the course. Keeping the left leg straight, raise the left leg in front of the body, ideally parallel to the floor. As the left leg is raised, reach across the body with the right arm so that the right hand touches the left foot. Alternate sides until the desired distance has been covered.
Inchworms	Assume the push-up position. The head should face the course. Keeping the legs straight, walk the feet up to the hands. Once the feet reach the hands, walk the hands out until the body is back in the push-up position. Repeat until the desired distance has been covered.
Stability ball hip raises	Lie face up on the ground, arms should be at the sides. With the legs straight, the heels should be supported by a stability ball. Keeping the legs straight, lift the hips up into the air until the hips are fully extended. Lower and repeat for the desired number of repetitions.
Stability ball leg curl	Lie face up on the ground, arms should be at the sides. With the legs straight, the heels should be supported by a stability ball. Keeping the legs straight, lift the hips up into the air until the hips are fully extended. With the hips in the air, flex the knees bringing the stability ball towards the body. Extend the knees and repeat for the desired number of repetitions.

Tendinitis

Tendons attach muscles to bones. As such they are important for transmitting force to the bone to allow for movement. Due to overuse, they can become inflamed or suffer small tears, which cause pain. It is not uncommon for athletes who participate in jumping, running, or heavy lifting to develop tendinitis at the tendons that inserts the quadriceps group and the patella into the shin.

Tendinitis is treated with a mixture of rest, ice, and anti-inflammatories. In extreme situations, surgery may be required. Once the symptoms resolve, it is addressed through a combination of stretching and strengthening of the muscles that surround the knee, especially eccentric strengthening.

194

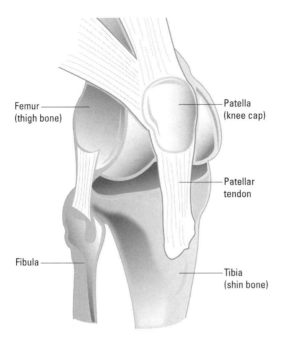

Figure 9.3 Patellar and quadriceps tendon.

Training through this injury can be done in the short term, but it will make the situation worse. If the athlete must train around the injury, it is important to get as much blood to the area as possible. This means a warm-up focusing on activities such as the stationary bicycle, dynamic flexibility exercises, and low-intensity activities prior to the main efforts.

Ligament injuries

There are several ligaments that are commonly injured in the knee. These include:

- anterior cruciate ligament;
- posterior cruciate ligament;
- medial collateral ligament;
- lateral collateral ligament.

Anterior cruciate ligament

The anterior cruciate ligament (ACL) connects the femur to the tibia and resists the forward movement of the tibia in relation to the femur. According to Lohmander *et al.* (2007), the ACL is the most commonly disrupted knee ligament. ACL injuries are the

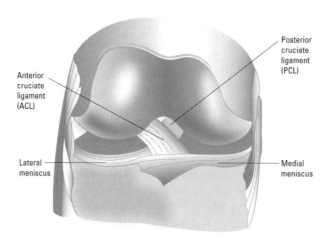

Figure 9.4 Anterior and posterior cruciate ligaments.

result of a twisting motion, a blow to the knee, or from landing improperly. Shimokochi and Shultz (2008) report that ACL injuries frequently occur when the knee is in shallow flexion (less than 20 degrees) or hyperextension, and when the quadriceps forces are not balanced out by a strong hamstring co-contraction. In addition to the short-term disruption that an ACL injury will cause to performance, it can also lead to long-term degenerative changes to the knee such as osteoarthritis (Lohmander et al., 2007).

Women are two to eight times more prone to ACL injuries than males. There are a number of theories about why this is the case including the presence of estrogen, width of the hips, and a lack of hamstring strength that affect both change of direction and landing mechanics (Beaulieu et al., 2008; Ebben et al., 2010).

ACL sprains will require rest, ice, and anti-inflammatories. ACL tears require surgery followed by a long period of rehabilitation.

Contact injuries cannot really be prevented. Injuries resulting from a change of direction or from landing can be prevented both through improving technique and from strengthening the joint, with a focus on learning to use the hamstrings during landing.

Posterior cruciate ligament

The posterior cruciate ligament (PCL) connects the femur to the tibia and resists the backward movement of the tibia in relation to the femur. PCL injuries are rarer than ACL injuries and are usually the result of a blow to the tibia when the knee is flexed. As they are the result of contact, not a lot can be done to prevent these injuries.

PCL sprains will require rest, ice, and anti-inflammatories. PCL tears require surgery to fix followed by a period of rehabilitation.

Medial and lateral collateral ligaments

These ligaments restrain valgus (knock-kneed, the medial ligament) and varus (bow-legged, the lateral ligament) movements. Injuries to these ligaments are generally the result of a blow and they are frequently injured along with the ACL and PCL. As it is the result of contact, not a lot can be done to prevent these injuries. As with the ACL and PCL injuries, they are usually treated with rest, ice, anti-inflammatories, and surgery, if the injury is severe enough, all followed by a period of rehabilitation.

Injuries to the ACL, PCL, and medial/lateral collateral ligaments can be trained around, depending upon severity, but they will severely limit athletic performance. It is not uncommon for individuals to live with complete tears to these ligaments, but it is impossible to rapidly change directions without them. Many of the lower-body exercises outlined in Chapter Two can be performed without these ligaments by wrapping or bracing the knee.

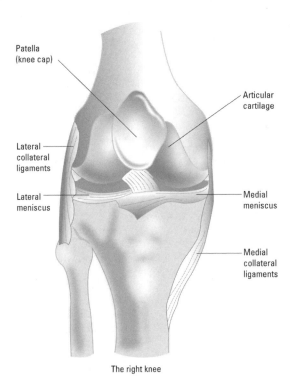

Patella (knee cap)

Articular cartilage

Lateral collateral ligaments

Lateral meniscus

Medial meniscus

Medial collateral ligaments

The right knee

Figure 9.5 Medial and lateral collateral ligaments, meniscus.

Open-chain exercises seem to provide more strain to the ACL and PCL than closed-chain exercises due to the lack of muscular co-contraction, this suggests that they should be avoided during an ACL or PCL injury unless they are part of a supervised rehabilitation program. By contrast, closed-chain exercises performed at greater than 50–60 degrees of knee flexion stress the PCL, which suggests that that deep closed-chain exercises should be avoided during a PCL injury.

Meniscus injuries

The meniscus sits on top of the tibia and serves as a shock absorber, preventing bone-to-bone contact between the femur and the tibia. Tears to the meniscus are typically caused by twisting motions. It is not unusual for a meniscus injury to accompany an ACL injury (Lohmander et al., 2007). They result in pain, catching, and locking sensations.

Meniscus injuries heal with difficulty, due to the fact that much of the meniscus lacks a direct blood supply, instead relying on diffusion (Jarit and Bosco, 2010). With this in mind, it is important for an athlete with a meniscus injury to avoid weight-bearing exercises and to focus on cardiovascular exercises such as the stationary bicycle and open kinetic-chain exercises such as leg extensions.

Table 9.5 provides a summary of modifications to exercises that can be done to account for tendonitis and meniscal injuries.

Table 9.5 Modifications to exercises to account for knee injuries

Injury	Exercise	Modification
Tendonitis	Sprinting, jogging	Stationary bicycle.
	Squats/leg presses	Limit descent to 50–60 degrees of knee flexion or pain-free range-of-motion.
	Leg extensions	Avoid.
	Plyometrics	Avoid.
	Power cleans/snatches	Avoid squat versions of the lifts, limit knee flexion to 50–60 degrees or pain-free range-of-motion when receiving the barbell
Meniscus	Sprinting, jogging	Stationary bicycle.
	Squats/leg press	Limit knee flexion to 50–60 degrees during descent. If this is not pain-free then substitute with leg extensions.
	Plyometrics	Avoid.
	Power cleans/snatches	Avoid squat versions of the lifts, limit knee flexion to 50–60 degrees or pain-free range-of-motion.

injuries

GROIN INJURIES

Hip-adductor (i.e., groin) muscle strains are the most common injury in hockey and occur more often in hockey and soccer than in other sports (Nicholas and Tyler, 2002). The adductor muscles consist of the pectineus, adductor longus, adductor brevis, adductor magnus, gracilis, and obturator eternus. The adductor longus is believed to be the muscle that is most frequently injured.

Once a groin injury has occurred, depending upon the severity, it is addressed by a combination of rest, ice, and anti-inflammatories. There is then a progressive period of rehabilitation focusing on strengthening the abductors/adductors, balance training, abdominal training, and slide-board training, progressively leading back to sport-specific training (ibid.).

There is believed to be a relationship between the ratio of adductor strength to abductor strength and being at greater risk of a groin injury. Those athletes with less adductor strength are more at risk. Exercises such as sumo squats, side lunges, ball squeezes, and adduction performed against resistance are all methods to improve adduction strength and could help prevent injuries.

SHIN SPLINTS

Shin splints are also known as medial tibial stress syndrome and are manifested as pain along the posterior medial side of the mid-to-distant tibia. There is no clear consensus on which muscles are responsible for shin splints, with the soleus, tibialis posterior, and flexor digitorun longus all being implicated in the literature (Moen et al., 2009). Many athletes experience shin splints when they perform sprinting or jogging programs. Shin splints are thought to be a result of increasing volume too soon, running surfaces (for example concrete or artificial turf), improper footwear, or genetics.

Shin splints are treated with a combination of rest, ice, and anti-inflammatories. The factors that could have contributed to the shin splints need to be addressed (footwear, volume, etc.) to the extent possible. As the athlete resumes activities, a progressive strengthening program should be implemented.

Shin splints are challenging to train around. The athlete is going to be unable to sprint or jog without aggravating the injury, which means that fitness must be maintained with exercises such as the stationary bicycle and the elliptical cross-trainer. In the short term, this will allow for the athlete's fitness to be maintained, but if the athlete requires eight or more weeks of time off, then their fitness will suffer.

Table 9.6 provides a summary of exercises that can be used to help prevent shin splints. Normally, these are performed as part of a cool-down following a running or sprinting workout.

Table 9.6 Sample shin splint prevention exercises

Exercise	Description
Walk on toes	Drill is performed barefoot. Plantarflex the ankles. Walk the desired distance, do not let the heels touch the ground.
Walk on heels	Drill is performed barefoot. Dorsiflex the ankles. Walk the desired distance, do not let the balls of the feet touch the ground.
Walk toes in	Drill is performed barefoot. Plantarflex the ankles. Turn the toes in. Walk the desired distance with the ankles plantarflexed and the toes in.
Walk toes out	Drill is performed barefoot. Plantarflex the ankles. Turn the toes out. Walk the desired distance with the ankles plantarflexed and the toes out.
Walk on inside of feet	Drill is performed barefoot. Evert the ankles. Walk the desired distance with the ankles everted.
Walk on outside of feet	Drill is performed barefoot. Invert the ankles. Walk the desired distance with the ankles inverted.
Stand on one foot, medicine-ball chest pass	Drill is performed barefoot. Stand on one foot. Face partner. Perform chest passes with the medicine-ball.
Stand on one foot, varied medicine-ball throws	Drill is performed barefoot. Stand on one foot. Face partner. Perform medicine-ball throws to shoulder, chest, waist, and knee height.
Stand on one foot, medicine-ball throws, unstable surface.	Perform any of the medicine-ball drills while standing on one foot on an unstable surface.

ANKLE INJURIES

Ankle-ligament sprains are one of the most common injuries in sports. Most ankle sprains are a result of an inversion injury, with damage to the anterior talofibular ligament or the calcaneofibular ligament being the most likely culprits (Hancock, 2008).

Ankle-ligament sprains are treated with a combination of rest, ice, compression, and anti-inflammatories. Rehabilitation focuses on progressively reducing swelling, increasing range of motion, increasing proprioception, increasing strength, and gradually preparing the athlete for sport-specific training (ibid.).

A strength and conditioning program is probably not going to prevent ankle sprains resulting from contact or from a bad landing, though it is conceivable that it could reduce the severity of the injury, but this is impossible to substantiate. If a coach wanted to design a program to help prevent ankle injuries, the focus should be on proprioception (i.e., balance) exercises combined with strengthening the muscles that act on the ankle.

To a point, an ankle injury can be trained around, though it may make the injury worse. This is usually done by taping or bracing the ankle to improve its stability. An ankle injury is going to make changing directions and landing very difficult, though many strength-training exercises could still be performed even with the injury.

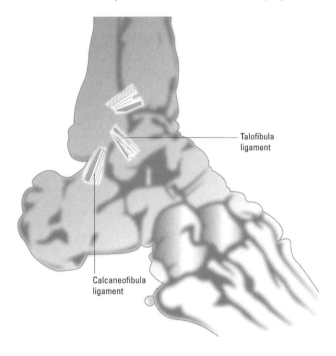

Talofibula ligament

Calcaneofibula ligament

Figure 9.6 Lateral ankle ligaments.

KEY READINGS

McKenzie, R.A. (1998) *The Lumbar Spine: Mechanical Diagnosis and Therapy*, Spinal Publications: Wellington, New Zealand.

The use of exercise in the treatment of lower-back injuries is contentious. This book, now in multiple editions, promotes the use of lumbar-extension exercises to strengthen the muscles along the spine and to help relieve lower back pain. It's important for the strength and conditioning professional to be familiar with it as it is one of the foundational books using exercise as therapy.

Escamilla, R.F., Fleisig, G.S., Zheng, N., Lander, J.E., Barrentine, S.W., Andrews, J.R., Bergemann, B.W., and Moorman III, C.T. (2001) Effects of technique variation on knee biomechanics during the squat and leg press, *Medicine and Science in Sports and Exercise*, 33(9): 1552–66.

Escamilla *et al.* (2001) studied the effects of the squat and leg-press exercise on how the knee experiences these exercises. It is an important study, and relevant to this chapter, because it reveals during which parts of each exercise various structures are loaded more or less. It also helped to disprove the idea that the squat exercise stresses the anterior cruciate ligament.

CHAPTER TEN

AGE AND TRAINING

Most strength and conditioning research, guidelines, and publications are geared towards an 18–30-year-old population. This should make sense as this population represents the bulk of elite athletes and college students, which are the primary focus of most research and coaching publications. Unfortunately, many individuals do not fall into either group. This makes applying strength and conditioning research and recommendations challenging as people that are older or younger will respond differently to training and will have different needs. This chapter will address two different age groups (youth and masters) and discuss how strength and conditioning is different for each age group.

OUTLINE

Youth

Masters

Key readings

YOUTH

Individuals under the age of 18 represent a large segment of the sporting population. It is not unusual for coaches, parents, and the athletes themselves to want to engage in strength and conditioning to improve performance, prevent injuries, enhance fitness, and improve body image. With the youth population, there are concerns about both the safety and the effectiveness of strength and conditioning.

With regards to safety, the primary concern deals with potential injuries to the athlete's *growth plates*. The growth plates are located at the ends of the long bones. As a youth grows, cartilage is deposited at the growth plate, which lengthens the bone. This cartilage is then transformed into bone. It needs to be kept in mind that young athletes have skeletons that are still growing. Kemper (2000) reports that peak bone mass is achieved between 16 and 23 for females and between 16 and 25 for males. Theoretically, overhead lifts and maximal lifts could result in a fracture to one of the growth plates, which could impact the growth of a young athlete's skeleton.

Faigenbaum et al., in a 2009 position statement, report that there are no documentable growth-cartilage injuries from strength training. There are, however, other injuries to youth from strength training. Myer et al. (2009) examined three years of United States emergency-room visits and found that the bulk of strength training-related injuries are accidents, primarily to the feet (i.e., something is dropped on the foot) or strains/sprains.

The effectiveness of strength training for youth has also been called into question. This is logical as youths do not have the anabolic hormones to increase muscle mass as a result of strength training. A number of studies find that age-appropriate strength and conditioning is effective for five-year-old children and up for increasing strength, bone mineral density, vertical jump, sprinting speed, and shuttle run speed (De Renne et al., 1996; Faigenbaum et al., 2001; Faigenbaum et al., 2002; Wong et al., 2010).

Before designing a strength and conditioning program for youth, it needs to be kept in mind that they are not simply tiny adults; there are some fundamental differences in their physiology and this will impact the effectiveness of a strength and conditioning program. First, boys and girls are similar in terms of 10-meter and 30-meter sprinting velocities and both upper-body and abdominal muscular endurance until somewhere between the ages of 12 and 16 (Castro-Pinero et al., 2009; Papaiakovou et al., 2009). These differences suggest that they may respond in a similar manner up until the ages of 12–16, at which time it may be appropriate to differentiate the programs based upon differences in athletic performance measures.

Not only are the similarities and differences between the genders important to factor in, but youth of different ages will also experience training differently. For example, Gabbett et al. (2008b) compared 14-year-old rugby players to 17-year-old ones. None of the players had previous experience with strength training. The athletes performed ten weeks of periodized, total-body strength training. The authors found that the younger athletes had greater improvements in speed, muscular power, upper-body muscular endurance, and maximal aerobic power than did the older athletes.

A second important difference is that youths do not respond to adult volume and intensity recommendations in the same manner as adults. The research that has been done indicates that youth aged 5 to 13 make the best increases in strength when exposed to moderate volumes (10–15 repetitions per set) and moderate intensities (50–100 percent of 10-RM) (De Renne et al., 1996; Faigenbaum et al., 2001). This is very different when compared to adults that need lower volumes and much greater intensities for increases in strength.

A final difference is that youths do not require free weights or special selectorized equipment to make improvements. Wong et al. (2010) studied 62 Chinese soccer players (around 13 years old) and found that 12 weeks of strength and power training using medicine balls, sand bags, and body weight resulted in 5 to 6 percent improvements in vertical jump, soccer-ball speed, and ten-meter sprints, and a 20 percent improvement in shuttle run time.

With the above in mind, a number of guidelines can be presented regarding the strength and conditioning of youth:

- Proper supervision is important for creating a safe and effective experience.
- One to two strength-training sessions a week is plenty for five- to 12-year-olds; older athletes can progress to three sessions per week.
- Exercises should focus on one to two sets of 10–15 repetitions at 50–100 percent of 10-RM intensity for five to 12-year-olds; older athletes can progress to three sets and greater intensities.
- Youth will receive benefit from all modes of strength training including medicine balls and sand bags.
- Sprinting, agility, and plyometrics are appropriate for youth, provided that proper supervision exists, technique is emphasized, and the volume and intensity are controlled.
- For youth to have a successful experience, strength and conditioning must be a fun and rewarding experience, otherwise the coach will never hold their interest. This requires approaching the training very differently than with adults or elite athletes.

Table 10.1 compares age-appropriate strength training sessions with the above guidelines in mind. The first age group (5–13) focuses primarily on bodyweight and medicine-ball exercises with a very low volume (typically one set per exercise). The second age group (14–16) incorporates a combination of free-weight, medicine-ball, and body-weight exercises. The volume is greater than with the first age group. The final age group (17+) uses free weights on all the exercises, trains with three or more sets per exercise, and is able to train at a percentage of 1-RM on appropriate exercises.

MASTERS

Aging in a non-active population results in a number of changes that affect an individual's ability to go through the activities of daily life (ADL). These include an atrophy of fast-twitch muscle fibers, a reduced ability to generate force, a reduction in rates of force development, reduced power, reduced speed, and reduced stride length (walking and running).

Many of these changes can be positively influenced by strength-training programs. A number of studies looking at previously inactive populations show that 12–24 weeks of

Table 10.1 Age-appropriate strength-training sessions

Age 5–13	Age 14–16	Age 17+
Dynamic flexibility exercises, 5–10 minutes.	Dynamic flexibility exercises, 5–10 minutes.	Dynamic flexibility exercises, 5–10 minutes.
Medicine ball power clean and press, × 10–15.	Medicine ball power clean and press, 2 × 10–15.	Power clean, 3 × 6 × 60%.
Squat jumps, × 10–15.	Back squats, 2 × 12–15.	Back squats, 3 × 8–12 × 80%.
Squats, medicine ball held in front of body, × 10–15.	Inchworms, 10 meters.	Romanian deadlifts, 3 × 8–12.
Inchworms, 10 meters.	Bench press, 3 × 12–15.	Bench press, 3 × 8–12 × 80%.
Wheelbarrows, 10 meters.	Pull-ups.	Bent-over rows, 3 × 8–12.
Push-ups, 1 × max.		Military press, 3 × 8–12.
Pull-ups, 1 × max.		

strength training results in significant increases in strength, rate of force development, vertical jump, stride length, fast-twitch muscle-fiber area, and gait speed (Caserotti *et al.*, 2008; DeBeliso *et al.*, 2005; Hakkinen *et al.*, 2001; Hanson *et al.*, 2009; Harris *et al.*, 2004; Persch *et al.*, 2009). Hurley and Roth (2000) state that decades of age-related loss in strength and muscle mass can be regained in the first few months of a strength-training program.

Research investigating strength training and the normal older population reveals that many approaches to strength training are effective. For example, Harris *et al.* (2004) had 76 subjects, with a mean age of 71.2, perform one of three selectorized strength-training workouts twice a week with two to three minutes' rest in between sets for 18 weeks:

Group A: 2 × 15 RM
Group B: 3 × 9 RM
Group C: 4 × 6 RM

At the end of the 18 weeks, all three groups significantly improved in terms of upper-body and lower-body strength, but there was no statistically significant difference between them.

DeBeliso *et al.* (2005) had 60 subjects with a mean age of 71.6 perform 18 weeks of selectorized strength training, twice a week. One group performed 3 × 9 RM on each exercise, the other performed a periodized program with six weeks of 2 × 15 RM, six weeks of 3 × 9 RM, and six weeks of 4 × 6 RM. Both groups significantly improved upper- and lower-body strength with no statistically significant difference between the groups.

Based upon these studies and others, a few recommendations can be developed regarding strength training and older individuals:

- Proper supervision is important for creating a safe and effective experience.
- Two sessions a week, at least for the first six months of training, are adequate for increasing strength and muscle mass.
- Moderate volume and intensity are very effective at increasing strength and muscle mass in older individuals. Sets of eight to 15 are appropriate.
- Most studies examine the effects of selectorized strength training on older adults. Free weights will certainly be effective, but these should be used after giving the individuals a chance to get into shape with the selectorized equipment.

Table 10.2 compares a week of workouts for active 18–30-year-olds with a week of workouts for an adult 65+. The younger adult is working out five times a week on a push/pull/lower-body split. When appropriate, they are training at a percentage of 1-RM. The older adult is training twice per week, focusing on the whole body during each session. The volume (two sets per exercise) is considerably lower than for the younger adult, as is the intensity level.

The above assumes a typically inactive older adult. What about masters athletes? Research on masters weightlifters and sprinters shows an inevitable age-related decline in performance. Table 10.3 shows the average annual decline in weightlifting total (snatch plus clean and jerk) for masters weightlifters by decade. Notice that it is not a linear decline; there are two periods, 50–60, and 70+ where the rate of decline accelerates.

Table 10.4 shows the age-related decline in factors affecting sprinting performance in masters sprinters aged 30-plus. The table reveals a steady decline in strength, stride length/frequency, velocity, performance, vertical jump, and fast-twitch fiber area despite the activity level of the athletes. In addition, Korhonen et al. (2005) report that elite master sprinters suffer an age-related decline in peak lactic acid following 100-meter, 200-meter, and 400-meter sprints, and Hamilton (1993) reports that elite master sprinters have a reduced hip and knee range of motion during the sprint, which impacts their ability to exert force against the ground.

Strength training can address some of these declines in masters athletes. Cristea et al. (2008) studied masters sprinters (mean age 66) and had them perform a strength and conditioning program that included squats, variations of the Olympic lifts, Romanian deadlifts, and plyoemtrics for 20 weeks. At the end of that time, the athletes increased their back squat 1-RM by almost 30 percent, their squat jump height by almost 10 percent, and their fast-twitch muscle fiber area by almost 20 percent.

Regardless of training status, there will be an age-related decline in performance as an athlete ages. Some of that can be minimized with strength training, but it cannot be halted. This age-related decline will not be a linear one, but will have periods where it will accelerate.

Table 10.2 Comparison of workouts for active 18–30-year-olds with older adults

	18–30	65+
Monday	Bench press, 3 × 8–12 × 80% Dumbbell incline press, 3 × 8–12 Dumbbell flies, 3 × 12–15 Military press, 3 × 8–12 Triceps pushdowns, 3 × 12–15	Leg press, 2 × 12–15 Lunges, 2 × 12–15 Leg curls, 2 × 12–15 Dumbbell bench press, 2 × 12–15 Lat pull-downs, 2 × 12–15 Dumbbell shoulder press, 2 × 12–15
Tuesday	Lat pull-downs, 3 × 8–12 Bent-over rows, 3 × 8–12 One-arm dumbbell rows, 3 × 8–12 Shrugs, 3 × 8–12 Biceps curls, 3 × 12–15	
Wednesday	Back squats, 3 × 8–12 × 80% Leg press, 3 × 8–12 Leg extensions, 3 × 12–15 Calf raises, 3 × 12–15	
Thursday	Off	Leg extensions, 2 × 12–15 Back squats, 2 × 12–15 Romanian deadlifts, 2 × 12–15 Dumbbell incline press, 2 × 12–15 One-arm dumbbell rows, 2 × 12–15 Dumbbell shoulder press, 2 × 12–15
Friday	Incline press, 3 × 12–15 Pull-ups, 3 × 12–15 Upright rows, 3 × 12–15 Triceps extensions, 3 × 12–15 Dumbbell curls, 3 × 12–15	
Saturday	Front squats, 3 × 4–6 × 80% Romanian deadlifts, 3 × 8–12 Leg curls, 3 × 12–15 Calf raises, 3 × 12–15	

Table 10.3 Age-related declines in two-lift total in masters weightlifters

Decades	Average annual decline in two-lift total
40–50 years	1.03%
50–60 years	1.85%
60–70 years	1.30%
70+ years	3.05%

Source: Adapted from Meltzer 1994.

age and training

Table 10.4 Age-related declines in sprinting performance in master sprinters

Variable	Average decline per decade
60m-sprint time	6%
100m-sprint time	7%
Maximum velocity	5–6%
Stride length	4–5%
Stride frequency	1–2%
Type II fiber area	7%
Type I fiber area	No change
Maximum strength	9%
Vertical jump	11%

Source: Adapted from Korhonen *et al.* 2003, Korhonen *et al.* 2009, Rearburn and Dascombe 2009.

Table 10.5 compares the training week of an 18–30-year-old sprinter with a masters sprinter. The week for the 18–30-year-old sprinter represents a typical week of training for the off-season. Speed work is divided into acceleration (Monday), maximal velocity (Wednesday), and speed endurance (Friday) sessions. Strength work is divided into maximal strength (Monday, links with acceleration), hypertrophy (Wednesday and Friday, links with maximal velocity and speed endurance), and power (Tuesday and Thursday, links with plyometrics) sessions. The masters sprinter does not perform as much strength-training work, only three sessions per week with a reduced volume and intensity, though many of the exercises are similar (note that one session consists entirely of body-weight exercises performed in a circuit). Speed work is only performed twice per week, focusing on acceleration (Tuesday) and maximal velocity. The masters athlete also has a cardio-vascular exercise session to help the muscles of the lower body recover from the training.

KEY READINGS

Korhonen, M.T., Mero, A.A., Alen, M., Sipila, S., Hakkinen, K., Liikavainio, T., Viitasalo, J.T., Haverinen, M.T. and Suominen, H. (2009) Biomechanical and skeletal muscle determinants of maximum running speed with aging, *Medicine and Science in Sports and Exercise*, 41(4): 844–56.

Korhonen, M.T., Mero, A. and Suominen, H. (2003) Age-related differences in 100–m sprint performance in male and female master runners, *Medicine and Science in Sports and Exercise*, 35(8): 1419–28.

Meltzer, D.E. (1994) Age dependence of Olympic weightlifting ability, *Medicine and Science in Sports and Exercise*, 26(8): 1053–67.

Table 10.5 Comparing the weekly training of an 18–30-year-old sprinter with a masters sprinter

	18–30	65+
Monday	Strength: Back squats, 3 × 3–6 × 90% Romanian deadlifts, 3 × 3–6 Bench press, 3 × 4–8 × 90% Bent-over rows, 3 × 4–8 Military press, 3 × 4–8 Speed: Block starts, 3 × 4 × 20 meters	Strength: Back squats, 3 × 6–10 × 80% Romanian deadlifts, 3 × 6–10 Bench press, 3 × 6–10 × 80% Pull-ups, 3 × 6–10 Military press, 3 × 6–10
Tuesday	Strength: Power clean, 3 × 3 × 60% Split jerk, 3 × 3 × 60% Clean pulls, 3 × 4 × 65% Plyometrics: Standing long jump, 3 × 5 Box jumps (1), 3 × 5 Counter-movement jumps, 3 × 5	Speed: Standing starts, 5 × 60 meters
Wednesday	Strength: Dumbbell bench press, 3 × 12–15 Dips, 3 × Max Pull-ups, 3 × Max Dumbbell shoulder press, 3 × 12–15 Biceps, 3 × 12–15 Triceps, 3 × 12–15 Speed: Standing starts, 3 × 3 × 60 meters	Strength (circuit approach, perform each exercise for 30 seconds, no rest; repeat 3×): Body-weight squats Lunges Inchworms Walking on toes Walking on heels Push-ups Dips Pull-ups Crunches Cardiovascular: Stationary bicycle, 20 minutes
Thursday	Strength: Power snatch, 3 × 3 × 60% Snatch pulls, 3 × 4 × 65% Dumbbell split clean, 3 × 4 Plyometrics: Standing triple jump, 3 × 5 Hurdle hops, 3 × 10 meters Pike jumps, 3 × 10	Plyometrics: Standing long jump, 3 × 10 Hurdle hops, 3 × 10 meters Counter-movement jump, 3 × 10
Friday	Strength: Front squats, 3 × 4–6 × 80% Lunges, 3 × 12–15 Good mornings, 3 × 12–15 Leg curls, 3 × 12–15 Calves, 3 × 12–15 Speed: Standing starts, 4 × 300 meters	Strength: Power clean, 3 × 3 × 60% Split jerk, 3 × 3 × 60% Clean pulls, 3 × 4 × 65% Speed: Block starts, 5 × 20 meters

age and training

Rearburn, P. and Dascombe, B. (2009) Anaerobic performance in masters adults, *European Reviews of Aging and Physical Activity*, 6: 39–53.

The above studies are important ones for any strength and conditioning professional who works with masters athletes. Each study tracks changes in performance over time. It needs to be pointed out that while these studies demonstrate non-linear declines in performance over time, they have limitations. None of these studies follows a group of masters athletes over time, so they are only snapshots of where the athletes were during the study. This means that the reader is unable to evaluate how each athlete's performance has changed over a 20–60-year period.

Cristea, A., Korhonen, M.T., Hakkinen, K., Mero, A., Alen, M., Sipila, S., Viitasalo, J.T., Koljonen, M.J., Suominen, H., and Larsson, L. (2008) Effects of combined strength and sprint training on regulation of muscle contraction at the whole-muscle and single-fibre levels in elite master sprinters, *Acta Physiologica*, 193: 275–289.

Cristea et al. (2008) is interesting from several standpoints. First, it demonstrates that age-related declines in athletic performance can be reversed. Second, it establishes that masters athletes are able to tolerate the same training methods that younger athletes can, though there are volume and intensity reductions. Third, it studies athletes, so presumably this population entered the study at a higher fitness level than an untrained older population.

CHAPTER ELEVEN

LEVEL OF COMPETITION AND TRAINING

Athletes who are competing at different levels have different training experiences, are at different points in terms of their genetic potential, respond to exercise differently, have different strength and conditioning needs, and have very different competition schedules. All of these considerations should influence a strength and conditioning program. With this in mind, this chapter is going to describe strength and conditioning for beginners, national-caliber athletes, and elite/professional athletes.

OUTLINE

Beginners

- Considerations
- Program design

National-caliber athletes

- Considerations
- Program design

Elite/professional athletes

- Considerations
- Program design

Key readings

BEGINNERS

Beginners are athletes that are new to sports, new to strength and conditioning programs, or not talented enough to become nationally competitive.

Considerations

There are a number of considerations with regards to a beginner's strength and conditioning program. These include:

- Training experiences. Beginners tend to have very limited training experience. Assumptions with regards to fitness and exercise techniques cannot be made. As a result, the focus of the training is going to need to be on a multifaceted approach to the development of athletic fitness that focuses on teaching foundational techniques.
- Development. Due to their limited training experience, beginners will not be very far along towards their genetic potential. As a result, highly specialized strength and conditioning exercises will not be beneficial.
- Exercise effectiveness. At this point in the athlete's development, everything is effective. The athlete will make improvements in performance from general, fundamental exercises and will not require advanced training tools.
- Strength and conditioning needs. A beginner needs to develop a fitness and skill base in their training. This refers to foundational exercises that teach basic technique, technique drills in the speed training combined with an emphasis on sprinting various distances, conditioning, and fundamental agility skills occasionally combined with other skills.
- Competition schedule. Beginners have a limited competition schedule especially compared to more advanced athletes. Very simple periodization models can be used to organize their programs with most of the training focused on preparation.

Program design

With the above in mind, beginning strength and conditioning programs will need to focus on the following: anatomical adaptations, athletic fitness, and technique.

Anatomic adaptations

This refers to getting muscles, joints, connective tissue, and the skeleton prepared to safely and effectively compete in the sport. This is achieved through multi-joint exercises, done with moderate repetitions/intensity, which train the entire body.

Athletic fitness

Beginners benefit from a broad strength and conditioning program that develops metabolic conditioning, strength, and limited power training. Two things should be kept in mind that at this stage: first, event/position-specific metabolic conditioning will not really be necessary. Second, power will increase as a result of the other training that is done, so it won't need a great deal of emphasis at this stage.

Technique

Without a long training background, it cannot be assumed that beginners understand how to perform many exercises properly. A strength and conditioning program for beginners is going to need to focus on teaching these techniques. Strength-training exercises focus on basic movements such as squats, deadlifts, Romanian deadlifts, presses, and the Olympic lifts from the hang. Speed training focuses on technique drills, starts, and sprints of various distances. Agility training focuses on the fundamental skills (start, stop, etc.).

The strength and conditioning program for a beginner will focus on a fairly simple periodization scheme, one which is organized as follows:

- Preparation period. The preparation period should make up the bulk of a beginner's training year. A beginner is not going to receive much benefit from highly specialized training; as a result, the primary focus of training is going to be on foundational, general exercises. The period should be designed around the following modes of exercise:
  - Strength training. Strength training should begin with high volume and lower intensities. As the period progresses, the volume should decrease while the intensity increases. Beginners will benefit from two to four strength-training sessions per week, depending upon how each session is organized.
  - Speed training. Speed training should begin with a focus on the dynamic warm-up and technique drills. As the period progresses, sprints of varying distances should be incorporated as well as a focus on teaching the athlete how to start explosively. It is appropriate to do one speed-training session a week for beginners, especially if agility training and metabolic conditioning will also be conducted.
  - Agility training. Agility training is going to focus on the fundamental skills. While the agility training is being conducted, the skills that are being taught in the speed-training workouts should be reinforced (i.e., start explosively, sprinting technique, etc.). Like with speed training, one session a week is appropriate for beginners.
  - Metabolic conditioning. Sprinting and circuit training are appropriate conditioning tools for beginners. As with the agility training, sprinting technique needs to be reinforced during the metabolic conditioning sessions for beginners. This type of training could be a major focus for a beginner, with up to three sessions a week.
- Competition period. Unlike more advanced athletes, the competitive period is going to be shorter, less focused on specifics, and more focused on fundamental skills.

214

Training may be cut back in favor of more focus on sport-skills training. The period should be designed around the following modes of exercise:

- Strength training. During the entire competitive period, strength training should focus on moderate volumes and intensities. Because beginners are increasing their strength so quickly, training at a prescribed percentage of 1-RM may not be optimal for many athletes. An alternative is to have the athletes focus on training at a repetition range (e.g., eight to 12 reps/set) and on increasing the number of repetitions performed at a given weight. Once the high end of the range is reached (e.g., 12 reps), the resistance is increased and the cycle begins again. Due to the focus on competitions and skills training, strength training may be reduced to two or three sessions per week.
- Speed training, agility training, and metabolic conditioning. All may be performed as in the preparatory period or the training may be radically abbreviated by combining it. For example, metabolic conditioning emphasizing sprinting also can develop speed training. Agility training performed over greater distances with limited rest also enhances metabolic conditioning.

NATIONAL-CALIBER ATHLETES

A national-caliber athlete is one who is talented enough to be competing at the national level. While genetic potential may mitigate some of this, it generally implies a history with training and competition prior to reaching this level.

Considerations

- Training experiences. A national-caliber athlete will have several years' experience with training and sports practice. They will have mastered many of the sport's fundamentals as well as the techniques for foundational exercises in a strength and conditioning program. This allows the strength and conditioning coach to begin adding more advanced exercises to a program.
- Development. Some individuals will peak at this level, others will pass through it to become an elite athlete. As a result, there is more variability at this level depending on where the athlete is in his/her genetic potential.
- Exercise effectiveness. The effectiveness of exercises is going to depend upon where the athlete is in his/her genetic potential. An athlete that is close to their peak is not going to continue responding positively to fundamental exercises. One who has not yet peaked will make gains in response to all types of exercise, including fundamental ones.
- Strength and conditioning needs. Due to a national-caliber athlete's training background, a wider variety of exercises will be used in terms of strength training, speed

training, and plyometrics. In addition, more advanced-agility drills incorporating combinations of exercises and an unpredictable element will be widely used.

■ Competition schedule. A national-caliber athlete spends more time in competition than a beginner. It may approach a quarter to half of an athlete's year. Less time is available for preparatory training and more time needs to be spent on event-specific training and peaking.

Program design

The strength and conditioning of national-caliber athletes needs to focus on anatomic adaptations, strength, power, speed, agility, sport/position-specific metabolic conditioning, and technique.

Anatomical adaptations

At this level, anatomical adaptations train ligaments and tendons, strengthen bones, and cause muscles to hypertrophy. This is achieved through multi-joint exercises, with moderate to high volumes and moderate intensities. To a point, a national-caliber athlete will benefit from additional hypertrophy in order to increase their strength and power.

Strength

Increases in strength can no longer be automatically assumed as a result of general strength training. A focus must be made on improving this quality through a combination of using appropriate exercises with low volumes and high intensities. Since the athlete will have a technical foundation already, some more advanced strength-training exercises can be used to help with strength development (e.g., pause or eccentric squats).

Power

Increases in power can no longer be assumed as a result of general training. As a result, greater emphasis must be put on the variations of the Olympic lifts and plyometrics must be introduced into the training.

Speed

For most athletes, the approaches to training used by beginners are going to continue to be effective at increasing speed. At this level, workouts may be differentiated and focused on either acceleration or maximum velocity.

Agility

Agility training is going to be a lot more important for national-caliber athletes than for beginners. Fundamental skills should be reinforced; intermediate and advanced drills should be conducted extensively.

Sport-/position-specific metabolic conditioning

This is the period in an athlete's career where sport-specific and, in some cases, position-specific metabolic conditioning should be performed. The training tools should be expanded to include strongman training in addition to sprints and circuit training.

Technique

Technique can never be assumed and should always be reinforced. The athlete will continue performing the fundamental exercises used as a beginner, but also will begin to integrate more advanced exercises and drills as their training progresses.

The strength and conditioning program for a national-caliber athlete will focus on a standard periodization scheme, one which can be organized as follows:

- General preparation phase:
  - Strength training. For this level of athlete, this phase lays the foundation for the rest of the year in terms of technique, anatomic adaptations, and strength. The strength training is designed around basic multi-joint exercises with a high to moderate volume and low to moderate intensity. As the phase progresses, the volume decreases while the intensity increases (the athlete is given a chance to adapt to the exercises and resistance before it is increased). Depending on the needs of the athlete, there may be three to five strength-training sessions per week.
  - Plyometric training. If plyometric training is included in this phase, it is generally simple double-leg exercises that teach the athlete how to explode and how to land. The volume will be low.
  - Speed training. Technique drills and sprints of varying distances will be the focus

217

of this phase of training. Volume will be low as the athlete works on technique and building a fitness base. Speed-training sessions will be organized around acceleration and/or maximal-velocity sessions. Depending on the needs of the athlete, there may be one to three speed-training sessions per week.

- Agility training. Most of this phase will be spent on fundamental skills and intermediate drills. Volume and intensity will be low as the athlete is building a technique and fitness base. Depending upon the needs of the athlete there may be one to three agility-training sessions per week.

- Metabolic conditioning. Metabolic conditioning may be a priority during this phase of training. For the national-caliber athlete, all approaches to metabolic conditioning may be used with one to four sessions per week being devoted to it depending upon need.

- Special preparation phase:

  - Strength training. This phase focuses on maximal strength and power development. Use of the Olympic lifts is expanded. Volume is moderate to low and the intensity is moderate to high. As the phase progresses, the intensity increases and the volume decreases. There may be two to four sessions per week depending upon need.

  - Plyometric training. Plyometric training may be expanded for this level of athlete, with a focus primarily on double-leg exercises although the range of exercises used may be expanded. Depending on need, there may be up to three sessions per week.

  - Speed training. Speed training will still focus on technique and building a fitness base. The number of sessions per week may be expanded depending upon the needs of the athlete.

  - Agility training. A national-caliber athlete should be able to focus agility training around intermediate drills with some reactive drills included during this phase of training. This means that the intensity will be greater than during the general preparation phase. Sessions will remain one to three per week.

  - Metabolic conditioning. Metabolic conditioning will be unchanged from the general preparation phase. It may fluctuate from one to four sessions per week depending upon the athlete's need.

- Pre-competition phase:

  - Strength training. For the national-caliber athlete, this phase should see the heaviest training of the year combined with a focus on power training. The volume will be moderate to light, with a moderate to high intensity. Sessions may be cut back to two to four per week to accommodate the greater intensity. This phase will see greater variety in terms of Olympic lifts and multi-joint exercises with tools such as bands, chains, pause lifts, and eccentric lifts employed.

  - Plyometric training. The volume and intensity of plyometric training will be increasing throughout this phase as the athlete prepares to peak. Double-leg

level of competition and training

exercises will still be the focus, but a greater variety of exercises will be used. Training may be conducted anywhere from one to three sessions per week.

■ Speed, agility, and metabolic conditioning training. Beginning with this phase, the nature of these training sessions will change. Depending on the sport, they may be combined to save time (e.g., training speed while performing agility drills). Intensity will be high with one to three training sessions per week. Agility training will primarily focus on intermediate and reactive drills.

■ Competition phase:

■ Strength training. Due to the rigors of competition and travel, strength training is cut back to two to three sessions per week with a moderate to low volume and moderate to high intensity. This serves to maintain strength and power during the competition phase. Combination and complex exercises are used to save time.

■ Plyometric training. While sessions of plyometric training could be performed, it is not unusual to combine them with strength training in the form of complex exercises to save time.

■ Speed, agility, and metabolic conditioning training. As with the pre-competition phase, these may be combined to save time (e.g., training speed while performing agility drills). Intensity will be high with one to three training sessions per week. Agility training will focus primarily on intermediate and reactive drills.

Table 11.1 summarizes differences between the beginner and the national-caliber athlete with regards to volume, intensity, and number of training sessions per week, depending on the phase of training.

ELITE/PROFESSIONAL ATHLETES

An elite/professional athlete is competing at the international level and at the peak of his or her sport. While there are always exceptions, in general this has been preceded by years of training and competition.

Considerations

■ Training experiences. Elite athletes have years and, in some cases, decades of experience. They should have a grasp of the fundamental techniques behind strength and conditioning and should have a thorough fitness base.

■ Development. Elite athletes will be close to their genetic potential in all aspects of their physical development. Improvements in strength, speed, and power will be very small and will take a great deal of effort to achieve.

■ Exercise effectiveness. The elite athlete will need to perform some of the

Table 11.1 Different approaches to training for beginner and national-caliber-athletes

Phase of training	Level of athlete	Exercise mode	Volume	Intensity	Frequency per week
General preparation	Beginner	Strength	H	L	2–4
		Plyometric	N/A	N/A	0
		Speed	L	L	1
		Agility	L	L	1
		Metabolic	M	M	1–3
	National	Strength	H	L	3–5
		Plyometric	L	L	0–1
		Speed	L	L	1–3
		Agility	L	L	1–3
		Metabolic	M	M	1–4
Special preparation	Beginner	Strength	H	L	2–4
		Plyometric	N/A	N/A	0
		Speed	L	L	1
		Agility	L	L	1
		Metabolic	M	M	1–3
	National	Strength	M	M/H	3–5
		Plyometric	L	L/M	0–3
		Speed	M	M/H	1–3
		Agility	M	M	1–3
		Metabolic	M	M/H	1–4
Pre-competition	Beginner	Strength	M	M	2–3
		Plyometric	N/A	N/A	0
		Speed	M	M	1–3
		Agility	M	M	1–3
		Metabolic	M	M	1–3
	National	Strength	M/L	M/H	2–4
		Plyometric	L/M	M/H	1–3
		Speed	L	H	1–3
		Agility	M	M	1–3
		Metabolic	M/L	M	1–3
Competition	Beginner	Strength	M	M	2–3
		Plyometric	N/A	N/A	0
		Speed	M	M	1–3
		Agility	M	M	1–3
		Metabolic	M	M	1–3
	National	Strength	M/L	M/H	1–3
		Plyometric	M/L	M/H	1–3
		Speed	L	H	1–3
		Agility	M/H	M/H	1–3
		Metabolic	M	M	1–3

fundamental exercises to maintain athletic fitness, but they will not be as effective as they would be with a beginner. At this point, the athlete will need to focus on advanced and event-specific exercises.

■ Strength and conditioning needs. Strength and conditioning programs will need to balance between the need for specificity and the need for variation. As the athlete will be close to his/her genetic potential, there is going to be a need to vary exercises on a regular basis (every two to four weeks). Advanced training tools such as extensive use of plyometrics, reactive agility training, and assisted/resisted speed training may all be employed successfully by elite athletes.

■ Competition schedule. For an elite athlete, the competition schedule may cover six to 12 months of the year. The athlete may not be competing every month, but there may be so many significant competitions spaced throughout the year that there may be no down time in terms of the athlete's training.

Program design

With elite athletes, training needs to take into account individual differences, the considerations described above, and the highly specific needs of the athlete's event/position. These factors will influence training approaches geared towards anatomic adaptations, strength, power, speed, agility, conditioning, and how the programs are periodized.

Anatomic adaptations

An elite athlete's training is going to be heavily focused on power and event-/position-specific training. There will be very little time in a training year to devote to anatomic adaptations. In addition to time constraints, two other things need to be recognized. First, the elite athlete will be close to their genetic limits in terms of the hypertrophy they need for the sport. Second, any additional muscle mass added through strength training may not have a positive impact on the sport as the athlete must be able to perform with the extra mass.

With this in mind, the focus of training changes so that there may be some training geared towards anatomic adaptations, but this will be more geared towards the rehabilitation or prevention of injuries.

Strength

This level of athlete will be close to their genetic potential in terms of strength. An enormous amount of time, energy, and effort must be spent to continue to increase strength and this effort carries heightened risks of injury from the training. At this level, it may not be worth the risks to continue aggressively attempting to increase the athlete's strength.

As a result, an elite athlete's training begins to focus on maintaining their already high levels of strength. This is done through a variety of exercises designed to keep the athlete interested and challenged as a result of training.

Power

Due to their long experience with training and their strength levels, elite athletes will spend the bulk of their time focusing on improving their power. At this level, a range of approaches is used to achieve this objective. These include the Olympic lifts and their variations, bands and chains on squats and bench presses, extensive use of plyometrics, complex training, and combined training.

Speed

The elite athlete may have performed speed training long enough that a plateau has been reached. This is the level where advanced training tools such as resisted and assisted sprinting, variable sprinting, and attempts to increase stride frequency and stride length would be appropriate.

Agility

Except as warm-up, elite athletes will not benefit from fundamental or intermediate agility skills. The focus of training will need to be on reactive drills that incorporate other athletes and implements such as balls.

Sport-/position-specific metabolic conditioning

At the elite level, conditioning is focused on the athlete's sport and on their position within the sport. These needs are determined precisely, based upon the needs of this level of competition, the athlete's performance in competition, and accounting for known challenges that specific opponents may provide. Conditioning will not be general in nature unless it is being used as a recovery modality, rather it will be as close to the athlete's event as possible.

Periodization

The classic periodization model does not serve elite athletes well. There are a number of reasons for this. First, training needs to be a lot more individualized than with other levels of athlete. This means that it needs to be structured according to the individual athlete's ability to recover and peak. Second, a long preparation phase is not going to benefit the athlete as they are already close to their genetic peak. Third, elite athletes spend a great part of the year in competition, which makes the traditional model's structure difficult.

With the exception of small periods of time, the athlete is going to be in highly specific training all year round. Due to their experience, it is best to modify the athlete's workouts every three to four weeks, depending on the athlete. At the very least the exercises should be changed every three to four weeks, if not the intensity and volume. This keeps the athlete engaged and challenged.

Table 11.2 summarizes much of the information provided in this chapter by showing how the exercises that are used will change depending upon the level of the athlete. The elite athlete has the greatest variety of exercises available to him or her, the beginner has the most basic selection of exercises.

Chapter Twelve will provide examples of periodized strength and conditioning programs for multiple levels of development that will illustrate many of the concepts covered in this chapter.

KEY READINGS

Bondarchuk, A. (1988) Constructing a training system, part I, *Track Technique*, 102: 3254–59, 3268.

Bondarchuk, A. (1988) Constructing a training system, part II, *Track Technique*, 103: 3286–88.

In these two articles, legendary throws coach Anatoli Bondarchuk describes how elite athletes are different than all other levels and how training needs to change as a result. These articles provide the foundation of the idea that for the elite athlete, training tools need to be changed regularly so that the athlete keeps progressing from training.

Cissik, J.M. (2000) Conditioning for hammer throwers, *Track and Field Coaches Review*, 73(1): 32–34.

In this short article, Cissik shows how to apply Bondarchuk's concepts to the training of the collegiate hammer thrower.

Table 11.2 Summary of differences between different levels of athletic development

Level of development	Physical quality	Exercises
Beginner	Strength	Back/front squats Deadlifts Romanian deadlifts Lunges Leg press Leg extension/curl Calf exercises Presses Rows Pulls Upper-body assistance Power clean (hang) Power snatch (hang) Jerk (all) Pulls
	Power	N/A
	Speed	Technique drills Sprints of varied distances
	Agility	Start Stop Back-pedal Shuffle Run curves Zig-zags
	Metabolic conditioning	Sprints Circuit training
National-caliber	Strength	Back/front squats Pause/eccentric squats Deadlifts Romanian deadlifts Good mornings Hyperextensions Lunges Leg press Leg extension/curl Calf exercises Presses Pause/eccentric presses Rows Pulls Upper-body assistance Power clean (hang, dumbbells, split) Power snatch (hang, dumbbells, split) Jerk (all) Pulls
	Power	Double-leg single-effort jumps Double-leg multiple-effort jumps Bounds Box jumps

Table 11.2 (continued)

Level of development	Physical quality	Exercises
	Speed	Technique drills Sprints of varied distances Varied-pace sprinting
	Agility	Fundamental skills Intermediate drills Some reactive drills
	Metabolic conditioning	Sprints Circuit training Strongman training
Elite	Strength	Back/front squats Pause/eccentric squats Squats with bands/chains Deadlifts Romanian deadlifts Good mornings Hyperextensions Lunges Leg press Leg extension/curl Calf exercises Presses Pause/eccentric presses Presses with bands/chains Rows Pulls Upper-body assistance Power clean (hang, dumbbells, split) Power snatch (hang, dumbbells, split) Jerk (all) Pulls
	Power	Double-/single-leg single-effort jumps Depth jumps Double-/single-leg multiple-effort jumps Bounds Box jumps
	Speed	Technique drills Sprints of varied distances Varied-pace sprinting Assisted/resisted sprinting
	Agility	Fundamental skills Intermediate drills Reactive drills
	Metabolic conditioning	Sprints Circuit training Strongman training

CHAPTER TWELVE

PUTTING IT ALL TOGETHER

This chapter will put together everything that has been covered in this book and apply it to the sport of soccer. It will show how the concepts apply and how they change depending upon the age and level of development of the athlete.

OUTLINE

The needs analysis

■ Needs of the sport
■ Needs of the position
■ Needs of the athlete

Beginners (pre-pubescent youth)

Beginners

National-caliber

■ Preparatory period
■ Competition period
■ Recovery period

Elite/professional

■ Preparatory period
■ Competition period

Master

Drills

Key readings

THE NEEDS ANALYSIS

Needs of the sport

Soccer is a sport played by an estimated 265 million people worldwide (Alentorn-Geli et al., 2009). It is a fast-paced, full-contact sport in which players may cover 10–12 kilometers, with as many as 1,300 activity changes in a game (Andersson et al., 2010; Bradley et al., 2010; Mohr et al., 2008). It is divided into two 45–minute halves and there is a tendency for players to cover less distance at slower speeds during the second half of play (Andersson et al., 2010; Mohr et al., 2008).

A number of authors have sought to analyze the movement patterns during the game of soccer. These movements are classified according to the speeds at which they are performed:

- standing;
- walking (6 km/hour or less);
- jogging or low-intensity running (6–12 km/hour);
- high-intensity running (12–25 km/hour);
- sprinting (25+ km/hour);
- backwards running (10 km/hour).

Table 12.1 provides a summary of some of the research looking at how much time in a game is spent performing each type of movement. While these percentages change depending upon the level of competition and domestic versus international games, and are affected by the position of the player, it is evident that the bulk of the time is spent between low-intensity activities like standing, walking, and jogging that are interspersed with short and intense sprints (Andersson et al., 2010; Bradley et al., 2010; Dellal et al., 2010; Di Salvo et al., 2007; Mohr et al., 2008).

Soccer is a contact sport, which means that players are injured as a result of participation. ACL tears, ankle sprains, overuse injuries to the lower leg and knee, contusions, and

Table 12.1 Movement patterns in soccer as a percentage of the game

Movement pattern	% of game
Standing	19.7
Walking	42.8
Jogging	27.15
High intensity running	4.4
Sprinting	0.78
Backward running	3.9

Source: Adapted from Andersson et al. 2010, Mohr et al. 2008.

concussions are common injuries (Alentorn-Geli et al., 2009; Faude et al., 2006; Hagglund et al., 2009; Junge and Dvorak, 2007; Steffen et al., 2009; Walden et al., 2007). There may be differences in injury patterns based upon the position played, with Faude et al. (2006) reporting that defenders and forwards suffer more injuries than goalkeepers and midfielders.

In addition to position, gender may influence injuries. According to Alentorn-Geli et al. (2009), female soccer players are up to six times more likely to suffer ACL injuries. With regards to other injuries, the literature is conflicted with regards to whether males and females suffer injuries at different rates. Walden et al. (2007) report no significant differences between men and women in terms of injury incidences whereas Hagglund et al. (2009) report that men are more likely to sustain hip/groin injuries with women being more likely to sustain knee injuries.

Soccer is a total-body activity with a variety of movement patterns required for success. Due to the distances covered and the variety of speeds of movement seen in the game, the soccer athlete is going to require a more well-rounded approach to strength and conditioning that emphasizes total-body strength and power training, agility, sprinting, and cardiovascular endurance. Attention will need to be paid to conditioning the knee and ankle to help prevent injuries to those areas.

Needs of the position

The main positions in soccer are the goalkeeper, the defender, the midfielder, and the forward. The goalkeepers are positioned in front of the goal and have the job of preventing shots from crossing the goal line. Defenders work mainly in the defensive third of the field and are focused on stopping the opponent's attack. Midfielders work in the middle third of the field between the defenders and the forwards. Their job is to link the defense to the offense through ball control and passing. The forwards work on the front third of the field and are responsible for most of the team's scoring.

Table 12.2 shows how the player's position influences the distances covered during a game. Notice that the midfielders cover the greatest distances at almost all speeds. Note that the level of the athlete, the nature of the competition (international versus domestic), and even gender may influence this information.

Needs of the athlete

The various soccer positions have different physiological characteristics depending upon the level of play. Table 12.3 outlines the differences for national-caliber soccer players by position. In general, goalkeepers tend to be taller, heavier, slower in terms of sprinting,

Table 12.2 Differences in movement pattern by position

	Defenders	Midfielders	Forwards
Total distance (km)	10.25	11.39	10.59
High-intensity running (km)	1.65	2.38	2.12
Sprinting (km)	0.35	0.48	0.49

Source: Adapted from Andersson *et al.* 2010, Bradley *et al.* 2010, Dellal *et al.* 2010, DiSalvo *et al.* 2007, Mohr *et al.* 2008.

Table 12.3 Physiological characteristics of national-caliber soccer players by position

	Goalkeepers	Defenders	Midfielders	Forwards
Weight (kg)	77.07	72.93	69.71	71.05
Height (cm)	179.43	177.45	174.43	176.21
Maximal oxygen consumption (ml/kg/min)	52.35	59.47	59.20	59.5
9.1-meter sprint (sec)	1.8	1.7	1.7	1.7
30-meter sprint (sec)	3.83	3.71	3.68	3.51
36.5-meter sprint (sec)	5.3	4.9	5	4.9
Squat jump (cm)	41.8	40	38.9	41.9
Counter-movement jump (cm)	48.05	52.82	51.39	53.48
Drop jump (cm)	42.9	41.35	42.26	43.46

Source: Adapted from Kaplan 2010, Silvestre *et al.* 2006.

have a lower maximal oxygen consumption, and be less explosive as measured by jumping ability. This trend continues with elite-level soccer players (Sporis *et al.*, 2009; Wong, 2008). Defenders, midfielders, and forwards tend to be very similar in terms of their physiological characteristics. This trend does not appear to continue at the elite level. At the elite level, the midfielders are shorter and lighter than the other positions and also have the greatest maximal oxygen consumption (Sporis *et al.*, 2009; Wong, 2008). At the elite level, the forwards have a slight edge on the defenders in terms of sprinting speed and jumping ability (Sporis *et al.*, 2009).

BEGINNERS (PRE-PUBESCENT YOUTH)

Due to the maturation process, beginners make increases in speed, jumping ability, and strength (Fernandez-Gonzalo *et al.*, 2010; Mirkov *et al.*, 2010; Mujika *et al.*, 2009). This increase declines as the athlete matures. For example, Mujika *et al.* studied 11–18-year-old soccer players and measured their mean 30-meter sprint time in a 6 × 30-meter sprint test. From the age of 11 to the age of 15, mean 30-meter sprint times improved by 3.5 percent per year. From the ages of 15–18, mean 30-meter sprint times only improved by only 0.8 percent per year.

At the beginner's level, there are no physiological differences between the various positions (Wong et al., 2009). This, combined with the lack of a need for a truly periodized program, means that this population can focus on a well-rounded general strength and conditioning program.

For pre-pubescent youth, a strength and conditioning program needs to focus on the following:

- a total-body approach to training;
- variety of implements – young athletes need variety to stay interested and to keep the experience fun;
- mastering fundamental skills;
- injury prevention – soccer players are likely to suffer sprains and strains particularly to the lower extremity; addressing these areas in the conditioning program may help to keep young athletes healthy;
- aerobic fitness base – more so than any other team sport, soccer players need an aerobic fitness base and this needs to be developed beginning at this level.

Table 12.4 provides a sample three-day per week conditioning program for pre-pubescent soccer players. This program is meant to be done on the soccer field in conjunction with practice and if done as written will take 20–60 minutes to complete. The last row in the table provides suggestions on how each workout can be modified to keep the athletes challenged over time.

BEGINNERS

As soccer is an international sport, it is challenging to lay out a beginner's soccer schedule. Some locations will take beginner's sport more seriously (and have more structure) than others. For the purposes of this book, these beginners are considered 14–18-year-old athletes (i.e., high-school age). The soccer season runs from January through March, with the play-offs occurring in April. Athletes play two games a week, on Tuesdays and Fridays.

Chapter Eleven covered the fact that a beginner's training will be largely general and multifaceted in nature. The program in this chapter is written as if this is the only activity that the athlete is participating in. If they are active in other sports, or play soccer outside of this season, this needs to be factored in to the athlete's program. If the athlete has a different season, the program will need to be modified accordingly.

Table 12.4 Sample workout program for pre-pubescent soccer players

	Day 1	Day 2	Day 3
Workout	Dynamic flexibility exercises, 5–10 minutes	Dynamic flexibility exercises, 5–10 minutes	Dynamic flexibility exercises, 5–10 minutes
	Medicine ball circuit with a partner (30 seconds each station; repeat circuit 3×): Chest pass Overhead chop pass Twisting throw Squats (hold ball in front of body) Lunges (hold ball overhead) Romanian deadlifts (hold ball in front of body) Crunches (hold ball in front of body) Leg raises (hold ball between feet)	Speed/agility circuit (30 seconds each station, repeat circuit 3×): Shin splint drills Ankling Heel to hip drills High knee drills A drills Shuffling Back-pedaling Start, stop, start	Total-body circuit (30 seconds each station, repeat circuit 3×): Bear crawl Push-ups Wheelbarrows Lunges Inchworms Crab walk Sit-ups Leg raises
		Sprint 30 meters, perform lunges back, sprint 30 meters, perform inchworms back, repeat 3×	Small-sided games: 20–30 minutes
	Medicine ball toss, forward (10×, throw, sprint to ball, throw again)		
	Medicine ball toss, backward (10×, throw, sprint to ball, throw again)		
Variations	Substitute sandbags, dumbbells, or kettle bells for medicine balls	Vary the times, repetitions, and number of sets	Vary the circuit exercises, times, repetitions, and number of sets
	Vary distances, times, number of repetitions, and number of sets	Vary the sprinting distances Vary the sprinting starting positions (standing start, crouching start, etc.)	Vary the rules, field size, and number of players for the small-sided games
	Vary the recovery movement with the medicine ball tosses	Vary the recovery movement with the 30-meter sprints	

Table 12.5 Organization of the beginner's year. For the periods, C refers to the Competition period, R to Recovery period, P the Preparatory period. For the phases, C refers to Competition phase, R to Recovery phase, GP to General Preparation phase, SP to Special Preparation phase, PC to Pre-competition phase

Month	J	F	M	A	M	J	J	A	S	O	N	D
Period	C	C	C	C/R	R	P	P	P	P	P	P	C
Phase	C	C	C	C/R	R	GP	GP	GP	GP	GP	SP	PC
Mesocycle	8	9	10	11	12	1	2	3	4	5	6	7

Table 12.5 provides the breakdown of the periods and phases for this soccer player. The competition phase runs for 14 weeks from January until mid-April. The athlete has six weeks of recovery after the end of the season. The preparatory phase lasts almost 24 weeks, primarily consisting of general preperation training. There are four weeks of pre-competition training in December. Table 12.5 also provides a mesocycle number under each phase of training.

Table 12.6 breaks down the first mesocycle of training. The following are the highlights of this mesocycle:

■ Free weights are introduced once per week and are designed to develop the athlete's musculo-skeletal base and teach fundamental techniques. The strength-training workouts have a moderate volume and short rest. As a result they are teamed up with small-sided games.
■ Speed, agility, and simple plyometrics are emphasized the second day of the workout program. In addition to reinforcing conditioning and enhancing speed/agility/power, these exercises also teach running, changing direction, and landing.
■ The third day is a multifaceted day that develops most qualities. Conditioning is developed by the circuit approach to the medicine-ball training as well as the small-sided games. The medicine-ball training will help to develop power, strength, and anatomical adaptations. In addition, many of the exercises will develop ankle strength by having the athlete perform the exercise on one leg at a time.

Mesocycle 1 was meant to be an introduction to organized training for the athlete. Mesocycles 2 through 5 are designed to further this, reinforce/develop techniques, and continue to expand the athlete's fitness base. Table 12.7 shows how training will be organized on a weekly basis for those mesocycles:

■ There is a focus on conditioning, in fact it is the most important aspect of this athlete's strength and conditioning program during this time. It is done three days a week. "Strength" training is put alongside conditioning. This type of training will still

232

Table 12.6 Mesocycle one, general preparation phase of training for a beginning soccer player

	Day 1	Day 2	Day 3
Workout	Dynamic flexibility exercises, 5–10 minutes	Dynamic flexibility exercises, 5–10 minutes	Dynamic flexibility exercises, 5–10 minutes
	Back squats, 2–3 × 8–15 Romanian deadlifts, 2–3 × 8–15 Bench press, 2–3 × 8–15 Bent-over rows, 2–3 × 8–15 Standing military press, 2–3 × 8–15	Speed/agility technique drills, 10 minutes	Medicine ball circuit (30 seconds each station, repeat circuit 3×): Clean and press Chest pass, stand on one leg
		Speed/agility circuit: Sprint 30 meters, shuffle back Sprint 30 meters, backpedal back, etc.	Overhead chop pass, stand on one leg Twist and throw, stand on one leg
	Small-sided games, 20–30 minutes	Plyometrics (10× each): Standing long jump Counter-movement jump Medicine ball toss, forward Medicine ball toss, backward	Squats, hold ball in front of body Romanian deadlifts, hold ball in front of body Lunges, hold ball overhead Crunches, hold ball in front of body Leg raises, hold ball in between feet
			Small-sided games, 20–30 minutes
Variations	Vary the number of sets, repetitions, and amount of weight.	Vary the number of sets, repetitions, distances, and number of sets.	Vary the number of sets, repetitions, distances, and number of sets.
	Use dumbbells instead of barbells.	Vary the recovery activity between sprints and plyometrics.	Vary the implements used in the medicine ball circuit.
	Vary the number of players, field size, number of balls, and time for the game.		Vary the number of players, field size, number of balls, and time for the game.

involve higher volumes and multiple modes of training, so it will not interfere with the conditioning training.

■ Speed, agility, and plyometrics are emphasized twice a week in between the conditioning/strength sessions. The focus is still on technique and developing a fitness base.

Table 12.7 Weekly organization of training, mesocycles 2 through 5, beginning soccer player

	Monday	Tuesday	Wednesday	Thursday	Friday
Strength	X		X		X
Speed		X		X	
Agility		X		X	
Plyometrics		X		X	
Conditioning	X		X		X

Table 12.8 provides sample workouts from each mesocycle in the general preparation phase of training (mesocycles 2 through 5). Over the course of these mesocycles, the athlete's training is evolving. Strength training will progress to the point where a 1-RM can be taken at the end of the third mesocycle, power cleans will be introduced in the fourth mesocycle, and there will be three days of weightroom strength training by the fourth mesocycle. Over the mesocycles, the conditioning evolves to focusing on sprints with varied distances and recovery schemes. By the fourth mesocycle, Friday becomes the small-sided game day as this is to prepare the athlete for Friday matches in the upcoming competitive season. Speed, agility, and plyometrics work will not change much over the course of these mesocycles as the focus is on technique and developing the athlete's fitness base.

Table 12.9 and 12.10 provide the weekly breakdowns for the special preparation/pre-competition phases of training (Table 12.9) and the competition phases of training (Table 12.10). During the special preparation and pre-competition phases (mesocycles 6 and 7), conditioning has been cut back to twice/week to allow for more of an emphasis on power training. Strength training remains at three times/week, one of the plyometrics sessions is moved to Friday to complement the strength training, and speed/agility will be largely unchanged.

During the competition phases (mesocycles 8 through 11), the games will be used to maintain the athlete's conditioning unless this is a deficiency. Strength training and plyometrics will be cut back to twice/week, with speed/agility reduced to once/week.

Table 12.11 provides sample workouts for mesocycles 6, 7, and 8 to demonstrate how training will evolve as the athlete begins competing. During these mesocycles, the strength training has progressed to the point where all the workouts are being performed in the weightroom. There is still a focus on basic exercises. By the competition phase (beginning with mesocycle 8), the athlete is performing more variations of the Olympic lifts and is training heavier than in the previous months. Due to this, the strength training is linked to the plyometrics beginning in mesocycle eight. Until the competition phase, the plyomeric workouts are the same as in the previous phases. Beginning in the competition phase, the plyometric exercises are not changed but they are used differently as they are complexed with strength training exercises to save on time.

Table 12.8 General preparation phase of training, mesocycles 2 through 5, beginning soccer player

	Mesocycle 2	Mesocycle 3	Mesocycle 4	Mesocycle 5
Monday	Dynamic flexibility exercises, 5–10 minutes	Dynamic flexibility exercises, 5–10 minutes	Dynamic flexibility exercises, 5–10 minutes	Dynamic flexibility exercises, 5–10 minutes
	Strength (rest 60 seconds between sets):	Strength (rest 60 seconds between sets):	Strength (rest 60 seconds between sets):	Strength (rest 60 seconds between sets):
	Back squats, 3 × 8–15	Back squats, 3 × 8–15	Power clean, h, AK, 3 × 6	Power clean, h, AK, 3 × 6 × 60%
	Romanian deadlifts, 3 × 8–15	Romanian deadlifts, 3 × 8–15	Back squats, 3 × 8–15 × 70%	Front squats, 3 × 8–12 × 75%
	Bench press, 3 × 8–15	Bench press, 3 × 8–15	Romanian deadlifts, 3 × 8–15-RM	Hyperextensions, 3 × 8–12-RM
	Bent-over rows, 3 × 8–15	Bent-over rows, 3 × 8–15	Bench press, 3 × 8–15 × 70%	Incline press, 3 × 8–12 × 75%
	Standing military press, 3 × 8–15	Standing military press, 3 × 8–15	Bent-over rows, 3 × 8–15-RM	One-arm dumbbell Rows, 3 × 8–12-RM
			Standing military press, 3 × 8–15-RM	Seated military press, 3 × 8–12-RM
	Conditioning:	Conditioning:	Conditioning:	Conditioning:
	10 × 30-meter sprints, 20 seconds walking recovery	11 × 35-meter sprints, 20 seconds walking recovery	12 × 40-meter sprints, 20 seconds walking recovery	2 × 10 × 20-meter sprints, 20 seconds walking recovery between sprints, 5' recovery between sets

235

Table 12.8 (continued)

	Mesocycle 2	Mesocycle 3	Mesocycle 4	Mesocycle 5
Tuesday	Dynamic flexibility exercises, 5–10 minutes	Dynamic flexibility exercises, 5–10 minutes	Dynamic flexibility exercises, 5–10 minutes	Dynamic flexibility exercises, 5–10 minutes
	Speed/agility technique drills, 10 minutes	Speed/agility technique drills, 10 minutes	Speed/agility technique drills, 10 minutes	Speed/agility technique drills, 10 minutes
	Speed/agility circuit: Sprint 30 meters, shuffle back Sprint 30 meters, back-pedal back, etc.	Speed/agility circuit: Sprint 30 meters, shuffle back Sprint 30 meters, back-pedal back, etc.	Speed/agility circuit: Sprint 30 meters, shuffle back Sprint 30 meters, back-pedal back, etc.	Speed/agility circuit: Sprint 30 meters, shuffle back Sprint 30 meters, back-pedal back, etc.
	Plyometrics (10× each): Standing long jump Counter-movement jump Medicine ball toss, forward Medicine ball toss, backward	Plyometrics (10× each): Standing long jump Counter-movement jump Medicine ball toss, forward Medicine ball toss, backward	Plyometrics (10× each): Standing long jump Counter-movement jump Medicine ball toss, forward Medicine ball toss, backward	Plyometrics (10× each): Standing long jump Counter-movement jump Medicine ball toss, forward Medicine ball toss, backward

Table 12.8 (continued)

	Mesocycle 2	Mesocycle 3	Mesocycle 4	Mesocycle 5
Wednesday	Dynamic flexibility exercises, 5–10 minutes	Dynamic flexibility exercises, 5–10 minutes	Dynamic flexibility exercises, 5–10 minutes	Dynamic flexibility exercises, 5–10 minutes
	Strength: Medicine ball circuit (30 seconds each station, repeat circuit 3×): Clean and press Chest pass, stand on one leg Overhead chop Pass, stand on one leg Twist and throw, stand on one leg Squats, hold ball in front of body Romanian deadlifts, hold ball in front of body Lunges, hold ball overhead Crunches, hold ball in front-of-body Leg raises, hold ball in between feet	Strength: Medicine ball circuit (30 seconds each station, repeat circuit 3×): Clean and press Chest pass, stand on one leg Overhead chop Pass, stand on one leg Twist and throw, Stand on one leg Squats, hold ball in front of body Romanian deadlifts, Hold ball in front of body Lunges, hold ball overhead Crunches, hold ball in front-of-body Leg raises, hold ball in between feet	Strength: Dumbbell bench press, 3 × 12–15-RM Dips, 3 × max Pull-Ups, 3 × max 3-in-1 Shoulders, 3 × 12–15-RM Biceps/triceps, 3 × 12–15-RM	Strength: Dumbbell bench press, 3 × 12–15-RM Dips, 3 × max Pull-ups, 3 × max 3-in-1 shoulders, 3 × 12–15-RM Biceps/triceps, 3 × 12–15-RM
	Conditioning: Small-sided games, 20–30 minutes	Conditioning: Small-sided games, 20–30 minutes	Conditioning: Sprinting circuit, (recovery until the next sprint): 1 × 20 meters (10 sec), 1 × 40 meters (20 sec), 1 × 60 meters (40 sec), 1 × 80 meters (60 sec), 2 × 100 meters (60 sec), 1 × 80 meters (60 sec), 1 × 60 meters (40 sec), 1 × 40 meters (20 sec), 1 × 20 meters	Conditioning: Sprinting circuit, (recovery until the next sprint): 1 × 20 meters (10 sec), 1 × 40 meters (20 sec), 1 × 60 meters (40 sec), 1 × 80 meters (60 sec), 2 × 100 meters (60 sec), 1 × 80 meters (60 sec), 1 × 60 meters (40 sec), 1 × 40 meters (20 sec), 1 × 20 meters

Table 12.8 (continued)

	Mesocycle 2	Mesocycle 3	Mesocycle 4	Mesocycle 5
Thursday	Dynamic flexibility exercises, 5–10 minutes	Dynamic flexibility exercises, 5–10 minutes	Dynamic flexibility exercises, 5–10 minutes	Dynamic flexibility exercises, 5–10 minutes
	Speed/agility technique drills, 10 minutes	Speed/agility technique drills, 10 minutes	Speed/agility technique drills, 10 minutes	Speed/agility technique drills, 10 minutes
	Speed/agility circuit: Sprint 30 meters, shuffle back Sprint 30 meters, back-pedal back, etc.	Speed/agility circuit: Sprint 30 meters, shuffle back Sprint 30 meters, back-pedal back, etc.	Speed/agility circuit: Sprint 30 meters, shuffle back Sprint 30 meters, back-pedal back, etc.	Speed/agility circuit: Sprint 30 meters, shuffle back Sprint 30 meters, back-pedal back, etc.
	Plyometrics (10× each): Standing long jump Counter-movement jump Medicine ball toss, forward Medicine ball toss, backward	Plyometrics (10× each): Standing long jump Counter-movement jump Medicine ball toss, forward Medicine ball toss, backward	Plyometrics (10× each): Standing long jump Counter-movement jump Medicine ball toss, forward Medicine ball toss, backward	Plyometrics (10× each): Standing long jump Counter-movement jump Medicine ball toss, forward Medicine ball toss, backward

238

putting it all together

Table 12.8 (continued)

	Mesocycle 2	Mesocycle 3	Mesocycle 4	Mesocycle 5
Friday	Dynamic flexibility exercises, 5–10 minutes	Dynamic flexibility exercises, 5–10 minutes	Dynamic flexibility exercises, 5–10 minutes	Dynamic flexibility exercises, 5–10 minutes
	Strength/ conditioning: Circuit training (perform each circuit for 30 seconds, sprint 30 seconds in-between, repeat 3×): Squats Front lunges Rear lunges Side lunges Inchworms Walk on toes Walk on heels Wheelbarrows Bear crawl Push-ups Pull-ups Dips	Strength/ conditioning: Circuit training (perform each circuit for 30 seconds, sprint 30 seconds in between, repeat 3×): Squats Front lunges Rear lunges Side lunges Inchworms Walk on toes Walk on heels Wheelbarrows Bear crawl Push-ups Pull-ups Dips	Strength: Back squats, 3 × 12–15 × 60% Lunges, 3 × 12–15-RM Good mornings, 3 × 12–15-RM Hyperextensions, 3 × 12–15-RM Calf raises, 3 × 12–15-RM	Strength: Back squats, 3 × 12–15 × 60% Lunges, 3 × 12–15-RM Good mornings, 3 × 12–15-RM Hyperextensions, 3 × 12–15-RM Calf raises, 3 × 12–15-RM
			Conditioning: Small-sided games, 20–30 minutes	Conditioning: Small-sided games, 20–30 minutes

239

putting it all together

Table 12.9 Weekly organization of training, mesocycles 6 and 7, beginning soccer player

	Monday	Tuesday	Wednesday	Thursday	Friday
Strength	X		X		X
Speed		X		X	
Agility		X		X	
Plyometrics		X			X
Conditioning	X		X		

Table 12.10 Weekly organization of training, mesocycles 8 through 11, beginning soccer player

	Monday	Tuesday	Wednesday	Thursday	Friday
Strength	X		X		
Speed			X		
Agility			X		
Plyometrics	X		X		
Conditioning		X			X
Game		X			X

Speed and agility are unchanged from the previous phases, the focus is still on technique and fitness.

Conditioning focuses on sprint-based conditioning until the competition phase. If it is not a weakness of the athlete, the intent is to use the game to maintain conditioning. If it is a weakness then this will need to be addressed.

Following the competition phases, the beginning athlete in this program should enter approximately six weeks of unstructured activity. The athlete should remain active, but should be encouraged to avoid soccer and structured conditioning.

At the conclusion of following a program like this for several years, a beginning soccer player will be well grounded in terms of techniques, will have a degree of anatomical adaptations, soccer-specific conditioning, and will be prepared to move to the next level.

NATIONAL-CALIBER

In the United States, this represents a collegiate athlete. Collegiate soccer is a sport played from mid-August through mid-November, depending upon post-season play. Athletes play two games a week, usually on Fridays and Sundays (women) or Wednesdays and Saturdays (men).

Table 12.11 Special preparation, pre-competition, and competition phases of training for the beginning soccer player. Mesocycles 6 through 8

	Mesocycle 6	Mesocycle 7	Mesocycle 8
Monday	Dynamic flexibility exercises, 5–10 minutes	Dynamic flexibility exercises, 5–10 minutes	Dynamic flexibility exercises, 5–10 minutes
	Strength: Dumbbell bench press, 3 × 8–12-RM Dips, 3 × max Pull-ups, 3 × max 3-in-1 shoulders, 3 × 8–12-RM Biceps/triceps, 3 × 8–12-RM	Strength: Dumbbell bench press, 3 × 8–12-RM Dips, 3 × max Pull-ups, 3 × max 3-in-1 shoulders, 3 × 8–12-RM Biceps/triceps, 3 × 8–12-RM	Strength: Back squats, 3 × 2–6 × 90% Romanian deadlifts, 3 × 2–6-RM Bench press, 3 × 2–6 × 90% Bent-over rows, 3 × 2–6-RM Standing dumbbell Shoulder press, 3 × 2–6-RM
	Conditioning: 2 × 10 × 20-meter sprints, 20 seconds walking recovery between sprints, 5′ recovery between sets	Conditioning: 2 × 10 × 30-meter sprints, 20 seconds walking recovery between sprints, 5′ recovery between sets	Plyometrics (10× each): Standing long jump Counter-movement jump Medicine ball toss, forward Medicine ball toss, backward
Tuesday	Dynamic flexibility exercises, 5–10 minutes	Dynamic flexibility exercises, 5–10 minutes	Game
	Speed/agility technique drills, 10 minutes	Speed/agility technique drills, 10 minutes	
	Speed/agility circuit: Sprint 30 meters, shuffle back Sprint 30 meters, back-pedal back, etc.	Speed/agility circuit: Sprint 30 meters, shuffle back Sprint 30 meters, back-pedal back, etc.	
	Plyometrics (10× each): Standing long jump Counter-movement jump Medicine ball toss, forward Medicine ball toss, backward	Plyometrics (10× each): Standing long jump Counter-movement jump Medicine ball toss, forward Medicine ball toss, backward	

Table 12.11 (continued)

	Mesocycle 6	Mesocycle 7	Mesocycle 8
Wednesday	Dynamic flexibility exercises, 5–10 minutes	Dynamic flexibility exercises, 5–10 minutes	Dynamic flexibility exercises, 5–10 minutes
	Strength: Back squats, 3 × 8–12 × 65% Lunges, 3 × 8–12-RM Good mornings, 3 × 8–12-RM Hyperextensions, 3 × 8–12-RM Calf raises, 3 × 12–15-RM	Strength: Back squats, 3 × 8–12 × 70% Lunges, 3 × 8–12-RM Good mornings, 3 × 8–12-RM Hyperextensions, 3 × 8–12-RM Calf raises, 3 × 12–15-RM	Strength/plyometrics: Power clean, h, K, 3 × 4 × 70% Clean pulls, h, AK + Counter-movement jumps, 3 × 4 × 75% + 10 jumps Front squats + squat jumps, 3 × 4 × 70% + 10 jumps Dumbbell bench press + MB chest pass, 3 × 4–8-RM + 10 throws Pull-ups + MB toss, behind, 3 × 4–8-RM + 10 throws
	Conditioning: Sprinting circuit: 1 × 20 meters (10 sec), 1 × 40 meters (20 sec), 1 × 60 meters (40 sec), 1 × 80 meters (60 sec), 2 × 100 meters (60 sec), 1 × 80 meters (60 sec), 1 × 60 meters (40 sec), 1 × 40 meters (20 sec), 1 × 20 meters	Conditioning: Sprinting circuit: 1 × 20 meters (10 sec), 1 × 40 meters (20 sec), 1 × 60 meters (40 sec), 1 × 80 meters (60 sec), 2 × 100 meters (60 sec), 1 × 80 meters (60 sec), 1 × 60 meters (40 sec), 1 × 40 meters (20 sec), 1 × 20 meters	Speed/agility technique drills, 10 minutes Speed/agility circuit: Sprint 30 meters, shuffle back Sprint 30 meters, back-pedal back, etc.
Thursday	Dynamic flexibility exercises, 5–10 minutes Speed/agility technique drills, 10 minutes Speed/agility circuit: Sprint 30 meters, shuffle back Sprint 30 meters, back-pedal back, etc.	Dynamic flexibility exercises, 5–10 minutes Speed/agility technique drills, 10 minutes Speed/agility circuit: Sprint 30 meters, shuffle back Sprint 30 meters, back-pedal back, etc.	Off

Table 12.11 (continued)

	Mesocycle 6	Mesocycle 7	Mesocycle 8
Friday	Dynamic flexibility exercises, 5–10 minutes	Dynamic flexibility exercises, 5–10 minutes	Game
	Strength (rest 60 seconds between sets): Power clean, h, K, 3 × 6 × 60% Front squats, 3 × 8–12 × 80% Hyperextensions, 3 × 8–12-RM Incline press, 3 × 8–12 × 80% One-arm dumbbell rows, 3 × 8–12-RM Seated military press, 3 × 8–12-RM	Strength (rest 60 seconds between sets): Power clean, h, K, 3 × 6 × 65% Front squats, 3 × 4–8 × 85% Hyperextensions, 3 × 4–8-RM Incline press, 3 × 4–8 × 85% One-arm dumbbell rows, 3 × 4–8-RM Seated military press, 3 × 4–8-RM	
	Plyometrics (10× each): Standing long jump Counter-movement jump Medicine ball toss, forward Medicine ball toss, backward	Plyometrics (10× each): Standing long jump Counter-movement jump Medicine ball toss, forward Medicine ball toss, backward	

There are a number of important differences between the national-caliber soccer player and the beginner:

- This will be the only sport that the athlete participates in.
- This is the level at which the positions need to be distinguished.
- The athlete has a history. Athletes will know how to perform exercises, have weaknesses and strengths, and have a history with injuries. All of these things will need to be accounted for.
- There is a need to individualize conditioning programs. Group conditioning programs will be too difficult for some players and not difficult enough for others, coaches must be able to modify the programs to the athlete's needs.

With the above in mind, the program is organized to build upon the beginner program. It is organized so that the competition period runs from August through mid-November,

Table 12.12 Organization of the national-caliber athlete's year

Month	J	F	M	A	M	J	J	A	S	O	N	D
Period	P	P	P	P	P	P	P	C	C	C	C/R	R
Phase	GP	GP	GP	GP	SP	SP	SP	PC	C	C	C/R	R
Mesocycle	1	2	3	4	5	6	7	8	9	10	11	12

the recovery period follows competition and runs through December, with the preparatory period running from January through July. Table 12.12 shows how the national-caliber soccer player's year is organized into periods, phases, and mesocycles.

Preparatory period

The preparatory period covers January through July and is divided into four general preparation phases and three special preparation phases. Table 12.13 provides the breakdown of a training week in the general preparation phases for the national-caliber athlete. The major foci are strength training and metabolic conditioning. Strength training is conducted three times per week, with conditioning being conducted twice. Speed, agility, and plyometrics will also be performed twice a week. Table 12.14 shows the details of the athlete's workouts during the general preparation phases of training. Essentially, this program begins where the beginner's preparatory training left off. As the general preparation phase progresses, the training becomes heavier and the strength-training exercises are varied. For the most part, speed, agility, and plyometrics is being performed in a manner that seeks to link the activities back to soccer so rarely are skills performed in isolation. Descriptions of the agility drills are at the end of the chapter. Conditioning relies on sprint-based conditioning and both the volume and the difficulty increase during the general preparation phase of training.

Table 12.13 Weekly organization of training, mesocycles 1 through 4, national-caliber soccer player

	Monday	Tuesday	Wednesday	Thursday	Friday
Strength	X		X		X
Speed		X		X	
Agility		X		X	
Plyometrics		X			X
Conditioning	X		X		

Table 12.14 Training during the general preparation phase of training, national-caliber athlete

	Mesocycle 1	Mesocycle 2	Mesocycle 3	Mesocycle 4
Monday	Strength: Back squats, 3 × 8–12 × 65% Lunges, 3 × 8–12-RM Good mornings, 3 × 8–12-RM Hyperextensions, 3 × 8–12-RM Calf raises, 3 × 12–15-RM Conditioning: Sprinting circuit: 1 × 20 meters (10 sec), 1 × 40 meters (20 sec), 1 × 60 meters (40 sec), 1 × 80 meters (60 sec), 2 × 100 meters (60 sec), 1 × 80 meters (60 sec), 1 × 60 meters (40 sec), 1 × 40 meters (20 sec), 1 × 20 meters	Strength: Back squats, 3 × 8–12 × 70% Lunges, 3 × 8–12-RM Good mornings, 3 × 8–12-RM Hyperextensions, 3 × 8–12-RM Calf raises, 3 × 12–15-RM Conditioning: Sprinting circuit: 1 × 20 meters (10 sec), 1 × 40 meters (20 sec), 1 × 60 meters (40 sec), 1 × 80 meters (60 sec), 2 × 100 meters (60 sec), 1 × 80 meters (60 sec), 1 × 60 meters (40 sec), 1 × 40 meters (20 sec), 1 × 20 meters	Strength: Front squats, 3 × 8–12 × 75% Reverse lunges, 3 × 8–12-RM Romanian deadlifts, 3 × 8–12-RM Hyperextensions, 3 × 8–12-RM Calf raises, 3 × 12–15-RM Conditioning: Sprinting circuit: 1 × 20 meters (8 sec), 1 × 40 meters (16 sec), 1 × 60 meters (32 sec), 1 × 80 meters (50 sec), 4 × 100 meters (60 sec), 1 × 80 meters (50 sec), 1 × 60 meters (32 sec), 1 × 40 meters (16 sec), 1 × 20 meters	Strength: Front squats, 3 × 6–10 × 80% Reverse lunges, 3 × 6–10-RM Romanian deadlifts, 3 × 6–10-RM Hyperextensions, 3 × 6–10-RM Calf raises, 3 × 12–15-RM Conditioning: Sprinting circuit: 1 × 20 meters (8 sec), 1 × 40 meters (16 sec), 1 × 60 meters (32 sec), 1 × 80 meters (50 sec), 4 × 100 meters (60 sec), 1 × 80 meters (50 sec), 1 × 60 meters (32 sec), 1 × 40 meters (16 sec), 1 × 20 meters

245

putting it all together

Table 12.14 (continued)

	Mesocycle 1	Mesocycle 2	Mesocycle 3	Mesocycle 4
Tuesday	Dynamic flexibility exercises, 5–10 minutes	Dynamic flexibility exercises, 5–10 minutes	Dynamic flexibility exercises, 5–10 minutes	Dynamic flexibility exercises, 5–10 minutes
	Speed/agility technique drills, 10 minutes	Speed/agility technique drills, 10 minutes	Speed/agility technique drills, 10 minutes	Speed/agility technique drills, 10 minutes
	Speed/agility circuit: Sprint 30 meters, shuffle back Sprint 30 meters, back-pedal back, etc.	Speed/agility combination drills: Drill #1, 3–5× Drill #2, 3–5× Drill #3, 3–5×	Speed/agility combination drills: Drill #1, 3–5× Drill #2, 3–5× Drill #3, 3–5×	Speed/agility combination drills: Drill #1, 3–5× Drill #2, 3–5× Drill #3, 3–5×
	Plyometrics (10× each): Standing long jump Counter-movement jump Medicine ball toss, forward Medicine ball toss, backward	Plyometrics (10× each): Standing long jump Counter-movement jump Medicine ball toss, forward Medicine ball toss, backward	Plyometrics: Standing long jump + 5-meter sprint, 3–5× Counter-movement jump + 5-meter sprint, 3–5× Medicine ball toss, forward + 5-meter sprint, 3–5× Medicine ball toss, backward + 5-meter sprint, 3–5×	Plyometrics: Standing long jump + 5-meter sprint, 3–5× Counter-movement jump + 5-meter sprint, 3–5× Medicine ball toss, forward + 5-meter sprint, 3–5× Medicine ball toss, backward + 5-meter sprint, 3–5×

putting it all together

Table 12.14 (continued)

	Mesocycle 1	Mesocycle 2	Mesocycle 3	Mesocycle 4
Wednesday	Dynamic flexibility exercises, 5–10 minutes	Dynamic flexibility exercises, 5–10 minutes	Dynamic flexibility exercises, 5–10 minutes	Dynamic flexibility exercises, 5–10 minutes
	Strength: Dumbbell bench Press, 3 × 8–12-RM Dips, 3 × max Pull-ups, 3 × max 3-in-1 shoulders, 3 × 8–12-RM Biceps/triceps, 3 × 8–12-RM	Strength: Dumbbell bench Press, 3 × 8–12-RM Dips, 3 × max Pull-ups, 3 × max 3-in-1 shoulders, 3 × 8–12-RM Biceps/triceps, 3 × 8–12-RM	Strength: Bench press, 3 × 8–12 × 70% Dumbbell incline press, 3 × 8–12-RM Bent-over rows, 3 × 8–12-RM Standing military press, 3 × 8–12-RM	Strength: Bench press, 3 × 8–12 × 75% Dumbbell incline press, 3 × 8–12-RM Bent-over rows, 3 × 8–12-RM Standing military press, 3 × 8–12-RM
	Conditioning: 2 × 10 × 20-meter sprints, 20 seconds walking recovery between sprints, 5' recovery between sets	Conditioning: 2 × 10 × 30-meter sprints, 20 seconds walking recovery between sprints, 5' recovery between sets	Conditioning: 2 × 10 × 40-meter sprints, 20 seconds walking recovery between sprints, 5' recovery between sets	Conditioning: 2 × 10 × 50-meter sprints, 20 seconds walking recovery between sprints, 5' recovery between sets
Thursday	Dynamic flexibility exercises, 5–10 minutes	Dynamic flexibility exercises, 5–10 minutes	Dynamic flexibility exercises, 5–10 minutes	Dynamic flexibility exercises, 5–10 minutes
	Speed/agility technique drills, 10 minutes	Speed/agility technique drills, 10 minutes	Speed/agility technique drills, 10 minutes	Speed/agility technique drills, 10 minutes
	Speed/agility circuit: Sprint 30 meters, shuffle back Sprint 30 meters, back-pedal back, etc.	Speed/agility circuit: Sprint 30 meters, shuffle back Sprint 30 meters, back-pedal back, etc.	Speed/agility circuit: Sprint 30 meters, shuffle back Sprint 30 meters, back-pedal back, etc.	Speed/agility circuit: Sprint 30 meters, shuffle back Sprint 30 meters, back-pedal back, etc.

putting it all together

Table 12.14 (continued)

	Mesocycle 1	Mesocycle 2	Mesocycle 3	Mesocycle 4
Friday	Dynamic flexibility exercises, 5–10 minutes	Dynamic flexibility exercises, 5–10 minutes	Dynamic flexibility exercises, 5–10 minutes	Dynamic flexibility exercises, 5–10 minutes
	Strength (rest 60 seconds between sets): Power clean, h, AK, $3 \times 6 \times 60\%$ Front squats, $3 \times 8–12 \times 80\%$ Hyperextensions, $3 \times 8–12$-RM Incline press, $3 \times 8–12 \times 80\%$ One-arm dumbbell rows, $3 \times 8–12$-RM Seated military press, $3 \times 8–12$-RM	Strength (rest 60 seconds between sets): Power clean, h, K, $3 \times 6 \times 60\%$ Front squats, $3 \times 8–12 \times 80\%$ Hyperextensions, $3 \times 8–12$-RM Incline press, $3 \times 8–12 \times 80\%$ One-arm dumbbell rows, $3 \times 8–12$-RM Seated military press, $3 \times 8–12$-RM	Strength (rest 60 seconds between sets): Power clean, h, BK, $3 \times 6 \times 65\%$ Back squats, $3 \times 4–8 \times 85\%$ Deadlifts, $3 \times 4–6$ Dumbbell bench press, $3 \times 4–8$-RM Pull-ups, $3 \times 4–8$-RM Seated dumbbell shoulder press, $3 \times 4–8$-RM	Strength (rest 60 seconds between sets): Power clean, $3 \times 4 \times 70\%$ Back squats, $3 \times 2–6 \times 90\%$ Deadlifts, $3 \times 2–6$ Dumbbell bench press, $3 \times 2–6$-RM Pull-ups, $3 \times 2–6$-RM Seated dumbbell shoulder press, $3 \times 2–6$-RM
	Plyometrics ($10\times$ each): Standing long jump Counter-movement jump Medicine ball toss, forward Medicine ball toss, backward	Plyometrics ($10\times$ each): Standing long jump Counter-movement jump Medicine ball toss, forward Medicine ball toss, backward	Plyometrics ($10\times$ each): Tuck jump Cone jump (over 10 meters) Medicine ball toss, forward Medicine ball toss, backward	Plyometrics ($10\times$ each): Tuck jump Cone jump (over 10 meters) Medicine ball toss, forward Medicine ball toss, backward

248

putting it all together

At this level, it is appropriate to begin distinguishing between positions on the workouts. The first mesocycle should see all the athletes perform the workouts as written. After that the programs may be varied based upon positions:

■ Goalkeepers: Goalkeeper workouts could be reorganized to focus less on conditioning and more on strength/power. This could be accomplished by organizing the workouts as follows:
  ■ Monday: strength/plyometrics
  ■ Tuesday: speed/agility
  ■ Wednesday: strength/plyometrics
  ■ Thursday: speed/agility
  ■ Friday: strength/conditioning
■ Midfielders: The volume of the conditioning workouts could be increased by 5–10%/week, up to 1,200 meters per session. In addition, the recovery can gradually be modified to focus on slow jogging as recovery as opposed to walking.
■ Defenders/forwards: A greater emphasis can be placed on sprinting that is performed in conjunction with other skills. This can be done by increasing the distances on the three agility drills to allow for more sprinting and increasing the distances of the sprints following plyometrics.

Table 12.15 provides an overview of the weekly organization of training during the special preparation phases of training (mesocycles 5 through 7) and the precompetition phase of training. There are differences when comparing to the general preparation phases:

■ Strength and plyometrics training will be the major foci in these phases. As a result they will be emphasized three times per week.
■ Speed and agility will continue to be performed twice a week.
■ Conditioning will be performed twice a week in conjunction with speed/agility training.

Table 12.16 provides sample workouts for the special preparation phase of training. The strength-training workouts are progressively becoming heavier while the exercises are

Table 12.15 Weekly organization of training, mesocycles 5 through 7, national-caliber soccer player

	Monday	Tuesday	Wednesday	Thursday	Friday
Strength	X		X		X
Speed		X		X	
Agility		X		X	
Plyometrics	X		X		X
Conditioning		X		X	

Table 12.16 Training during the special preparation phase of training, national-caliber athlete

	Mesocycle 5	Mesocycle 6	Mesocycle 7
Monday	Dynamic flexibility exercises, 5–10 minutes	Dynamic flexibility exercises, 5–10 minutes	Dynamic flexibility exercises, 5–10 minutes
	Strength (rest 2 minutes between sets):	Strength (rest 2 minutes between sets):	Strength/plyometrics (rest 2 minutes between sets):
	Power clean, 3 × 4 × 70%	Power clean, 3 × 4 × 75%	Power clean + split jerk,
	Push jerk, 3 × 4 × 70%	Split jerk, 3 × 4 × 75%	3 × 3 + 2 × 80%
	Pause squats, 3 × 4 × 70%	Eccentric squats, 3 × 4 × 70%	Clean pulls + counter-movement jump,
	Romanian deadlifts, 3 × 6–10-RM	Good mornings, 3 × 6–10-RM	3 × 4 × 85% + 10 Jumps
			Pause split squats + squat jump, 3 ×
	Plyometrics:	Plyometrics:	4–8 + 10 jumps
	Standing long jump, 3–5×	Standing long jump, 3–5×	Romanian deadlifts + MB toss, forward,
	Counter-movement jump, 3–5×	Counter-movement jump, 3–5×	3 × 4–8-RM + 10 throws
	Medicine ball toss, forward, 3–5×	Medicine ball toss, forward, 3–5×	
	Medicine ball toss, backward, 3–5×	Medicine ball toss, backward, 3–5×	

Table 12.16 (continued)

	Mesocycle 5	Mesocycle 6	Mesocycle 7
Tuesday	Dynamic flexibility exercises, 5–10 minutes	Dynamic flexibility exercises, 5–10 minutes	Dynamic flexibility exercises, 5–10 minutes
	Speed/agility technique drills, 10 minutes	Speed/agility technique drills, 10 minutes	Speed/agility technique drills, 10 minutes
	Speed/agility: Drill #1, 3–5× Drill #2, 3–5× Drill #3, 3–5×	Speed/agility: Drill #1, 3–5× Drill #2, 1× Drill #4, 3–5× Drill #3, 3–5×	Speed/agility: Drill #1, 1 Drill #2, 1× Drill #4, 3–5× Drill #5, 3–5× Drill #3, 3–5×
	Conditioning: Sprinting circuit 1 × 20 meters (8 sec), 1 × 40 meters (16 sec), 1 × 60 meters (32 sec), 1 × 80 meters (50 sec), 4 × 100 meters (60 sec), 1 × 80 meters (50 sec), 1 × 60 meters (32 sec), 1 × 40 meters (16 sec), 1 × 20 meters	Conditioning: Sprinting circuit 1 × 20 meters (8 sec), 1 × 40 meters (16 sec), 1 × 60 meters (32 sec), 1 × 80 meters (50 sec), 4 × 100 meters (60 sec), 1 × 80 meters (50 sec), 1 × 60 meters (32 sec), 1 × 40 meters (16 sec), 1 × 20 meters	Conditioning: Sprinting circuit 1 × 20 meters (8 sec), 1 × 40 meters (16 sec), 1 × 60 meters (32 sec), 1 × 80 meters (50 sec), 4 × 100 meters (60 sec), 1 × 80 meters (50 sec), 1 × 60 meters (32 sec), 1 × 40 meters (16 sec), 1 × 20 meters

Table 12.16 (continued)

	Mesocycle 5	Mesocycle 6	Mesocycle 7
Wednesday	Dynamic flexibility exercises, 5–10 minutes	Dynamic flexibility exercises, 5–10 minutes	Dynamic flexibility exercises, 5–10 minutes
	Strength (rest 2 minutes between sets): Snatch pulls, 3 × 4 × 50% of power clean 1-RM Pause bench press, 3 × 4 × 70% One-arm dumbbell rows, 3 × 6–10-RM Seated military press, 3 × 6–10-RM	Strength (rest 2 minutes between sets): Snatch pulls, 3 × 4 × 60% of power clean 1-RM Eccentric bench press, 3 × 4 × 75% One-arm dumbbell rows, 3 × 6–10-RM Seated military press, 3 × 6–10-RM	Strength/plyometrics (rest 2 minutes between sets): Snatch pulls, 3 × 4 × 70% of power clean 1-RM Pause bench press + clapping push-ups, 3 × 3 × 80% + 10 push-ups One-arm dumbbell rows + MB toss, behind, 3 × 6–10-RM + 10 throws Seated military press, 3 × 6–10-RM
	Plyometrics (perform each 10×): MB chest pass MB chest pass, stand on one leg (10× each side) MB side toss, stand on one leg (10× each side)	Plyometrics (perform each 10×): MB chest pass MB chest pass, stand on one leg (10× each side) MB side toss, stand on one leg (10× each side)	

Table 12.16 (continued)

	Mesocycle 5	Mesocycle 6	Mesocycle 7
Thursday	Dynamic flexibility exercises, 5–10 minutes	Dynamic flexibility exercises, 5–10 minutes	Dynamic flexibility exercises, 5–10 minutes
	Speed/agility technique drills, 10 minutes	Speed/agility technique drills, 10 minutes	Speed/agility technique drills, 10 minutes
	Speed/agility circuit (perform each for 20 meters, no rest during the circuit, 2 minutes walking recovery, repeat): Sprint Back-pedal Shuffle right Sprint Shuffle left Sprint Zig-zags Sprint	Speed/agility circuit (perform each for 20 meters, no rest during the circuit, 2 minutes walking recovery, repeat): Sprint Back-pedal Shuffle right Sprint Shuffle left Sprint Zig-zags Sprint	Speed/agility circuit (perform each for 20 meters, no rest during the circuit, 2 minutes walking recovery, perform 3×): Sprint Back-pedal Shuffle right Sprint Shuffle left Sprint Zig-zags Sprint
	Conditioning: 2 × 10 × 50-meter sprints, 20 seconds walking recovery between sprints, 5' recovery between sets	Conditioning: 2 × 10 × 50-meter sprints, 20 seconds walking recovery between sprints, 5' recovery between sets	Conditioning: 2 × 10 × 50-meter sprints, 20 seconds walking recovery between sprints, 5' recovery between sets

Table 12.16 (continued)

	Mesocycle 5	Mesocycle 6	Mesocycle 7
Friday	Dynamic flexibility exercises, 5–10 minutes	Dynamic flexibility exercises, 5–10 minutes	Dynamic flexibility exercises, 5–10 minutes
	Strength (rest 2 minutes between sets):	Strength (rest 2 minutes between sets):	Strength/plyometrics (rest 2 minutes between sets):
	Split clean, h, AK + push jerk, 3 × 3+2 × 50%	Split clean, h, K + push jerk, 3 × 3+2 × 60%	Split clean + push jerk, 3 × 3+2 × 70%
	Front squats, 3 × 6 × 60%	Front squats, 3 × 6 × 65%	Clean pulls + tuck jump, 3 × 5 × 75% + 10 jumps
	Incline press, 3 × 8–12-RM	Incline press, 3 × 8–12-RM	Pause incline press + MB Drop pass, 3 × 4–8 + 10 throws
	Pull-ups, 3 × 8–12-RM	Pull-ups, 3 × 8–12-RM	Pull-ups, 3 × 8–12-RM
	Plyometrics (10× each):	Plyometrics (10× each):	
	Tuck jump	Tuck jump	
	Cone jump (over 10 meters)	Cone jump (over 10 meters)	
	Medicine ball toss, forward	Medicine ball toss, forward	
	Medicine ball toss, backward	Medicine ball toss, backward	

becoming more advanced. Plyometric exercises are also becoming more advanced as the special preparation phase progresses. By the last mesocycle, the strength training and plyometrics are being complexed to save time. Agility drills are becoming faster, more reactive, and more complicated. On Thursday the agility drills are used as a supplement to the conditioning workout. Conditioning is maintained in this phase unless it is a weakness of the athlete.

During the special preparation phase, the programs may be varied based upon positions:

- Goalkeepers: Goalkeeper workouts could be reorganized to focus less on conditioning and more on strength/power. This could be accomplished by organizing the workouts as follows:
  - Monday: strength/plyometrics
  - Tuesday: strength/plyometrics
  - Wednesday: speed/agility/conditioning
  - Thursday: strength/plyometrics
  - Friday: strength/plyometrics
- Midfielders: The volume of the conditioning workouts could be increased by 5–10%/week, up to 1,400 meters per session. In addition, jogging can be used as recovery.
- Defenders/forwards: A greater emphasis can be placed on sprinting that is performed in conjunction with other skills.

Competition period

The competition period runs from August through mid-November and is organized into one pre-competition phase and three competition phases. Tables 12.17 and 12.18 show the weekly organizations of training during the competition period for female athletes (Table 12.17) and male athletes (Table 12.18). There are some differences due to the fact that males and females have games on different days.

Table 12.17 Weekly organization of training, mesocycles 8 through 11, national-caliber soccer player (female)

	Monday	Tuesday	Wednesday	Thursday	Friday	Saturday	Sunday
Strength	X	X		X			
Speed			X				
Agility			X				
Plyometrics		X					
Conditioning	X				X		X
Game					X		X

Table 12.18 Weekly organization of training, mesocycles 8 through 11, national-caliber soccer player (male)

	Monday	Tuesday	Wednesday	Thursday	Friday	Saturday	Sunday
Strength	X	X			X		
Speed				X			
Agility				X			
Plyometrics		X					
Conditioning	X		X			X	
Game			X			X	

For both, conditioning is largely maintained with games being used as the conditioning workouts. There is one conditioning workout a week in addition to games. Strength is trained three times per week, Monday/Tuesday and either Thursday or Friday (i.e., the day before a game). Speed and agility are maintained with one session per week unless these are weaknesses. Finally, plyometrics are performed once a week in conjunction with the second strength training session.

Table 12.19 provides sample workouts during the competition period. It is written for the female athletes, but can easily be modified for the male athlete's schedule. The workouts are meant to be brief, to maintain the athlete's overall fitness, focus on developing power, and prepare the athlete for competition. Note that the workouts change every mesocycle, these workouts resemble what the elite athlete's workouts look like.

As with the preparatory period of training, workouts can be modified by playing position:

- Goalkeepers: Depending upon how the athlete responds to strength training before a match, the last day of strength training can be modified to resemble the second to increase the emphasis on this quality.
- Midfielders: These athletes can incorporate a second conditioning workout on Wednesday if there is a desire to emphasize this more.
- Defenders/forwards: These can expand the volume of speed/agility work on Wednesday and can modify the distances on the agility drills to allow for more sprinting during those drills.

Recovery period

The recovery period runs from mid-November through December. During this time the athlete should avoid soccer or structured training, but should engage in activity three to five times per week. This could include other sports, the swimming pool, body-weight circuits, etc. The idea is to give the athlete a mental and physical break, while maintaining fitness, so that the athlete returns in January healthy and refreshed to begin the training process again.

Table 12.19 Training during the competition period of training, national-caliber athlete

	Mesocycle 8	Mesocycle 9	Mesocycle 10	Mesocycle 11
Monday	Dynamic flexibility exercises, 5–10 minutes	Dynamic flexibility exercises, 5–10 minutes	Dynamic flexibility exercises, 5–10 minutes	Dynamic flexibility exercises, 5–10 minutes
	Strength (rest 2 minutes between sets):	Strength (rest 2 minutes between sets):	Strength (rest 2 minutes between sets):	Strength (rest 2 minutes between sets):
	Eccentric squats, 3 × 4 × 70%	Pause front squats, 3 × 4 × 70%	Eccentric front squats, 3 × 4 × 70%	Back squats, 3 × 2 × 90%
	Romanian deadlifts, 3 × 4–8-RM	Good mornings, 3 × 4–8-RM	Hyperextensions, 3 × 4–8-RM	Romanian deadlifts, 3 × 2–6-RM
	Eccentric bench Press, 3 × 4 × 70%	Pause bench press, 3 × 4 × 70%	Eccentric incline press, 3 × 4	Bench press, 3 × 2 × 90%
	Bent-over rows, 3 × 4–8-RM	Pull-ups, 3 × 4–8-RM	One-arm dumbbell rows, 3 × 4–8-RM	Pull-ups, 3 × 2–6-RM
	Conditioning: 2 × 10 × 50-meter sprints, 20 seconds walking recovery between sprints, 5′ recovery between sets	Conditioning: Sprinting circuit 1 × 20 meters (8 sec), 1 × 40 meters (16 sec), 1 × 60 meters (32 sec), 1 × 80 meters (50 sec), 4 × 100 meters (60 sec), 1 × 80 meters (50 sec), 1 × 60 meters (32 sec), 1 × 40 meters (16 sec), 1 × 20 meters	Conditioning: 2 × 10 × 50-meter sprints, 20 seconds walking recovery between sprints, 5′ recovery between sets	Conditioning: Sprinting circuit 1 × 20 meters (8 sec), 1 × 40 meters (16 sec), 1 × 60 meters (32 sec), 1 × 80 meters (50 sec), 4 × 100 meters (60 sec), 1 × 80 meters (50 sec), 1 × 60 meters (32 sec), 1 × 40 meters (16 sec), 1 × 20 meters

Table 12.19 (continued)

	Mesocycle 8	Mesocycle 9	Mesocycle 10	Mesocycle 11
Tuesday	Dynamic flexibility exercises, 5–10 minutes	Dynamic flexibility exercises, 5–10 minutes	Dynamic flexibility exercises, 5–10 minutes	Dynamic flexibility exercises, 5–10 minutes
	Strength/plyometrics (rest 2 minutes between sets): Snatch pull + tuck jump, 3 × 4 × 60% + 10 jumps Split clean + push jerk + cone jump, 3 × 3+2 × 60% + 10 cones	Strength/plyometrics (rest 2 minutes between sets): Power clean + split jerk, 3 × 3+2 × 60% Clean pulls + counter-movement jump, 3 × 4 × 65%+10 jumps Dumbbell push jerk + tuck jump, 3 × 4+10 jumps	Strength/plyometrics (rest 2 minutes between sets): Power clean, 3 × 2+2 × 80%+60% Push jerk + standing long jump, 3 × 3 × 60% + 10 jumps Snatch pulls + cone jump, 3 × 4 × 60% + 10 cones	Strength/plyometrics (rest 2 minutes between sets): Clean pulls + split clean + push jerk, 3 × 3+2+2 × 60%
Wednesday	Dynamic flexibility exercises, 5–10 minutes	Dynamic flexibility exercises, 5–10 minutes	Dynamic flexibility exercises, 5–10 minutes	Dynamic flexibility exercises, 5–10 minutes
	Speed/agility technique drills, 10 minutes	Speed/agility technique drills, 10 minutes	Speed/agility technique drills, 10 minutes	Speed/agility technique drills, 10 minutes
	Speed/agility: Drill #3, 3× Drill #5, 3×	Speed/agility: Drill #4, 3× Drill #5, 3×	Speed/agility: Drill #1, 1× Drill #2, 1× Drill #3, 1× Drill #4, 1× Drill #5, 1×	Speed/agility: Drill #5, 5×

Table 12.19 (continued)

	Mesocycle 8	Mesocycle 9	Mesocycle 10	Mesocycle 11
Thursday	Dynamic flexibility exercises, 5–10 minutes Strength (rest 2 minutes between sets): Power clean, 3 × 3 × 70% Back squats, 3 × 4 × 70%	Dynamic flexibility exercises, 5–10 minutes Strength (rest 2 minutes between sets): Split clean, 3 × 3 × 70% Front squats, 3 × 3 × 70%	Dynamic flexibility exercises, 5–10 minutes Strength (rest 2 minutes between sets): Snatch pulls, 3 × 3 × 60% Back squats, 3 × 4 × 70%	Dynamic flexibility exercises, 5–10 minutes Strength (rest 2 minutes between sets): Power clean, 3 × 3 × 70% Front squats, 3 × 3 × 70%
Friday	Conditioning/game	Conditioning/game	Conditioning/game	Conditioning/game
Saturday	Off	Off	Off	Off
Sunday	Conditioning/game	Conditioning/game	Conditioning/game	Conditioning/game

ELITE/PROFESSIONAL

There are a number of important considerations for the elite soccer player:

- The athlete has a history.
- All workouts will need to be individualized.
- The athlete plays a specific position and is unlikely to change at this level.
- The athlete will need frequent changes to his/her training program: elite athletes are masters at adapting to exercise, their ability to recover is one of the things that makes them elite. Each of them will adapt to exercises at different speeds, so the mesocycles will need to be shorter to accommodate this.
- Almost all training is going to be event/position-specific in nature.

With the above in mind, our sample elite soccer player plays for the Barclay Premier League. For the sake of this example he is a midfielder, has no weaknesses, and responds best to three week-long mesocycles. Table 12.20 shows a breakdown of the elite athlete's year into periods and phases. August through May is spent in competition, leaving only June and July for other types of training. With a new mesocycle every three weeks, this means there will be 17 mesocycles during the course of the year, with the first one beginning in mid-May.

Table 12.20 Organization of the elite athlete's year, athlete plays in the Barclay Premier League

Month	J	F	M	A	M	J	J	A	S	O	N	D
Period	C	C	C	C	C	P	C	C	C	C	C	C
Phase	C	C	C	C	C	R/GP	PC	C	C	C	C	C

The 2009/2010 season ended on May 15 for our athlete. This will allow us to have a recovery period that begins on May 17 and runs through May 30. During that time, the athlete will take a break from soccer and from organized activity.

Preparatory period

The preparatory period runs from May 31 until July 4 and will consist of two, three-week mesocycles (numbers 2 and 3). This will be the only general-type training of the year. Table 12.21 details the training for this athlete during the preparatory period. Training is organized around strength training and plyometrics occurring on Monday, Wednesday, and Friday. Conditioning is performed on Tuesday, Thursday, and Saturday. Speed and agility training is also conducted on Tuesday, Thursday, and Saturday. Sunday is a day off during the preparatory period.

Table 12.21 Training during the preparatory period of training, elite athlete

	Mesocycle 2	Mesocycle 3
Monday	Dynamic flexibility exercises, 10–20 minutes	Dynamic flexibility exercises, 10–20 minutes
	Strength (rest 2 minutes between each set): Back squats, 3 × 6–10 × 80% Reverse hyperextensions, 3 × 6–10-RM Bench press, 3 × 6–10 × 80% Pull-ups, 3 × 6–10-RM Standing military press, 3 × 6–10-RM	Strength (rest 2 minutes between each set): Front squats, 3 × 6–10 × 80% Hyperextensions, 3 × 6–10-RM Incline press, 3 × 6–10-RM Bent-over rows, 3 × 6–10-RM Seated military press, 3 × 6–10-RM
	Plyometrics (perform each 10×): Squat jump Pike jump MB toss, forward MB toss, backward	Plyometrics (perform each 10×): Counter-movement jump Cone jump (10 meters) MB toss, forward MB toss, backward
Tuesday	Dynamic flexibility exercises, 10–20 minutes	Dynamic flexibility exercises, 10–20 minutes
	Speed/agility technique drills, 10 minutes	Speed/agility technique drills, 10 minutes
	Speed/agility: Drills 1–5, 1× each	Speed/agility: Drills 1–5, 1× each, performed with the soccer ball
	Conditioning: 3 × 10 × 50-meter sprints, 20-second jogging recovery between sprints, 5-minute walking recovery between sets	Conditioning: 3 × 10 × 50 meter sprints, 20-second jogging recovery between sprints, 5-minute walking recovery between sets

Table 12.21 (continued)

	Mesocycle 2	Mesocycle 3
Wednesday	Dynamic flexibility exercises, 10–20 minutes	Dynamic flexibility exercises, 10–20 minutes
	Strength (rest 2 minutes between sets): Power clean, 3 × 3 × 70% Push jerk, 3 × 3 × 70% Clean pulls, 3 × 4 × 75%	Strength (rest 2 minutes between sets): Split clean, 3 × 3 × 70% Push jerk, 3 × 3 × 70% Clean pulls, 3 × 4 × 75%
	Plyometrics (perform each 10 times): Tuck jump Standing long jump Box jump (1)	Plyometrics (perform each 10 times): Squat jump Hurdle jump (10 meters) Box jump (2)
Thursday	Dynamic flexibility exercises, 10–20 minutes	Dynamic flexibility exercises, 10–20 minutes
	Speed/agility technique drills, 10 minutes	Speed/agility technique drills, 10 minutes
	Speed/agility circuit (perform each for 20 meters, no rest during the circuit, 2 minutes walking recovery, repeat): Sprint Back-pedal Shuffle right Sprint Shuffle left Sprint Zig-zags Sprint	Speed/agility circuit (perform each for 20 meters, no rest during the circuit, 2 minutes jogging recovery, repeat): Sprint Back-pedal Shuffle right Sprint Shuffle left Sprint Zig-zags Sprint
	Conditioning: Small-sided games, 30 minutes	Conditioning: Small-sided games, 30 minutes

Table 12.21 (continued)

	Mesocycle 2	Mesocycle 3
Friday	Dynamic flexibility exercises, 10–20 minutes	Dynamic flexibility exercises, 10–20 minutes
	Strength/plyometrics (rest 2 minutes between sets): Pause squats + squat jump, 3 × 3 × 70% + 5 jumps Deadlifts + MB toss, forward, 3 × 4 × 70% + 5 throws Bench press + MB chest pass, 3 × 4 × 70%+10% in chains + 5 throws One-arm dumbbell rows, 3 × 4–8-RM	Strength/plyometrics (rest 2 minutes between sets): Eccentric squats + counter-movement jumps, 3 × 3 × 70% + 5 jumps Romanian deadlifts + MB toss, backward, 3 × 4–8-RM + 5 throws Eccentric bench press + MB chest pass, 3 × 4 × 70%+5 throws Pull-ups, 3 × 4–8-RM
Saturday	Dynamic flexibility exercises, 10–20 minutes	Dynamic flexibility exercises, 10–20 minutes
	Speed/agility technique drills, 10 minutes	Speed/agility technique drills, 10 minutes
	Speed/agility: Drill 1, 1× Drill 2, 1× Drill 3–5, 3× each with soccer ball	Speed/agility: Drill 1, 1× Drill 2, 1× Drill 3–5, 3× each with soccer ball
	Conditioning: Sprinting circuit while dribbling soccer ball 1 × 20 meters (8 sec), 1 × 40 meters (16 sec), 1 × 60 meters (32 sec), 1 × 80 meters (50 sec), 4 × 100 meters (60 sec), 1 × 80 meters (50 sec), 1 × 60 meters (32 sec), 1 × 40 meters (16 sec), 1 × 20 meters	Conditioning: Sprinting circuit while dribbling soccer ball 1 × 20 meters (8 sec), 1 × 40 meters (16 sec), 1 × 60 meters (32 sec), 1 × 80 meters (50 sec), 4 × 100 meters (60 sec), 1 × 80 meters (50 sec), 1 × 60 meters (32 sec), 1 × 40 meters (16 sec), 1 × 20 meters
Sunday	Off	Off

263

putting it all together

In the preparatory period, the strength training focuses on a heavier day (Monday), an explosive day (Wednesday), and a day that focuses on both (Friday). Plyometrics are performed in conjunction with each strength training session, on Friday they are complexed with the strength training. As the athlete is near his genetic potential, there is not a great emphasis on increasing strength or hypertrophy. Instead the focus is on applying that strength and hypertrophy.

Speed, agility, and conditioning is being done in the most sport-specific environment possible. When possible, the soccer ball is used to add complexity and specificity to the exercises. The midfielder is jogging for recovery between drills, rather than walking and the volume of conditioning is greater than it would be for other positions.

Competition period

This chapter is going to cover the first two mesocycles of the athlete's competition period for the 2010/2011 season. The 2010/2011 season begins July 5, with the fourth meso-cycle. This mesocycle runs from July 5 through July 25 and will include pre-season games on the 17 and 23 (Saturday and Friday). The fifth mesocycle of the year will run from July 26 through August 15 and will include pre-season games on the 1st (Sunday), 4th (Wednesday), 8th (Sunday), and the first match on the 14 (Saturday).

Games must be factored into the elite athlete's training schedule. With that in mind, three different training week templates will be developed depending upon the athlete's schedule:

- One game/week:
    - Day before the game. This will be a speed/agility workout. This will enable the athlete to get speed and agility work in without fatiguing him for the upcoming game.
    - Day of the game. The match will be considered a conditioning workout. Strength training and plyometrics will be conducted the day of the match in the morning to prime the athlete's nervous system.
    - Day after the match. This day will be a recovery day.
- Two games/week:
    - Day before the game. This will be a speed/agility workout.
    - Day of the game. The match will be considered a conditioning workout. Strength training and plyometrics will be conducted the day of the match in the morning.
    - Day after the game. This will be a speed/agility workout.
- No games: Training will be organized as it was in the preparatory period.

Table 12.22 details the workouts in the fourth mesocycle. The fourth mesocycle makes extensive use of complexes to maximize the athlete's training time. The focus on the

Table 12.22 Mesocycle 4 (July 5–July 25), elite soccer player

	Week of July 5	Week of July 12	Week of July 19
Monday	Dynamic flexibility exercises, 10–20 minutes	Dynamic flexibility exercises, 10–20 minutes	Dynamic flexibility exercises, 10–20 minutes
	Strength/plyometrics (rest 2 minutes between sets): Front squats + depth jumps, 3×2–$4 \times 90\% + 5$ jumps Deadlifts + counter-movement jumps, 3×2–$4 \times 80\% + 5$ jumps Bench press + clapping push-ups, 3×2–$4 \times 70\%$ + 10% with chains + 5 push-ups Bent-over rows, 3×4–8-RM	Strength/plyometrics (rest 2 minutes between sets): Front squats + depth jumps, 3×2–$4 \times 92.5\% + 5$ jumps Deadlifts + counter-movement jumps, 3×2–$4 \times 82.5\% + 5$ jumps Bench press + clapping push-ups, 3×2–$4 \times 72.5\%$ + 10% with chains + 5 push-ups Bent-over rows, 3×4–8-RM	Strength/plyometrics (rest 2 minutes between sets): Front squats + depth jumps, 3×1–$3 \times 95\% + 5$ jumps Deadlifts + counter-movement jumps, 3×1–$3 \times 85\% + 5$ jumps Bench press + clapping push-ups, 3×1–$3 \times 75\%$ + 10% with chains+ 5 push-ups Bent-over rows, 3×4–8-RM
Tuesday	Dynamic flexibility exercises, 10–20 minutes	Dynamic flexibility exercises, 10–20 minutes	Dynamic flexibility exercises, 10–20 minutes
	Speed/agility technique drills, 10 minutes	Speed/agility technique drills, 10 minutes	Speed/agility technique drills, 10 minutes
	Speed/agility: Drills 1–5, 1× each, against opponent and with ball (reactive)	Speed/agility: Drills 1–5, 1× each, against opponent and with ball (reactive)	Speed/agility: Drills 1–5, 1× each, against opponent and with ball (reactive)
	Conditioning: $3 \times 10 \times 50$-meter sprints, 20-second jogging recovery between sprints, 5-minute walking recovery between sets	Conditioning: $3 \times 10 \times 50$-meter sprints, 20-second jogging recovery between sprints, 5-minute walking recovery between sets	Conditioning: $3 \times 10 \times 50$-meter sprints, 20-second jogging recovery between sprints, 5-minute walking recovery between sets

Table 12.22 (continued)

	Week of July 5	Week of July 12	Week of July 19
Wednesday	Dynamic flexibility exercises, 10–20 minutes	Dynamic flexibility exercises, 10–20 minutes	Dynamic flexibility exercises, 10–20 minutes
	Strength/plyometrics (rest 2 minutes between sets): Split clean + box jump (1), 3 × 3–4 × 60% + 5 jumps Push jerk + tuck jump, 3 × 3–4 × 60% + 5 jumps Clean pulls, h, AK + counter-movement jumps, 3 × 4–6 × 65% + 5 jumps	Strength/plyometrics (rest 2 minutes between sets): Split clean + box jump (1), 3 × 3–4 × 62.5% + 5 jumps Push jerk + tuck jump, 3 × 3–4 × 62.5% + 5 jumps Clean pulls, h, AK + counter-movement jumps, 3 × 4–6 × 67.5% + 5 jumps	Strength/plyometrics (rest 2 minutes between sets): Split clean + box jump (1), 3 × 3–4 × 65% + 5 jumps Push jerk + tuck jump, 3 × 3–4 × 65% + 5 jumps Clean pulls, h, AK + counter-movement jumps, 3 × 4–6 × 70% + 5 jumps

putting it all together

Table 12.22 (continued)

	Week of July 5	Week of July 12	Week of July 19
Thursday	Dynamic flexibility exercises, 10–20 minutes	Dynamic flexibility exercises, 10–20 minutes	Dynamic flexibility exercises, 10–20 minutes
	Speed/agility technique drills, 10 minutes	Speed/agility technique drills, 10 minutes	Speed/agility technique drills, 10 minutes
	Speed/agility circuit (all exercises are done with the ball; perform each for 20 meters, no rest during the circuit, 2 minutes jogging recovery, repeat): Sprint Back-pedal Shuffle right Sprint Shuffle left Sprint Zig-zags Sprint	Speed/agility circuit (all exercises are done with the ball; perform each for 20 meters, no rest during the circuit, 2 minutes jogging recovery, repeat): Sprint Back-pedal Shuffle right Sprint Shuffle left Sprint Zig-zags Sprint	Speed/agility (all with ball and reacting to an opponent): Drill 1, 1× Drill 2, 1× Drill 3–5, 3× each
	Conditioning: Small-sided games, 30 minutes	Conditioning: Small-sided games, 30 minutes	

putting it all together

Table 12.22 (continued)

	Week of July 5	Week of July 12	Week of July 19
Friday	Dynamic flexibility exercises, 10–20 minutes	Dynamic flexibility exercises, 10–20 minutes	Dynamic flexibility exercises, 10–20 minutes
	Strength/plyometrics (rest 2 minutes between sets): Pause back squats + pike jumps, 3 × 2–4 × 60% + 10% chains + 5 jumps Good mornings + box jump (2), 3 × 4–8-RM + 5 jumps Pause bench press + MB chest pass, 3 × 2–4 × 70% + 5 throws	Speed/agility technique drills, 10 minutes Speed/agility (all with ball and reacting to an opponent): Drill 1, 1× Drill 2, 1× Drill 3–5, 3× each Conditioning: Sprinting circuit while dribbling soccer ball 1 × 20 meters (8 sec), 1 × 40 meters (16 sec), 1 × 60 meters (32 sec), 1 × 80 meters (50 sec), 4 × 100 meters (60 sec), 1 × 80 meters (50 sec), 1 × 60 meters (32 sec), 1 × 40 meters (16 sec), 1 × 20 meters	Strength/plyometrics (done in a.m.; rest 2 minutes between sets): Pause back squats + pike jumps, 3 × 2–4 × 60% + 10% chains + 5 jumps Good mornings + box jump (2), 3 × 4–8-RM + 5 jumps Pause bench press + MB Chest pass, 3 × 2–4 × 70% + 5 throws Game

Table 12.22 (continued)

	Week of July 5	Week of July 12	Week of July 19
Saturday	Dynamic flexibility exercises, 10–20 minutes	Dynamic flexibility exercises, 10–20 minutes	Off
	Speed/Agility Technique Drills, 10 minutes	Strength/Plyometrics (done in a.m.; rest 2 minutes between sets): Pause back squats + pike jumps, 3 ×	
	Speed/Agility (all with ball and reacting to an opponent): Drill 1, 1× Drill 2, 1× Drill 3–5, 3× each	2–4 × 60% + 10% chains + 5 jumps Good mornings + box jump (2), 3 × 4–8-RM + 5 jumps Pause bench press + MB chest pass, 3 × 2–4 × 70% + 5 throws	
	Conditioning: Sprinting circuit while dribbling soccer ball 1 × 20 meters (8 sec), 1 × 40 meters (16 sec), 1 × 60 meters (32 sec), 1 × 80 meters (50 sec), 4 × 100 meters (60 sec), 1 × 80 meters (50 sec), 1 × 60 meters (32 sec), 1 × 40 meters (16 sec), 1 × 20 meters	Game	

putting it all together

Table 12.22 (continued)

	Week of July 5	Week of July 12	Week of July 19
Sunday	Off	Off	Dynamic flexibility exercises, 10–20 minutes Speed/agility technique drills, 10 minutes Conditioning: Sprinting circuit while dribbling soccer ball 1 × 20 meters (8 sec), 1 × 40 meters (16 sec), 1 × 60 meters (32 sec), 1 × 80 meters (50 sec), 4 × 100 meters (60 sec), 1 × 80 meters (50 sec), 1 × 60 meters (32 sec), 1 × 40 meters (16 sec), 1 × 20 meters

strength and plyometrics is on power development and maximal strength maintenance. All exercises and training modalities are used in an elite athlete's training. Note that over the course of the mesocycle training gradually becomes heavier. Speed, agility, and conditioning are as sport-specific as possible. The ball, opponents, and jogging recoveries are used. For these examples, only the five agility drills are being used to keep things simple. In reality, there would be a much more extensive selection of agility tools to chose from.

Table 12.23 details the fifth mesocycle. It shows how the presence of multiple games during a week, or games on odd days requires the shifting around of the workouts. The presence of multiple games over this three-week period means that the athlete won't have much time for rest and recovery, this will have to be accounted for in future mesocycles.

MASTER

There are a number of important considerations for the masters athlete:

■ The masters athlete will have a reduced recovery ability. Due to this, frequency and volume will be greatly reduced compared to beginners, national caliber, and elite athletes. This also means that when changes are made in a program they must be balanced out across all the exercise modes.
■ Masters soccer is recreational. The masters athlete may not view it this way, but compared to the national caliber and elite athlete this will be less structured. A formal periodization program will not be necessary with this athlete provided that training is structured and progressive.
■ The athlete has a history.
■ There will not be a need to distinguish between the positions when designing the strength and conditioning program.

With the above in mind, Table 12.24 presents a sample week of workouts for the masters athlete. The week is organized into two strength-training sessions, both focusing on the athlete's entire body while minimizing the volume. Conditioning is performed once a week and is geared around small-sided games. This is to minimize the athlete's exposure to sprints and give his/her legs a chance to stay fresh. Plyometrics are performed once a week and are combined with very short sprints to make them more relevant to the athlete. Speed and agility work is performed once a week and, as has been the case at all levels in this chapter, focuses on making the exercises relevant to the sport of soccer.

Table 12.23 Mesocycle 5 (July 26–August 15), elite soccer player

	Week of July 26	Week of August 2	Week of August 9
Monday	Dynamic flexibility exercises, 10–20 minutes	Dynamic flexibility exercises, 10–20 minutes	Dynamic flexibility exercises, 10–20 minutes
	Strength/plyometrics (rest 2 minutes between sets): Split squats + squat jumps, 3 × 4–6 × 80% + 5 jumps One-legged Romanian deadlifts + standing long jump (land on one leg), 3 × 4–6+6 jumps Incline press + lying MB chest pass, 3 × 4–6 × 80% + 5 throws Pull-ups, 3 × 4-8-RM	Strength/plyometrics (rest 2 minutes between sets): Split squats + squat jumps, 3 × 4–6 × 82.5% + 5 jumps One-legged Romanian deadlifts + standing long jump (land on one leg), 3 × 4–6+6 jumps Incline press + lying MB chest pass, 3 × 4–6 × 82.5% + 5 throws Pull-ups, 3 × 4-8-RM	Speed/agility technique drills, 10 minutes Speed/agility: Drills 1–5, 1× each, against opponent and with ball (reactive)
Tuesday	Dynamic flexibility exercises, 10–20 minutes	Dynamic flexibility exercises, 10–20 minutes	Dynamic flexibility exercises, 10–20 minutes
	Speed/agility technique drills, 10 minutes Speed/agility: Drills 1–5, 1× each, against opponent and with ball (reactive) Conditioning: 2 × 15 × 40-meter sprints, 20-second jogging recovery between sprints, 5-minute walking recovery between sets	Speed/agility technique drills, 10 minutes Speed/agility: Drills 1–5, 1× each, against opponent and with ball (reactive) Conditioning: 2 × 15 × 40-meter sprints, 20-second jogging recovery between sprints, 5-minute walking recovery between sets	Strength/plyometrics (rest 2 minutes between sets): Split squats + squat jumps, 3 × 4–6 × 85% + 5 jumps One-legged Romanian deadlifts + standing long jump (land on one leg), 3 × 4–6+6 jumps Incline press + lying MB Chest pass, 3 × 4–6 × 85% + 5 throws Pull-ups, 3 × 4-8-RM

Table 12.23 (continued)

	Week of July 26	Week of August 2	Week of August 9
Wednesday	Dynamic flexibility exercises, 10–20 minutes	Dynamic flexibility exercises, 10–20 minutes	Dynamic flexibility exercises, 10–20 minutes
	Strength/plyometrics (rest 2 minutes between sets): Power clean + box jump (2), 3 × 3–4 × 60% + 5 jumps Split jerk + pike jump, 3 × 3–4 × 60% + 5 jumps	Power clean, 3 × 2 + 2 × 80% + 60% Eccentric squats + squat jumps, 3 × 3 × 70% + 5 jumps Eccentric bench press + MB chest pass, 3 × 4 × 70% + 5 throws	2 × 15 × 40-meter sprints, 20-second jogging recovery between sprints, 5-minute walking recovery between sets
	Clean pulls, h, K + counter-movement jumps (jump off one leg, land on both), 3 × 4–6 × 65% + 5 jumps	Game	

Table 12.23 (continued)

	Week of July 26	Week of August 2	Week of August 9
Thursday	Dynamic flexibility exercises, 10–20 minutes	Dynamic flexibility exercises, 10–20 minutes	Dynamic flexibility exercises, 10–20 minutes
	Speed/agility technique drills, 10 minutes	Speed/agility technique drills, 10 minutes	Power clean + box jump (2), 3×3–$4 \times 60\%$ + 5 jumps
			Split Jerk + pike jump,
	Speed/agility circuit (all exercises are done with the ball; perform each for 40 meters, no rest during the circuit, 2 minutes jogging recovery, repeat):	Speed/agility circuit (all exercises are done with the ball; perform each for 20 meters, no rest during the circuit, 2 minutes jogging recovery, repeat):	3×3–$4 \times 60\%$ + 5 jumps
	Sprint	Sprint	Clean pulls, h, K + Counter-movement jumps (jump off one leg, land on both),
	Back-pedal	Back-pedal	3×4–$6 \times 65\%$ + 5 jumps
	Shuffle right	Shuffle right	
	Sprint	Sprint	
	Shuffle left	Shuffle left	
	Sprint	Sprint	
	Zig-zags	Zig-zags	
	Sprint	Sprint	
	Conditioning: Small-sided games, 30 minutes		

Table 12.23 (continued)

	Week of July 26	Week of August 2	Week of August 9
Friday	Off	Off	Dynamic flexibility exercises, 10–20 minutes Speed/agility technique drills, 10 minutes Speed/agility (all with ball and reacting to an opponent): Drill 1, 1× Drill 2, 1× Drill 3–5, 3× each
Saturday	Dynamic flexibility exercises, 10–20 minutes Speed/agility technique drills, 10 minutes Speed/agility: Resisted starts, 10-meter sprints, 5× Stride-length drills, 5 × 20 meters Stride-frequency drills, 5 × 20 meters	Dynamic flexibility exercises, 10–20 minutes Speed/agility technique drills, 10 minutes Speed/agility: Resisted starts, 10-meter sprints, 5× Stride-length drills, 5 × 20 meters Stride-frequency drills, 5 × 20 meters	Dynamic flexibility exercises, 10–20 minutes Strength/plyometrics (rest 2 minutes between sets): Power clean, 3 × 2+2 × 80%+60% Eccentric squats + squat jumps, 3 × 3 × 70% + 5 jumps Eccentric bench press + MB chest pass, 3 × 4 × 70% + 5 throws Game

Table 12.23 (continued)

	Week of July 26	Week of August 2	Week of August 9
Sunday	Dynamic flexibility exercises, 10–20 minutes	Dynamic flexibility exercises, 10–20 minutes	Dynamic flexibility exercises, 10–20 minutes
	Strength/plyometrics (rest 2 minutes between sets): Power clean, 3 × 2+2 × 80%+60% Eccentric squats + squat jumps, 3 × 3 × 70% + 5 jumps Eccentric bench press + MB chest pass, 3 × 4 × 70% + 5 throws	Strength/plyometrics (rest 2 minutes between sets): Power clean, 3 × 2+2 × 80%+60% Eccentric squats + squat jumps, 3 × 3 × 70% + 5 jumps Eccentric bench press + MB chest pass, 3 × 4 × 70% + 5 throws	Speed/agility technique drills, 10 minutes
			Conditioning: Sprinting circuit while dribbling soccer ball 1 × 20 meters (8 sec), 1 × 40 meters (16 sec), 1 × 60 meters (32 sec), 1 × 80 meters (50 sec), 4 × 100 meters (60 sec), 1 × 80 meters (50 sec), 1 × 60 meters (32 sec), 1 × 40 meters (16 sec), 1 × 20 meters a
	Game	Game	

Table 12.24 Sample week of workouts for the masters soccer player

Day	Workout
Monday	Dynamic flexibility exercises, 10–20 minutes
	Strength: Back squats, 3 × 4–8 × 80% Lunges, 3 × 6–10 Romanian deadlifts, 3 × 6–10 Bench press, 3 × 4–8 × 80% Bent-over rows, 3 × 6–10 Seated military press, 3 × 6–10
Tuesday	Dynamic flexibility exercises, 10–20 minutes
	Conditioning: Small-sided games, 20 minutes
Wednesday	Dynamic flexibility exercises, 10–20 minutes
	Plyometrics: Counter-movement jump + 5-meter sprint, 5× Standing long jump + 5-meter sprint, 5× MB toss, forward + 5-meter sprint, 5× MB toss, backward + 5-meter sprint, 5×
Thursday	Off
Friday	Dynamic flexibility exercises, 10–20 minutes
	Strength: Power clean + split jerk, 3 × 3+2 × 60% Clean pulls, 3 × 4 × 65% Pause squats, 3 × 4 × 60% Pause bench press, 3 × 4 × 60%
Saturday	Dynamic flexibility exercises, 10–20 minutes
	Speed/agility technique drills, 10 minutes
	Speed/agility: Drills 1–5, 1× each
Sunday	Off

DRILLS

Drill 1

- Objectives: starting, stopping, acceleration.
- Set-up: set up cones on the start line, 5 meters, and 10 meters.
- Execution:
  - Athlete begins at the start line, on command the athlete runs to the 5-meter line and stops.
  - After coming to a complete stop, the athlete runs through the 10-meter line to end the drill.
- Variation:
  - All movements can be done to command, whistle, or other stimulus (i.e., the athlete starts on command, stops when told to, starts when told to, etc.).
  - Perform the drill while dribbling a soccer ball.
  - Perform the drill reacting to an opposing player's movements.

Drill 2

- Objectives: starting, stopping, shuffling, change of direction, acceleration.
- Set-up: see Figure 12.1.
- Execution:
  - Begin at the start line.
  - On command, run to the first cone. Stop.
  - Shuffle to the right or left.
  - At the second cone, turn and sprint through the third cone.
- Variation:
  - All movements can be done to command, whistle, or other stimulus.
  - Perform the drill while dribbling a soccer ball.
  - Perform the drill reacting to an opposing player's movements.

Drill 3

- Objectives: starting, stopping, back-pedaling, change of direction, acceleration.
- Set-up: set up cones on the start line and every five meters through 25 meters.
- Execution:
  - The athlete begins at the start line.
  - On command, the athlete sprints forward 10 meters, then back-pedals 5 meters, then sprints forward 10 meters, then back-pedals 5 meters until the entire distance has been covered.

278

putting it all together

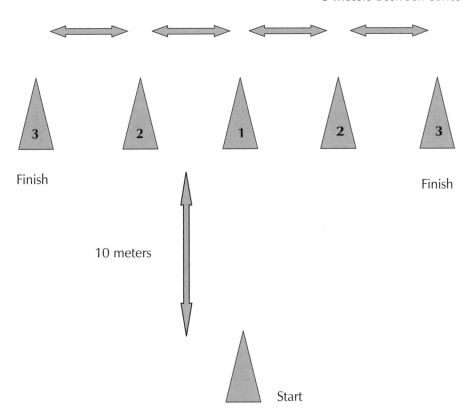

5 meters between cones

3 2 1 2 3

Finish   Finish

10 meters

Start

Figure 12.1 Drill 2.

- Variation:
  - All movements can be done to command, whistle, or other stimulus.
  - Perform the drill while dribbling a soccer ball.
  - Perform the drill reacting to an opposing player's movements.

Drill 4

- Objectives: starting, stopping, back-pedaling, shuffling, change of directions, acceleration, reacting, running curves.
- Set-up: see Figure 12.2. The distances between the cones should be varied.

- Execution:
  - Begin at the start (cone #1).
  - Sprint to cone #2.
  - Back-pedal to cone #1.
  - Change direction and sprint to cone #3.
  - Shuffle to cone #4.
  - Turn and sprint to cone #5.
  - Run around cone #5 to through the finish line.
- Variations:
  - All movements can be done to command, whistle, or other stimulus.
  - Perform the drill while dribbling a soccer ball.
  - Perform the drill reacting to an opposing player's movements.

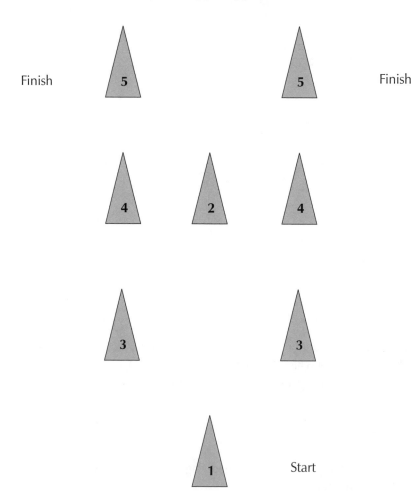

Figure 12.2 Drill 4.

Drill 5

- Objectives: starting, stopping, changing directions, running curves, zig-zagging, accelerating, reacting.
- Set-up: see Figure 12.3. The distance between the cones should be varied.
- Execution:
  - Begin at the start line (cone #1).
  - Sprint to cone #2. Stop.
  - Turn and sprint to cone #3.
  - Run around cone #3 towards the #4 cones.
  - Zig-zag through the #4 cones.
  - Sprint to cone #5 and the finish line.
- Variations:
  - All movements can be done to command, whistle, or other stimulus.
  - Perform the drill while dribbling a soccer ball.
  - Perform the drill reacting to an opposing player's movements.

KEY READINGS

Andersson, H.A., Randers, M.B., Heiner-Moller, A., Krustrup, P., and Mohr, M. (2010) Elite female soccer players perform more high-intensity running when playing in international games compared with domestic league games, *Journal of Strength and Conditioning Research*, 24(4): 912–19.

Bradley, P.S., Di Mascio, M., Peart, D., Olsen, P., and Sheldon, B. (2010) High-intensity activity profiles of elite soccer players at different performance levels, *Journal of Strength and Conditioning Research*, 24(9): 2343–51.

Dellal, A., Wong, D.P., Moalla, W., and Chamari, K. (2010) Physical and technical activity of soccer players in the French First League – with special reference to their playing position, *International Sports Medicine Journal*, 11(2): 278–90.

Di Salvo, V., Baron, R., Tschan, H., Calderon Montero, F.J., Bachl, N., and Pigozzi, F. (2007) Performance characteristics according to playing position in elite soccer, *International Journal of Sports Medicine*, 28: 222–27.

Mohr, M., Krustrup, P., Andersson, H., Kirkendal, D., and Bangsbo, J. (2008) Match activities of elite women soccer players at different performance levels, *Journal of Strength and Conditioning Research*, 22(2): 341–49.

The articles by Andersson *et al.* (2010), Bradley *et al.* (2010), Dellal *et al.* (2010), Di Salvo *et al.* (2007) and Mohr *et al.* (2008) are important articles for anyone that works with soccer players. These articles establish how to analyze performance in a soccer game to

Finish

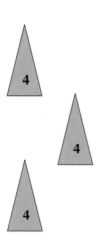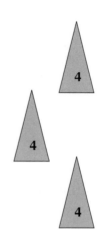

Start

Figure 12.3 Drill 5.

putting it all together

help design metabolic conditioning, speed training, and agility training in a way that has the best transfer to the sport. In addition, several of these articles demonstrate that the various positions do different things during the game. Each of these articles has limitations in that the specifics of the results applies only to the population studied, but the trends and the techniques can be studied and applied to other populations of athletes.

putting it all together

GLOSSARY

Acceleration – The process of increasing velocity.

Acromioclavicular joint – Part of the shoulder joint, where the clavicle connects to the scapula.

Actin – Also known as thin filaments, protein myofilament in the sarcomere. Myosin connects to actin and pulls it for the sarcomere to shorten.

Action potential – Electrochemical signal that changes the charge of the nerve and muscle fiber.

Adenosine triphosphate (ATP) – an adeonsine molecule bound to three phosphate groups, the compound that the body uses to fuel movement and chemical reactions.

Agonist – The muscle that performs the movement, also known as a prime mover.

Anabolic – A situation where tissue is added.

Annulus – In the intervertebral disc, the rough outer ring.

Antagonist – The muscle that opposes the movement.

Anterior cruciate ligament – Connects the femur to the tibia and resists the forward movement of the tibia in relation to the femur.

Basement membrane – Exterior of the endomysium.

Bone mineral density – The quantity of material in a given area of bone.

Bone modeling – Adaptation of bone to loading and unloading.

Bulging disc – In an intervertebral disc, the pushing out of the nucleus as a result of injury.

Casting – Dorsiflexing the ankle during sprinting.

Catabolic – A situation where tissue is degraded.

Co-activation – A situation where both the agonist and the antagonist are performing the movement.

Competition period – In periodization, the period during which the athlete is peaking.

Competition phase – In periodization, the phase in which the athlete is actually competing.

Complex training – Alternating between heavier strength training and similar plyometrics exercises on a set-for-set basis. A tool to help develop power.

Contrast training – Alternating between heavier and lighter loads. A tool to help develop power.

284

Corticospinal tract – Also known as the pyramidal pathway, the pathway from the motor cortex of the brain to the gray matter of the spinal cord.

Cortisol – Primary signaling hormone for carbohydrate metabolism, thought to be a marker for training intensity.

Creatine phosphate – Used to resynthesize ATP after it has been broken down.

Cross-bridge – Connection between actin and myosin during a muscular contraction.

Depolarization – Result of the actin potential, muscle fiber becomes positively charged inside.

Elastic energy – Energy stored in the tendon and elastic components of a muscle. Tapping into this results in increased force production.

Endomysium – The layer of connective tissue that surrounds each muscle fiber, consists of a basement membrane and a plasma membrane (also known as a sarcolemma).

Epimysium – The layer of connective tissue that surrounds the entire skeletal muscle.

Fasciculus – Bundles of muscle fibers located beneath the epimysium.

Fast-twitch muscle fibers – Capable of generating a large amount of force, quickly, but also fatigue quickly. They are larger than slow-twitch muscle fibers.

First pull – The period in a clean or snatch where the barbell is lifted from the floor to the height of the knees.

Free weights – Barbells, dumbbells, kettlebells, and body-weight exercises. These exercises are minimally limited by the design of a piece of equipment.

Frequency – How often one exercises.

General preparation phase – In periodization, the phase where the athlete broadly develops their fitness base.

General warm-up – The part of the warm-up that elevates heart rate gradually, increases blood flow to the tissues, and increases the temperature, allowing for more deformability of tissues.

Glenohumeral joint – Part of the shoulder joint, where the humerus connects to the scapula.

Growth hormone – Increases cellular amino acid uptake and protein synthesis. Also decreases glucose utilization, decreases glycogen synthesis, increases the utilization of fatty acids, and increases collagen synthesis.

Growth plate – Located at the end of long bones, where cartilage is deposited, which eventually causes the bones to lengthen.

Herniated disc – In an intervertebral disc, the rupturing of the annulus and the pushing out of the nucleus as a result of injury.

Hyperplasia – Increase in the number of muscle fibers.

Hypertrophy – Increase in the size of individual muscle fibers.

In series – Muscle-fiber orientation where the fibers run parallel to the tendon's line of pull.

Insulin-like growth factor – Has a controversial role in the regulation of hypertrophy.

Intensity – The quality of work done.

Lateral collateral ligament – Resist varus movement at the knee.

Macrocycle – In periodization, the period of time from the last peak through the next peak.

Maximal strength – The maximal amount of force that can be exerted.

Maximal velocity – The fastest an athlete can run.

Medial collateral ligament – Resist valgus movement at the knee.

Mesocycle – In periodization, subdivisions of the phase. Mesocycles usually last 2–4 weeks.

Metabolic conditioning – Getting an athlete in shape for the specific energy system demands of their sport or position.

Microcycle – In periodization, subdivisions of the mesocycle. Microcycles usually last one week.

Minimum essential strain – The threshold that initiates new bone formation.

Motor unit – The motor nerve and everything it innervates.

Myosin – Also known as think filaments, protein myofilament in the sarcomere. Connects to actin and pulls it for the sarcomere to shorten.

Muscle fibers – The cell of the muscle. Each muscle fiber runs the length of the muscle.

Needs analysis – The process of analyzing a sport and position to determine how the strength and conditioning program should be focused.

Neurons – Cell bodies located in the motor cortex of the brain that extend into the spinal cord and terminate in the spinal cord's gray matter.

Nucleus – In the intervertebral disc, the inner core.

One repetition maximum (1-RM) – The amount of weight that an athlete can lift at one time.

Overload – Principle of exercise that states that since the body adapts to exercise, it must be challenged to keep it adapting.

Patellofemoral compression – Refers to the patella acting on the femur.

Pennate muscle fibers – Muscle-fiber orientation where the fibers run obliquely to the tendon's line of pull.

Perimysium – The layer of connective tissue that surrounds each fasciculus.

Period – In periodization, subdivisions of the macrocycle. There is a preparatory period, competition period, and recovery period.

Periodization – A systematic, long-term planning process.

Periosteum – Outer surface of the bone, where new bone formation occurs.

Phase – In periodization, subdivisions of the period.

Plasma membrane – Interior of the endomysium, also known as the sarcolemma.

Posterior cruciate ligament – Connects the femur to the tibia and resists the backward movement of the tibia in relation to the femur.

Power – The ability to exert force quickly.

Pre-competition phase – In periodization, the phase that sees a sharp increase in intensity prior to the main competitions.

Preparatory period – In periodization, the period during which the athlete gets in shape for the sport.

Progression – Principle of exercise that states that exercise should be approached in a stepwise fashion, where each step builds upon the one that came before it.

Pronated – An overhand grip, i.e., the palms face down.

Pyramidal pathway – Also known as the corticospinal tract, the pathway from the motor cortex of the brain to the gray matter of the spinal cord.

Rate of force development – The speed with which muscle fibers can be recruited to produce force.

Repetition – A complete exercise movement from start to finish.

Repolarization – Result of the termination of the action potential, muscle fiber becomes negatively charged inside.

Rest – The amount of time between each set of exercises.

Sarcolemma – Interior of the endomysium, also known as the plasma membrane.

Sarcomere – Contractile unit of the muscle.

Sarcoplasmic reticulum – Interlocking tubular channels surrounding the sarcomere.

Satellite cells – Located between the basement membrane and plasma membrane, thought to help mediate hypertrophy.

Scapulothoracic joint – Part of the shoulder joint, the interaction between the fascia of the muscle and the thorax.

Second pull – The period of a clean or snatch where the barbell is lifted from the height of the knees until it reaches its maximum velocity, the explosive part of the lift.

Set – A group of repetitions.

Setting the back – Lifting strategy to protect the lower back, involves retracting the shoulder blades and puffing out the chest during lifting.

Size principle – Principle that states that the muscle fibers are recruited preferentially based upon their size, with the smaller fibers being recruited first.

Slow-twitch muscle fibers – Capable of generating a small amount of force, slowly, but are extremely resistant to fatigue.

Special preparation phase – In periodization, the phase where the athlete's fitness is applied to the sport.

Specific warm-up – The part of the warm-up that trains the muscles and joints in a manner similar to how they will be trained in the workout, allows for skills to be practiced and for intensity to be gradually increased.

Specificity – Principle of exercise that states that the body adapts to exercise according to how one exercises it.

Speed endurance – The ability to maintain maximal velocity.

Spondylolisthesis – Where a stress fracture weakens a vertebrae to the point where it shifts out of place.

Spondylolysis – A stress fracture in one of the spinal column's vertebrae.

Sprains – Overstretching and tearing of ligaments.

Sternoclavicular joint – Part of the shoulder joint, where the clavicle connects to the sternum.

Strains – Overstretching and tearing of muscles.

Striated muscle – Skeletal muscle, called striated because of its alternating light and dark bands.

Stride frequency – The number of strides per unit of time during sprinting, running, or walking.

Stride length – The distance between strides during running, sprinting, or walking.

Tendons – Connective tissue that attaches muscle to bone.

Testosterone – The primary anabolic hormone.

Tibifemoral compression – Compression of the femur on the tibia. Prevents the tibia from moving forwards and backwards, protects the cruciate ligaments.

Valgus – inward movement of the knees, knock-kneed.

Varus – Outward movement of the knees, bow-legged.

Velocity specificity – A concept that states that the body adapts to exercise at the velocities at which the exercise occurs.

Volume – The quantity of work done.

BIBLIOGRAPHY

Abdelkrim, N.B., Castagna, C., Jabri, I., Battikh, T., El Fazaa, S. and El Ati, J. (2010a) Activity profile and physiological requirements of junior elite basketball players in relation to aerobic-anaerobic fitness, *Journal of Strength and Conditioning Research*, 24(9): 2330–42.

Abdelkrim, N.B., Chaouachi, A., Chamari, K., Chtara, M. and Castagna, C. (2010b) Positional role and competitive level differences in elite-level men's basketball players, *Journal of Strength and Conditioning Research*, 24(5): 1346–55.

Abe, T., Brown, J.B. and Brechue, W.F. (1999) Architectural characteristics of skeletal muscle in black and white college football players, *Medicine and Science in Sports and Exercise*, 31: 1448–52.

Abe, T., Kumagai, K. and Brechue, W.F. (2000) Fascicle length of leg muscles is greater in sprinters than distance runners, *Medicine and Science in Sports and Exercise*, 32(6): 1125–9.

Adams, G.R. (2006) Satellite cell proliferation and skeletal muscle hypertrophy, *Applied Physiology, Nutrition, and Metabolism*, 31: 782–90.

Ahtiainen, J.P., Pakarinen, A., Alen, M., Kraemer, W.J. and Haakkinen, K. (2005) Short vs. long rest period between the sets in hypertrophyic resistance training: influence on muscle strength, size, and hormonal adaptations in trained men, *Journal of Strength and Conditioning Research*, 19(3): 572–82.

Alcaraz, P.E., Palao, J.M. and Elvira, J.L.L. (2009) Determining the optimal load for resisted sprint training with sled towing, *Journal of Strength and Conditioning Research*, 23(2): 480–5.

Alcaraz, P.E., Palao, J.M., Elvira, J.L.L. and Linthorne, N.P. (2008) Effects of three types of resisted sprint training devices on the kinematics of sprinting at maximum velocity, *Journal of Strength and Conditioning Research*, 22(3): 890–7.

Alentorn-Geli, E., Myer, G.D., Silvers, H.J., Samitier, G., Romero, D., Lazaro-Haro, C., and Cugat, R. (2009) Prevention of non-contact anterior cruciate ligament injuries in soccer players. Part 2: A review of prevention programs aimed to modify risk factors and to reduce injury rates, *Knee Surgery, Sports Traumatology, Arthoscopy*, 17: 859–79.

Alves, J.M.V.M., Rebelo, A.N., Abrantes, C. and Sampaio, J. (2010) Short-term effects of complex and contrast training in soccer players' vertical jump, sprint, and agility abilities, *Journal of Strength and Conditioning Research*, 24(4): 936–41.

Anderson, C.E., Sforzo, G.A. and Sigg, J.A. (2008) The effects of combining elastic and free weight resistance on strength and power in athletes, *Journal of Strength and Conditioning Research*, 22(2): 567–74.

Andersson, H.A., Randers, M.B., Heiner-Moller, A., Krustrup, P., and Mohr, M. (2010) Elite female soccer players perform more high-intensity running when playing in international games compared with domestic league games, *Journal of Strength and Conditioning Research*, 24(4): 912–19.

Baker, D. (2003) Acute effect of alternating heavy and light resistance on power output during upper-body complex power training, *Journal of Strength and Conditioning Research*, 17(3): 493–7.

Baker, D. and Nance, S. (1999) The relation between running speed and measures of strength and power in professional rugby league players, *Journal of Strength and Conditioning Research*, 13(3): 230–5.

Baker, D.G. and Newton, R.U. (2009) Effect of kinetically altering a repetition via the use of chain resistance on velocity during the bench press, *Journal of Strength and Conditioning Research*, 23(7): 1941–6.

Bakker, E.W., Verhagen, A.P., van Trijffel, E., Lucas, C., and Koes, B.W. (2009) Spinal mechanical load as a risk factor for low back pain, *Spine*, 34(8): E281–E293.

Balague, F., Bibbo, E., Melot, C., Szpalski, M., Gunzburg, R. and Keller, T.S. (2010) The association between isoinertial trunk muscle performance and low back pain in male adolescents, *European Spine Journal*, 19: 624–32.

Barnes, M. and Cissik, J. (2008) *Training for the 40-yard Dash*, Coaches Choice, Monterrey Bay, CA.

Barnett, A. (2006) Using recovery modalities between training sessions in elite athletes: Does it help? *Sports Medicine*, 36(9): 781–96.

Bauer, T., Thayer, R.E. and Baras, G. (1990) Comparison of training modalities for power development in the lower extremity, *Journal of Applied Sport Science Research*, 4(4): 115–21.

Beaulieu, M.L., Lamontagne, M., and Xu, L. (2008) Gender differences in tme-frequency EMG analysis of unanticipated cutting maneuvers, *Medicine and Science in Sports and Exercise*, 40(10): 1795–804.

Behm, D.G. (1995) Neuromuscular implications and applications of resistance training, *Journal of Strength and Conditioning Research*, 9(4): 264–74.

Behm, D.G. and Sale, D.G. (1993) Velocity specificity of resistance training, *Sports Medicine*, 15(6): 374–88.

Bellar, D.M., Muller, M.D., Barkley, J.E., Kim, C-H., Ida, K., Ryan, E.J., Bliss, M.V. and Glickman, E.L. (2010) The effects of combined elastic- and free-weight tension versus free-weight tension on one-repetition maximum strength in the bench press, *Journal of Strength and Conditioning Research*, 24.

Berg, K. and Latin, R.W. (1995) Comparison of physical and performance characteristics of NCAA Division I basketball and football players, *Journal of Strength and Conditioning Research*, 9(1): 22–26.

Berning, J.M., Coker, C.A. and Briggs, D. (2008) The biomechanical and perceptual influence of chain resistance on the performance of the Olympic clean, *Journal of Strength and Conditioning Research*, 22(2): 390–95.

Bird, S.P., Tarpenning, K.M. and Marino, F.E. (2005) Designing resistance training programmes to enhance muscular fitness, *Sports Medicine*, 35(10): 841–51.

Bishop, P.A., Jones, E. and Woods, A.K. (2008) Recovery from training: a brief review, *Journal of Strength and Conditioning Research*, 22(3): 1015–24.

Black, W. and Roundy, E. (1994) Comparisons of size, strength, speed, and power in NCAA Division 1-A football players, *Journal of Strength and Conditioning Research*, 8(2): 80–5.

Bompa, T.O. (1999) *Periodization: Theory and Methodology of Training*, 4th edn, Human Kinetics, Champaign, IL: 95–142.

Bondarchuk, A. (1988a) Constructing a training system, part I, *Track Technique*, 102: 3254–59, 3268.

Bondarchuk, A. (1988b) Constructing a training system, part II, *Track Technique*, 103: 3286–8.

Boraczynski, T. and Urniaz, J. (2008) The effect of plyometrics training on strength-speed abilities of basketball players, *Research Yearbook*, 14(1): 14–19.

Borowski, L.A., Yard, E.E., Fields, S.K. and Comstock, R.D. (2008) The epidemiology of U.S. high school basketball injuries, 2005–2007, *American Journal of Sports Medicine*, 36: 2328–35.

Bradley, P.S., Di Mascio, M., Peart, D., Olsen, P. and Sheldon, B. (2010) High-intensity activity profiles of elite soccer players at different performance levels, *Journal of Strength and Conditioning Research*, 24(9): 2343–51.

Brughelli, M. and Cronin, J. (2008) Preventing hamstring injuries in sport, *Strength and Conditioning* Journal, 30(1): 55–64.

Buresh, R., Berg, K. and French, J. (2009) The effect of resistive exercise rest interval on hormonal response, strength, and hypertrophy with training, *Journal of Strength and Conditioning Research*, 23(1): 62–71.

Calbet, J.A., Herrera, P.D. and Rodriguez, L.P. (1999) High bone mineral density in male elite professional volleyball players, *Osteoporosis International*, 10: 468–74.

Can, F., Yilmaz, I. and Erden, Z. (2004) Morphological characteristics and performance variables of women soccer players, *Journal of Strength and Conditioning Research*, 18(3): 480–5.

Carbuhn, A.F., Womack, J.W., Green, J.S., Morgan, K., Miller, G.S. and Crouse, S.F. (2008) Performance and blood pressure characteristics of first-year National Collegiate Athletic Association Division I football players, *Journal of Strength and Conditioning Research*, 22(4): 1347–54.

Carroll, T.J., Barton, J., Hsu, M. and Lee, M. (2009) The effect of strength training on the force of twitches evoked by corticospinal stimulation in humans, *Acta Physiologica*, 197: 161–73.

Caserotti, P., Aagaard, P., Larsen, J.B. and Puggaard, L. (2008) Explosive heavy-resistance training in old and very old adults: Changes in rapid muscle force, strength and power, *Scandinavian Journal of Medicine and Science in Sports*, 18: 773–82.

Castro-Pinero, J., Gonzalez-Montesinos, J.L., Mora, J., Keating, X.D., Girela-Rejon, M.J., Sjostrom, M. and Ruiz, J.R. (2009) Percentile values for muscular strength field tests in children aged 6 to 17 years: Influence of weight status, *Journal of Strength and Conditioning Research*, 23(8): 2295–310.

Chandler, T.J. Wilson, G.D., and Stone, M.H. (1989) The effect of the squat exercise on knee stability, *Medicine and Science in Sports and Exercise*, 21(3): 299–303.

Chappell, J.D. and Limpisvasti, O. (2008) Effect of a neuromuscular training program on the kinetics and kinematics of jumping tasks, *American Journal of Sports Medicine*, 36(6): 1081–6.

Chatzinikolaou, A., Fatouros, I.G., Gourgoulis, V., Avloniti, A., Jamurtas, A.Z., Nikolaidis, M.G., Douroudos, I., Michailidis, Y., Beneka, A., Malliou, P., Tofas, T., Georgiadis, I., Mandalidis, D. and Taxildaris, K. (2010) Time course of changes in performance and inflammatory responses after acute plyometrics exercise, *Journal of Strength and Conditioning Research*, 24(5): 1389–98.

Chang, D.E., Bushbacher, L.P. and Edlich, R.F. (1988) Limited joint mobility in power lifters, *American Journal of Sports Medicine*, 16(3): 280–4.

Cissik, J.M. (2000) Conditioning for hammer throwers, *Track and Field Coaches Review*, 73(1): 32–4.

Cissik, J.M. (2001) You need a needs analysis, *Track Coach*, 155: 4952–4.

Cissik, J.M. (2004) Means and methods of speed training, part I, *Strength and Conditioning Journal*, 26(4): 24–9.

Cissik, J.M. (2005) Means and methods of speed training, part II, *Strength and Conditioning Journal*, 27(1): 18–25.

Cissik, J.M. (2007) Program design: Linking it all together, *Track Coach*, 178: 5688–92.

Cissik, J.M. (2011) The role of core training in performance improvement, injury prevention, and injury treatment, *Strength and Conditioning Journal*, 33(1), 10–15.

Cissik, J.M. and Barnes, M. (2010) *Sport Speed and Agility Training*, 2nd edn, Coaches Choice, Monterey, CA: 37–67.

Cissik, J.M., Hedrick, A. and Barnes, M. (2008) Challenges applying the research on periodization, *Strength and Conditioning Journal*, 30(1): 45–51.

Clark, K.P., Stearne, D.J., Walts, C.T. and Miller, A.D. (2010) The longitudinal effects of resisted sprint training using weighted sleds vs. weighted vests, *Journal of Strength and Conditioning Research*, 24(12): 3287–95.

Coaching Education Committee (2001) *Coaching Education Program: Level II Course (Sprints, Hurdles, Relays)*, USA Track and Field.

Coh, M., Peharec, S., Bacic, P. and Kampmiller, T. (2009) Dynamic factors and electromyographic activity in a sprint start, *Biology of Sport*, 26(2): 137–47.

Coh, M. and Tomazin, K. (2005) Biomechanical characteristics of female sprinters during the acceleration phase and maximal speed phase, *Modern Athlete and Coach,* 43(4): 3–9.

Coh, M., Tomazin, K. and Rausavljevic, N. (2007) Differences in morphological and biodynamic characteristics of maximum speed and acceleration between two groups of female sprinters, *Biology of Sport*, 24(2): 115–28.

Comfort, P., Green, C.M. and Matthews, M. (2009) Training considerations after hamstring injury in athletes, *Strength and Conditioning Journal*, 31(1): 68–74.

Comyns, T.M., Harrison, A.J., Hennessy, L.K. and Jensen, R.L. (2006) The optimal complex training rest interval for athletes from anaerobic sports, *Journal of Strength and Conditioning Research*, 20(3): 471–6.

Cormie, P., McCaulley, G.O. and McBride, J.M. (2007a) Power versus strength-power jump squat training: influence on the load-power relationship, *Medicine and Science in Sports and Exercise*, 39(6): 996–1003.

Cormie, P., McCaulley, G.O., Triplett, N.T. and McBride, J.M. (2007b) Optimal loading for maximal power output during lower-body resistance exercise, *Medicine and Science in Sports and Exercise*, 39(2): 340–9.

Cormie, P., McGuigan, M.R. and Newton, R.U. (2010a) Adaptations in athletic performance after ballistic power versus strength training, *Medicine and Science in Sports and Exercise*, 42(8): 1582–98.

Cormie, P., McGuigan, M.R. and Newton, R.U. (2010b) Changes in the eccentric phase contribute to improved stretch-shorten cycle performance after training, *Medicine and Science in Sports and Exercise*, 42(9): 1731–44.

Cormie, P., McGuigan, M. and Newton, R.U. (2010c) Influence of strength on magnitude and mechanisms of adaptation to power training, *Medicine and Science in Sports and Exercise*, 42(8): 1566–81.

Cormie, P. McGuigan, M.R. and Newton, R.U. (2011) Developing maximal neuromuscular power. Part 1: biological basis of maximal power production. *Sports Medicine*, 41(1): 17–38.

Coyle, E.F., Coggan, A.R., Hooper, M.K. and Walters,T.J. (1988) Determinants of endurance in well-trained cyclists, *Journal of Applied Physiology*, 64(6): 2622–30.

Cristea, A., Korhonen, M.T., Hakkinen, K., Mero, A., Alen, M., Sipila, S., Viitasalo, J.T., Koljonen, M.J., Suominen, H. and Larsson, L. (2008) Effects of combined strength and sprint training on regulation of muscle contraction at the whole-muscle and single-fibre levels in elite master sprinters, *Acta Physiologica*, 193: 275–89.

Cronin, J.B. and Hansen, K.T. (2005) Strength and power predictors of sports speed, *Journal of Strength and Conditioning Research*, 19(2): 349–57.

Cronin, J.B., McNair, P.J. and Marshall, R.N. (2000) The role of maximal strength and load on initial power production, *Medicine and Science in Sports and Exercise*, 32(10): 1763–9.

Cronin, J., McNair, P.J. and Marshall, R.N. (2001) Velocity specificity, combination training and sport specific tasks, *Journal of Science and Medicine in Sport*, 4(2): 168–78.

DeBeliso, M., Harris, C., Spitzer-Gibson, T. and Adams, K.J. (2005) A comparison of periodised and fixed repetition training protocol in strength in older adults, *Journal of Science and Medicine in Sports*, 8(2): 190–9.

Delextrat, A. and Cohen, D. (2009) Strength, power, speed, and agility of women basketball players according to playing position, *Journal of Strength and Conditioning Research*, 23(7): 1974–81.

De Renne, C., Hetzler, R.K., Buxton, B.P. and Ho, K.W. (1996) Effects of training frequency on strength maintenance in pubescent baseball players, *Journal of Strength and Conditioning Research*, 10(1): 8–14.

de Souza, Jr., T.P., Fleck, S.J., Simao, R., Dubas, J.P., Pereira, B., Pacheco, E.M. de B., da Silva, A.C. and de Oliveira, P.R. (2010) Comparison between constant and decreasing rest intervals: influence on maximal strength and hypertrophy, *Journal of Strength and Conditioning Research* 24(7): 1843–50.

de Villarreal, E.S-S., Kellis, E., Kraemer, W.J. and Izquierdo, M. (2009) Determining variables of plyomeric training for improving vertical jump height performance: a meta-analysis, *Journal of Strength and Conditioning Research*, 23(2): 495–506.

Deitch, J.R., Starkey, C., Walters, S.L. and Moseley, J.B. (2006) Injury risk in professional basketball players: a comparison of Women's National Basketball Association and National Basketball Association athletes, *American Journal of Sports Medicine*, 34: 1077–83.

Dellal, A., Wong, D.P., Moalla, W., and Chamari, K. (2010) Physical and technical activity of soccer players in the French First League – with special reference to their playing position, *International Sports Medicine Journal*, 11(2): 278–90.

Deyo, R.A. (2004) 'Treatments for back pain: Can we get past trivial effects?' *Annals of Internal Medicine*, 141(12): 957–8.

Dick, F.W. (2002) *Sports Training Principles*, 4th edn. London: A&C Black, pp. 223–47.

Dick, R., Hertel, J., Agel, J., Grossman, J. and Marshall, S.W. (2007) Descriptive epidemiology of collegiate men's basketball injuries: National Collegiate Athletic Association injury surveillance system, 1988–1989 through 2003–2004, *Journal of Athletic Training*, 42(2): 194–201.

Di Salvo, V., Baron, R., Tschan, H., Calderon Montero, F.J., Bachl, N. and Pigozzi, F. (2007) Performance characteristics according to playing position in elite soccer, *International Journal of Sports Medicine*, 28: 222–7.

Dolgener, F.A. and Morien, A. (1993) The effect of massage on lactate disappearance, *Journal of Strength and Conditioning Research*, 7(3): 159–62.

Dupler, T.L., Amonette, W.E., Coleman, A.E., Hoffman, J.R. and Wenzel, T. (2010). Anthropometric and performance differences among high-school football players, *Journal of Strength and Conditioning Research*, 24(8): 1975–82.

Ebben, W.P., Fauth, M.L., Petushek, E.J., Garceau, L.R., Hsu, B.E., Lutsch, B.N. and Feldmann, C.R. (2010) Gender-based analysis of hamstring and quadriceps muscle activation during jump landings and cutting, *Journal of Strength and Conditioning Research*, 24(2): 408–15.

Ebben, W.P., Simenz, C. and Jensen, R.L. (2008) Evaluation of plyometrics intensity using electromyography, *Journal of Strength and Conditioning Research*, 22(3): 861–8.

Escamilla, R.F., Fleisig, G.S., Zheng, N., Lander, J.E., Barrentine, S.W., Andrews, J.R., Bergemann, B.W. and Moorman III, C.T. (2001) Effects of technique variation on knee biomechanics during the squat and leg press, *Medicine and Science in Sports and Exercise*, 33(9): 1552–66.

Faigenbaum, A.D., Kraemer, W.J., Blimkie, C.J.R., Jeffreys, I., Micheli, L.J., Nitka, M. and Rowland, T.W. (2009) Youth resistance training: updated position statement paper from the National Strength and Conditioning Association, *Journal of Strength and Conditioning Research*, 23(S5): S60–S79.

Faigenbaum, A.D., Loud, R.L., O'Connell, J., Glover, S., O'Connell, J. and Westcott, W.L. (2001) Effects of different resistance training protocols on upper-body strength and endurance development in children, *Journal of Strength and Conditioning Research*, 15(4): 459–65.

Faigenbaum, A.D., McFarland, J.E., Kelly, N.A., Ratamess, N.A., Kang, J. and Hoffman, J.R. (2010) Influence of recovery time on warm-up effects in male adolescent athletes, *Pediatric Exercise Science*, 22: 266–77.

Faigenbaum, A.D., Milliken, L.A., Loud, R.L., Burak, B.T., Doherty, C.L. and Westcott, W.L. (2002) Comparison of 1 and 2 days per week of strength training in children, *Research Quarterly for Exercise and Sport*, 73(4): 416–24.

Farrar, R.E., Mayhew, J.L. and Koch, A.J. (2010) Oxygen cost of kettlebell swings, *Journal of Strength and Conditioning Research*, 24(4): 1034–6.

Faude, O., Junge, A., Kindermann, W. and Dvorak, J. (2006) Risk factors for injuries in elite female soccer players, *British Journal of Sports Medicine*, 40: 785–90.

Fernandez-Gonzalo, R., De Souza-Teixeira, F., Bresciani, G., Garcia-Lopez, D., Hernandez-Murua, J.A., Jimenez-Jimenez, R. and De Paz, J.A. (2010) Comparison of technical and physiological characteristics of prepubescent soccer players of different ages, *Journal of Strength and Conditioning Research*, 24(7): 1790–8.

Fletcher, I.M. (2010) The effect of different dynamic stretch variables on jump performance, *European Journal of Applied Physiology*, 109: 491–8.

Fletcher, I.M. and Monte-Colombo, M.M. (2010) An investigation into the possible physiological mechanisms associated with changes in performance related to acute responses to different preactivity stretch modalities, *Applied Physiology Nutrition and Metabolism*, 35: 27–34.

Folland, J.P. and Williams, A.G. (2007) The adaptations to strength training, *Sports Medicine*, 37(2): 145–68.

Freeman, W. (1994) Coaching, periodization, and the battle of artist versus scientist, *Track Coach*, 127: 4054–7.

Gabbett, T.J. (2007) Physiological and anthropometric characteristics of elite women rugby league players, *Journal of Strength and Conditioning Research*, 21(3): 875–81.

Gabbett, T.J., Kelly, J.N. and Sheppard, J.M. (2008a) Speed, change of direction speed, and reactive agility of rugby league players, *Journal of Strength and Conditioning*

Research, 22(1): 174–81.

Gabbett, T.J., Johns, J. and Riemann, M. (2008b) Performance changes following training in junior rugby league players, *Journal of Strength and Conditioning Research*, 22(3): 910–7.

Gambetta, V. (1991) Some thoughts on new trends in training theory, *National Strength and Conditioning Association Journal*, 13(1): 24–6.

Garhammer, J. (1981) Force-velocity constraints and elastic energy utilization during multi-segment lifting/jumping activities, *Medicine and Science in Sports and Exercise*, 13(2): 96.

Garhammer, J. (1993) A review of power output studies of Olympic and powerlifting: methodology, performance prediction, and evaluation tests, *Journal of Strength and Conditioning Research*, 7(2): 76–89.

Garhammer, J. and Gregor, R. (1992) Propulsion forces as a function of intensity for weightlifting and vertical jumping, *Journal of Applied Sport Science Research*, 6(3): 129–34.

Gelen, E. (2010) Acute effects of different warm-up methods on sprint, slalom dribbling, and penalty kick performance in soccer players, *Journal of Strength and Conditioning Research*, 24(4): 950–6.

Goldby, L.J., Moore, A.P., Doust, J. and Trew, M.E. (2006) A randomized controlled trial investigating the efficiency of musculoskeletal physiotherapy on chronic low back disorder, *Spine*, 31(10): 1083–93.

Gollhofer, A. (2007) Adaptive responses of the neuromuscular system to training, *New Studies in Athletics*, 22(1): 23–30.

Goto, K., Nagasawa M., Yanagisawa O., Kizuka T., Ishii N., and Takamatsu, K. (2004) Muscular adaptations to combinations of high- and low-intensity resistance exercise, *Journal of Strength and Conditioning Research* 18(4): 730–7.

Greiwe, J.S., Hickner, R.C., Hansen, P.A., Racette, S.B., Chen, M. and Holloszy, J.O. (1999) Effects of endurance training on muscle glycogen accumulation in humans, *Journal of Applied Physiology*, 87(1): 222–6.

Hagglund, M., Walden, M. and Ekstrand, J. (2009) Injuries among male and female elite football players, *Scandinavian Journal of Medicine and Science in Sports*, 19: 819–27.

Hakkinen, K., Kraemer, W.J., Newton, R.U. and Alen, M. (2001) Changes in electromyographic activity, muscle fibre and force production characteristics during heavy resistance/power strength training in middle-aged and older men and women, *Acta Physiologica Scandinavica*, 171: 51–62.

Hamilton, N. (1993) Changes in sprint stride kinematics with age in masters athletes, *Journal of Applied Biomechanics*, 9: 15–26.

Hancock, D. (2008) The lateral ligament complex: insights and rehabilitation, *SportEX medicine*, 38: 14–19.

Hanson, E.D., Srivatsan, S.R., Agrawal, S., Menon, K.S., Delmonico, M.J., Wang, M.Q. and Hurley, B.F. (2009) Effects of strength training on physical functions: Influence of power, strength, and body composition, *Journal of Strength and Conditioning*

Research, 23(9): 2627–37.

Harre, D. (ed.) (1982) *Principles of Sports Training*, Berlin, Sportverlag: 47–72.

Harris, C., DeBeliso, M.A., Spitzer-Gibson, T.A. and Adams, K.J. (2004) 'The effect of resistance-training intensity on strength-gain response in the older adult', *Journal of Strength and Conditioning Research*, 18(4): 833–8.

Harris, G.R., Stone, M.H., O'Bryant, H.S., Proulx, C.M. and Johnson, R.L. (2000) Short-term performance effects of high power, high force, or combined weight-training methods, *Journal of Strength and Conditioning Research*, 14(1): 14–20.

Hawley, J.A. (2009) Molecular responses to strength and endurance training: Are they incompatible? *Applied Physiology, Nutrition, and Metabolism*, 34: 355–61.

Heuch, I., Hagen, K., Heuch, I., Nygaard, O. and Zwart, J-A. (2010) The impact of body mass index on the prevalence of low back pain, *Spine*, 35(7): 764–8.

Hides, J.A., Jull, G.A. and Richardson, C.A. (2001) Long-term effects of specific stabilizing exercises for first-episode low back pain, *Spine*, 26(11): E243–E248.

Higgins, T.R., Heazlewood, I.T. and Climstein, M. (2010) A random control trial of contrast baths and ice baths for recovery during competition in U/20 rugby union, *Journal of Strength and Conditioning Research*.

Hoffman, J.R., Vazquez, J., Pichardo, N. and Tennenbaum, G. (2009) Anthropometric and performance comparisons in professional baseball players, *Journal of Strength and Conditioning Research*, 23(8): 2173–8.

Holm, L., Reitelseder, S., Pedersen, T.G., Doessing, S., Petersen, S.G., Flyvbjerg, A., Andersen, J.L., Aagaard, P. and Kjaer, M. (2008) Changes in muscle size and MHC composition in response to resistance exercise with heavy and light loading intensity, *Journal of Applied Physiology*, 105: 1454–61.

Howarth, K.R., Phillips, S.M., MacDonald, M.J., Richards, D., Moreau, N.A. and Gibala, M.J. (2010) Effect of glycogen availability on human skeletal muscle protein turnover during exercise and recovery, *Journal of Applied Physiology*, 109(2): 431–8.

Howatson, G., Gaze, D. and van Someren, K.A. (2005) The efficacy of ice massage in the treatment of exercise-induced muscle damage, *Scandinavian Journal of Medicine and Science in Sports*, 15: 416–22.

Hoyt, T. (2009) Skeletal muscle benefits of endurance training: Mitochondrial adaptations, *AMAA Journal*, 22(3): 14–16.

Hrysomallis, C. and Kidgell, D. (2001) Effect of heavy dynamic resistive exercise on acute upper-body power, *Journal of Strength and Conditioning Research*, 15(4): 426–30.

Hurley, B.F. and Roth, S.M. (2000) Strength training in the elderly: effects on risk factors for age-related diseases, *Sports Medicine*, 30(4): 249–68.

Izquierdo, M., Hakkinen, K., Ibanez, J., Garrues, M., Anton, A., Zuniga, A., Larrion, J.L. and Gorostiaga, E.M. (2001) Effects of strength training on muscle power and serum hormones in middle-aged and older men, *Journal of Applied Physiology*, 90: 1497–1507.

Jakalski, K. (2000) Parachutes, tubing, and towing, in Jarver, J. (ed.) *Sprints and Relays*, 5th edn, TAFNEWS Press, Mountain View, CA: 95–100.

Jakalski, K. (2002) Contemporary research and sprinting: reconsidering the conceptual paradigm of running mechanics, *Track and Field Coaches Review*, 75(1): 21–2.

Jarit, G.J. and Bosco, J.A. (2010) Meniscal repair and reconstruction, *Bulletin of the NYU Hospital for Joint Diseases*, 68(2): 84–90.

Jelicic, M., Trninic, M. and Jelaska, I. (2010) Differences between three types of basketball players on the basis of situation-related efficiency, *Acta Kinesiologica*, 4: 82–9.

Jensen J.L., Marstrand, P.C.D. and Nielsen, J.B. (2005) Motor skill training and strength training are associated with different plastic changes in the central nervous system, *Journal of Applied Physiology*, 99: 1558–68.

Junge, A. and Dvorak, J. (2007) Injuries in female football players in top-level international tournaments, *British Journal of Sports Medicine*, 41(S I): i3–i7.

Kanehisa, H. and Miyashita, M. (1983) Specificity of velocity in strength training, *European Journal of Applied Physiology*, 52: 104–6.

Kaplan, T., Erkmen, N. and Taskin, H. (2009) The evaluation of the running speed and agility performance in professional and amateur soccer players, *Journal of Strength and Conditioning Research*, 23(3): 774–8.

Kawakami, Y., Abe, T., Kuno, S.Y. and Fukunaga, T. (1995) Training-induced changes in muscle architecture and specific tension, *European Journal of Applied Physiology*, 72: 37–43.

Kawamori, N. and Haff, G.G. (2004) The optimal training load for the development of muscular power, *Journal of Strength and Conditioning Research*, 18(3): 675–84.

Kell, R.T. and Asmundson, G.J.G. (2009) A comparison of two forms of periodized exercise rehabilitation programs in the management of chronic nonspecific low-back pain, *Journal of Strength and Conditioning Research*, 23(2): 513–23.

Keller, A., Hayden, J., Bombardier, C. and van Tulder, M. (2007) Effect sizes of non-surgical treatments of non-specific low-back pain, *European Spine Journal*, 16: 1776–88.

Kemper, H.C.G. (2000) Skeletal development during childhood and adolescence and the effects of physical activity, *Pediatric Exercise Science*, 12: 198–216.

Kilduff, L.P., Bevan, H., Owen, N., Kingsley, M.I.C., Bunce, P., Bennett M. and Cunningham, D. (2007) Optimal loading for peak power output during the hang power clean in professional rugby players, *International Journal of Sports Physiology and Performance*, 2: 260–9.

Kilduff, L.P., Owen, N., Bevan, H., Bennett, M., Kingsley, M.I.C. and Cunningham, D. (2008) Influence of recovery time on post-activation potentiation in professional rugby players, *Journal of Sports Sciences*, 26(8): 795–802.

Kivi, D.M.R. and Alexander, M.J.L. (2000) A kinematic comparison of the running A and B drills with sprinting, *Track Coach*, 150: 4782–3, 4788.

Klein, K.K. (1961) The deep squat exercise as utilized in weight training for athletics and its effect on the ligaments of the knee, *Journal of the Association of Physical and Mental Rehabilitation*, 15(1): 6–11, 23.

Knight, C.A. and Kamen, G. (2001) Adaptations in muscular activation of the knee extensor muscles with strength training in young and older adults, *Journal of Electromyography and Kinesiology*, 11: 405–12.

Komi, P.V. (1979) Neuromuscular performance: Factors influencing force and speed production, *Scandinavian Journal of Sports Science*, 1: 2–15.

Korhonen, M.T., Mero, A. and Suominen, H. (2003) Age-related differences in 100-m sprint performance in male and female master runners, *Medicine and Science in Sports and Exercise*, 35(8): 1419–28.

Korhonen, M.T., Suominen, H. and Mero, A. (2005) Age and sex differences in blood lactate response in sprint running in elite master athletes, *Canadian Journal of Applied Physiology*, 30(6): 647–65.

Korhonen, M.T., Mero, A.A., Alen, M., Sipila, S., Hakkinen, K., Liikavainio, T., Viitasalo, J.T., Haverinen, M.T. and Suominen, H. (2009) Biomechanical and skeletal muscle determinants of maximum running speed with aging, *Medicine and Science in Sports and Exercise*, 41(4): 844–56.

Kraemer, W.J. (2000) Endocrine responses to resistance exercise, in Baechle, T.R. and Earle, R.W. (eds) *Essentials of Strength Training and Conditioning*, 2nd edn, Champaign, IL: Human Kinetics, pp. 91–114.

Krieger, J.W. (2010) Single vs. multiple sets of resistance exercise for muscle hypertrophy: a meta-analysis, *Journal of Strength and Conditioning Research* 24(4): 1150–9.

Kubo, K., Ikebukuro, T., Yata, H., Tsunoda, N. and Kanehisa, H. (2010) Time course of changes in muscle and tendon properties during strength training and detraining, *Journal of Strength and Conditioning Research*, 24(2): 322–31.

Kumagai, K., Abe, T., Brechue, W.F., Ryushi, T., Takano, S. and Mizuno, M. (2000) Sprint performance is related to muscle fascicle length in male 100-m sprinters, *Journal of Applied Physiology*, 88(3), 811–16.

Kumar, S., Sharma, V.P. and Negi, M.P.S. (2009) Efficacy of dynamic muscular stabilization techniques over conventional techniques in rehabilitation of chronic low back pain, *Journal of Strength and Conditioning Research*, 23(9): 2651–9.

Kurz, T. (1991) *Science of Sports Training: How to Plan and Control Training for Peak Performance*, Island Pond, VT: Stadion Publishing Company, pp. 84–101, 231–41.

Kuznyetsov, V.V., Petrovskiy, V. and Schustin, B.N. (1983) The model for sprinters, in Jarver, J. (ed.) *Sprints and Relays*, 2nd edn, Mountain View, CA, TAFNEWS Press: 30–1.

Latin, R.W., Berg, K. and Baechle, T. (1994) Physical and performance characteristics of NCAA Division I male basketball players, *Journal of Strength and Conditioning Research*, 8(4): 214–18.

Lawton, T., Cronin, J., Drinkwater, E., Lindsell, R. and Pyne, D. (2004) The effect of continuous repetition training and intra-set rest training on bench press strength and power, *Journal of Sports Medicine and Physical Fitness*, 44(4): 361–7.

Letzelter, M., Sauerwein, G. and Burger, R. (1995) Resistance runs in speed development, in Jarver, J. (ed.) *Sprints and Relays*, 4th edn, Mountain View, CA: TAFNEWS Press, pp. 82–6.

Letzelter, S. (2006) The development of velocity and acceleration in sprints: A comparison of elite and juvenile female sprinters, *New Studies in Athletics*, 21(3): 15–22.

Little, T. and Williams, A.G. (2005) Specificity of acceleration, maximum speed, and agility in professional soccer players, *Journal of Strength and Conditioning Research*, 19(1): 76–8.

Lockie, R.G., Murphy, A.J. and Spinks, C.D. (2003) Effects of resisted sled towing on sprint kinematics in field-sport athletes, *Journal of Strength and Conditioning Research*, 17(4): 760–7.

Lohmander, L.S., Englund, P.M., Dahl, L.L. and Roos, E.M. (2007) The long-term consequences of anterior cruciate ligament and meniscus injuries, *American Journal of Sports Medicine*, 35(10): 1756–69.

Mackala, K. (2007) Optimisation of performance through kinematic analysis of the different phases of the 100 metres, *New Studies in Athletics*, 22(2): 7–16.

Makaruk, H. and Sacewicz, T. (2010) Effects of plyometric training on maximal power output and jumping ability, *Human Movement*, 11(1): 17–22.

Manoel, M.E., Harris-Love, M.O., Danoff, J.V. and Miller, T.A. (2008) Acute effects of static, dynamic, and proprioceptive neuromuscular facilitation stretching on muscle power in women, *Journal of Strength and Conditioning Research*, 22(5): 1528–34.

Markovic, G. (2007) Poor relationship between strength and power qualities and agility performance, *Journal of Sports Medicine and Physical Fitness*, 47(3): 276–83.

Matveyev, L. (1981) *Fundamentals of Sports Training*, Moscow, Progress Publishers, pp. 6–85, 166–85.

Maulder, P.S., Bradshaw, E.J. and Keogh, J.W.L. (2008) Kinematic alterations due to different loading schemes in early acceleration sprint performance from starting blocks, *Journal of Strength and Conditioning Research*, 22(6): 1992–2002.

McCall, G.E., Byrnes, W.C., Fleck, S.J., Dickinson, A. and Kraemer, W.J. (1999) Acute and chronic hormonal response to resistance training designed to promote muscle hypertrophy, *Canadian Journal of Applied Physiology*, 24(1): 96–107.

McCaw, S.T. and Friday, J.J. (1994) A comparison of muscle activity between a free weight and machine bench press, *Journal of Strength and Conditioning Research*, 8(4): 259–64.

McCurdy, K., Langford, G., Ernest, J., Jenkerson, D. and Doscher, M. (2009) Comparison of chain- and plate-loaded bench press training on strength, joint pain, and muscle soreness in Division II baseball players, *Journal of Strength and Conditioning Research*, 23(1): 187–95.

McFarlane, B. (1993) A basic and advanced technical model for speed, *National Strength and Conditioning Association Journal*, 15(5): 57–61.

McGill, S. (2010) Core training: Evidence translating to better performance and injury prevention, *Strength and Conditioning Journal*, 32(3): 33–46.

McKenzie, R.A. (1998) *The Lumbar Spine: Mechanical Diagnosis and Therapy*, Wellington, New Zealand: Spinal Publications.

McMillian, D.J., Moore, J.H., Hatler, B.S. and Taylor, D.C. (2006) Dynamic vs. static-stretching warm up: the effect on power and agility performance, *Journal of Strength and Conditioning Research*, 20(3): 492–9.

Medvedev, A.S. (1989) *A System of Multi-year Training in Weightlifting*, Livonia, MI, Sportivny Press, pp. 82–4.

Meir, R., Newton, R., Curtis, E., Fardell, M. and Butler, B. (2001) Physical fitness qualities of professional rugby league football players: determination of positional differences, *Journal of Strength and Conditioning Research*, 15(4): 450–8.

Meltzer, D.E. (1994) Age dependence of Olympic weightlifting ability, *Medicine and Science in Sports and Exercise*, 26(8): 1053–67.

Meyers, E.J. (1971) Effect of selected excercise variables on ligament stability and flexibility of the knee, *Research Quarterly*, 42(4): 411–22.

Mirkov, D.M., Kukoij, M., Ugarkovic, D., Koprivica, V.J. and Jaric, S. (2010) Development of anthropometric and physical performance profiles of young elite male soccer players: a longitudinal study, *Journal of Strength and Conditioning Research*, 24(10): 2677–82.

Moen, M.H., Tol, J.L., Weir, A., Steunebrink, M. and De Winter, T.C. (2009) Medial tibial stress syndrome: a critical review, *Sports Medicine*, 39(7): 523–46.

Mohr, M., Krustrup, P., Andersson, H., Kirkendal, D. and Bangsbo, J. (2008) Match activities of elite women soccer players at different performance levels, *Journal of Strength and Conditioning Research*, 22(2): 341–9.

Moir, G., Sanders, R., Button, C. and Glaister, M. (2007) The effect of periodized resistance training on accelerative sprint performance, *Sports Biomechanics*, 6(3): 285–300.

Morrissey, M.C., Hooper, D.M., Drechsler, W.I., Hill, H.J. and Bucknill, T. (2000) Velocity specificity in early training of the knee extensors after anterior cruciate ligament reconstruction, *European Journal of Applied Physiology*, 81: 493–6.

Mujika, I., Spencer, M., Santisteban, J., Goiriena, J.J. and Bishop, D. (2009) Age-related differences in repeated-sprint agility in highly trained youth football players, *Journal of Sports Sciences*, 27(14): 1581–90.

Myer, G.D., Quatman, C.E., Khoury, J., Wall, E.J. and Hewett, T.E. (2009) Youth versus adult "weightlifting" injuries presenting to Unites States emergency rooms: Accidental versus nonaccidental injury mechanisms, *Journal of Strength and Conditioning Research*, 23(7): 2054–60.

Narici, M. (1999) Human skeletal muscle architecture studied in vivo by non-invasive imaging techniques: functional significance and applications, *Journal of Electromyography and Kinesiology*, 9: 97–103.

Neelly, K.R., Terry, J.G. and Morris, M.J. (2010) A mechanical comparison of linear and double-looped hung supplemental heavy chain resistance to the back squat: a case study, *Journal of Strength and Conditioning Research*, 24(1): 278–81.

Nesser, T.W., Huxel, K.C., Tincher, J.L. and Okada, T. (2008) The relationship between core stability and performance in Division I football players, *Journal of Strength and Conditioning Research*, 22(6): 1750–4.

Nicholas, S.J. and Tyler, T.F. (2002) Adductor muscle strains in sport, *Sports Medicine*, 32(5): 339–44.

Nimphius, S., McGuigan, M.R. and Newton, R.U. (2010) Relationship between strength, power, speed, and change of direction performance in female soccer players, *Journal of Strength and Conditioning Research*, 24(4): 885–95.

Ostojic, S.M., Mazic, S. and Dikic, N. (2006) Profiling in basketball: physical and physiological characteristics of elite players, *Journal of Strength and Conditioning Research*, 20(4): 740–4.

Ozolin, N. (1978) How to improve speed, in Jarver, J. (ed.) *Sprints and Relays*, Mountain View, CA: TAFNEWS Press, pp. 55–6.

Papaiakovou, G., Giannakos, A., Michailidis, C., Patikas, D., Bassa, E., Kalopisis, V., Anthrakidis, N. and Kotzamanidis, C. (2009) The effect of chronological age and gender on the development of sprint performance during childhood and puberty, *Journal of Strength and Conditioning Research*, 23(9): 2568–73.

Perry, C.G, Heigenhauser, G.J., Bonen, A. and Spriet, L.L. (2008) High-intensity aerobic interval training increases fat and carbohydrate metabolic capacities in human skeletal muscle, *Applied Physiology, Nutrition, and Metabolism*, 33: 1112–23.

Persch, L.N., Ugrinowitsch, C., Pereira, G., and Rodacki, A.L. (2009) Strength training improves fall-related gait kinematics in the elderly: a randomized controlled trial, *Clinical Biomechanics*, 24: 819–25.

Petrella, J.K., Kim, J-S., Mayhew, D.L., Cross, J.M. and Bamman, M.M. (2008) Potent myofiber hypertrophy during resistance training in humans is associated with satellite cell-mediated myonuclear addition: a cluster analysis, *Journal of Applied Physiology*, 104: 1736–42.

Plisk, S.S. (2001) Muscular strength and stamina, in Foran, B. (ed.) *High-performance Sports Conditioning*, Champaign, IL: Human Kinetics, pp. 63–82.

Rearburn, P. and Dascombe, B. (2009) Anaerobic performance in masters adults, *European Reviews of Aging and Physical Activity*, 6: 39–53.

Sabo, D., Bernd, L., Pfeil, J. and Reiter, A. (1996) Bone quality in the lumbar spine in high-performance athletes, *European Spine Journal*, 5: 258–63.

Sahlin, K., Tonkonogi, M. and Soderlund, K. (1998) Energy supply and muscle fatigue in humans, *Acta Physiologica Scandinavica*, 162: 261–6.

Sampaio, J., Janeira, M., Ibanez, S. and Lorenzo, A. (2006) Discriminant analysis of game-related statistics between basketball guards, forwards and centres in three professional leagues, *European Journal of Sport Science*, 6(3): 173–8.

Samuel, M.N., Holcomb, W.R., Guadagnoli, M.A., Rubley, M.D. and Wallmann, H. (2008) Acute effects of static and ballistic stretching on measures of strength and power, *Journal of Strength and Conditioning Research*, 22(5): 1422–8.

Sassi, R.H., Dardouri, W., Yahmed, M.H., Gmada, N., Mahfoudhi, M.E. and Gharbi, Z. (2009) Relative and absolute reliability of a modified agility t-test and its relationship with vertical jump and straight sprint, *Journal of Strength and Conditioning Research*, 23(6): 1644–51.

Sato, K. and Mokha, M. (2009) Does core strength training influence running kinetics, lower-extremity stability, and 5000-m performance in runners? *Journal of Strength and Conditioning Research*, 23(1): 133–40.

Schmolinsky, G. (1996) *Track and Field: The East German Textbook of Athletics*, Toronto: Sports Books Publisher, pp. 136–41.

Schwanbeck, S., Chilibeck, P.D. and Binsted, G. (2009) A comparison of free weight squat to smith machine squat using electromyography, *Journal of Strength and Conditioning Research*, 23(9): 2588–91.

Secora, C.A., Latin, R.W., Berg, K.E. and Noble, J.M. (2004) Comparison of physical and performance characteristics of NCAA Division I football players: 1987 and 2000, *Journal of Strength and Conditioning Research*, 18(2): 286–91.

Seynnes, O.R., de Boer, M. and Narici, M.V. (2007) Early skeletal muscle hypertrophy and architectural changes in response to high-intensity resistance training, *Journal of Applied Physiology*, 102: 368–73.

Sheppard, J., Hobson, S., Barker, M., Taylor, K., Chapman, D., McGuigan, M. and Newton, R. (2008) The effect of training with accentuated eccentric load counter-movement jumps on strength and power characteristics of high-performance volleyball players, *International Journal of Sports Sciences and Coaching*, 3(3): 355–63.

Shimokochi, Y. and Shultz, S.J. (2008) Mechanisms of noncontact anterior cruciate ligament injury, *Journal of Athletic Training*, 43(4): 396–408.

Shirazi-Adl, A. (1989) Strains in fibers of a lumbar disc: analysis of the role of lifting in producing disc prolapsed, *Spine*, 14(1): 96–103.

Sierer, S.P., Battaglini, C.L., Mihalik, J.P., Shields, E.W. and Tomasini, N.T. (2008) The National Football League combine: Performance differences between drafted and nondrafted players entering the 2004 and 2005 drafts, *Journal of Strength and Conditioning Research*, 22(1): 6–12.

Silvestre, R., West, C., Maresh, C.M. and Kraemer, W.J. (2006) Body composition and physical performance in men's soccer: A study of a National Collegiate Athletic Association Division I team, *Journal of Strength and Conditioning Research*, 20(1): 177–83.

Smilios, I., Piliandis, T., Karamouzis, M. and Tokmakidis, S.P. (2003) Hormonal response after various resistance exercise protocols, *Medicine and Science in Sports and Exercise*, 35(4): 644–54.

Spangenburg, E.E. (2009) Changes in muscle mass with mechanical load: possible cellular mechanisms, *Applied Physiology, Nutrition, and Metabolism*, 34: 328–35.

Spennewyn, K.C. (2008) Strength outcomes in fixed versus free-form resistance equipment, *Journal of Strength and Conditioning Research*, 22(1): 75–81.

Spinks, C.D., Murphy, A.J., Spinks, W.L. and Lockie, R.G. (2007) The effects of resisted sprint training on acceleration performance and kinematics in soccer, rugby union, and Australian football players, *Journal of Strength and Conditioning Research*, 21(1): 77–85.

Sporis, G., Jukic, I., Ostojic, S.M. and Milanovic, D. (2009) Fitness profiling in soccer: Physical and physiologic characteristics of elite players, *Journal of Strength and Conditioning Research*, 23(7): 1947–53.

Stanton, R., Reaburn, P.R. and Humphries, B. (2004) The effect of short-term Swiss ball training on core stability and running economy, *Journal of Strength and Conditioning Research*, 19(3): 522–8.

Staron, R.S. (1997) Human skeletal muscle fiber types: delineation, development, and distribution, *Canadian Journal of Applied Physiology*, 22(4): 307–27.

Steffen, K., Pensgaard, A.M. and Bahr, R. (2009) Self-reported psychological characteristics as risk factors for injuries in female youth football, *Scandinavian Journal of Medicine and Science in Sports*, 19: 442–51.

Stone, M.H., Sands, W.A., Pierce, K.C., Ramsey, M.W. and Haff, G. (2008) Power and power potentiation among strength-power athletes: preliminary study, *International Journal of Sports Physiology and Performance*, 3: 55–67.

Tan, B. (1999) Manipulating resistance training program variables to optimize maximum strength in men: a review, *Journal of Strength and Conditioning Research*, 13(3): 289–304.

Tessitore, A., Meeusen, R., Cortis, C. and Capranica, L. (2007) Effects of different recovery interventions on anaerobic performances following preseason soccer training, *Journal of Strength and Conditioning Research*, 21(3): 745–50.

Tse, M.A., McManus, A.M. and Masters, R.S.W. (2004) Development and validation of a core endurance intervention program: implications for performance in college-age rowers, *Journal of Strength and Conditioning Research*, 19(3): 547–52.

Vaile, J.M., Gill, N.D. and Blazevich, A.J. (2007) The effect of contrast water therapy on symptoms of delayed onset muscle soreness, *Journal of Strength and Conditioning Research*, 21(3): 697–702.

van Middelkoop, M., Rubinstein, S.M., Verhagen, A.P., Koes, B.W. and van Tulder, M.W. (2010) Exercise therapy for chronic nonspecific low-back pain, *Best Practice and Research Clinical Rheumatology*, 24: 193–204.

Verchoshanskij, J.V. (1999) The end of 'periodization' of training in top-class sport, *New Studies in Athletics*, 14(1): 47–55.

Vescovi, J.D. and McGuigan, M.R. (2008) Relationships between sprinting, agility, and jump ability in female athletes, *Journal of Sports Sciences*, 26(1): 97–107.

Walden, M., Hagglund, M., and Ekstrand, J. (2007) Football injuries during European Championships 2004–2005, *Knee Surgery, Sports Traumatology, Arthoscopy*, 15: 1155–62.

Weiner, B.K. (2007) Difficult medical problems: on explanatory models and a pragmatic alternative, *Medical Hypotheses*, 68: 474–9.

Wernbom, M., Augustsson, J. and Thomee, R. (2007) The influence of frequency, intensity, volume, and mode of strength training on whole muscle cross-sectional area in humans, *Sports Medicine*, 37(3): 225–64.

West, T. and Robson, S. (2000) Running drills – Are we reaping the benefits? in Jarver, J.

(ed.) *Sprints and Relays*, 5th edn, Mountain View, CA: TAFNEWS Press, pp. 64–7.

Wilborn, C.D., Taylor, L.W., Greenwood, M., Kreider, R.B. and Willoughby, D.S. (2009) Effects of different intensities of resistance exercise on regulators of myogenesis, *Journal of Strength and Conditioning Research*, 23(8): 2179–87.

Wong, D. (2008) Characteristics of World Cup soccer players, *Soccer Journal*, Jan/Feb: 57–62.

Wong, P.-L., Chamari, K., Dellal, A. and Wisloff, U. (2009) Relationship between anthropometric and physiological characteristics in youth soccer players, *Journal of Strength and Conditioning Research*, 23(4): 1204–10.

Wong, P.-L., Chamari, K. and Wisloff, U. (2010) Effects of 12-week on-field combined strength and power training on physical performance among U-14 young soccer players, *Journal of Strength and Conditioning Research*, 24(3): 644–52.

Wretenberg, P., Feng, Y. and Arborelius, U.P. (1996) High- and low-bar squatting techniques during weight-training, *Medicine and Science in Sports and Exercise*, 28(2), 218–24.

Yeo, W.K., Paton, C.D., Garnham, A.P., Burke, L.M., Carey, A.L. and Hawley, J.A. (2008) Skeletal muscle adaptation and performance responses to once a day versus twice every second day endurance training regimens, *Journal of Applied Physiology*, 105: 1462–70.

Young, W.B. (2006) Transfer of strength and power training to sports performance, *International Journal of Sports Physiology and Performance*, 1: 74–83.

Young, W.B., McDowell, M.H. and Scarlett, B.J. (2001) Specificity of sprint and agility training methods, *Journal of Strength and Conditioning Research*, 15(3): 315–319.

Zatsiorsky, V.M. (1995) *Science and Practice of Strength Training*, Champaign, IL: Human Kinetics, pp. 200–22.

INDEX

217–18; for beginner athletes 214; for elite soccer players 260–4; for national-caliber soccer players 244–55

presses 53–60

pro-agility test 80

progression in exercise 127–9, 131, 133

pull-downs 64–5

pull-ups 63–4, 129–32

push jerks 37

quadriceps 11

Radcliffe, J.C. 120

Rearburn, P. 211

recovery methods 118–19

recovery time 126, 163, 178, 256

research: gaps in 3–4, 185; generalisability of 203

resistance, effect of increases in 125

rest periods 126, 150

reverse hyperextension exercise 52–3

Romanian deadlifts (RDLs) 49–50, 129

rotator-cuff injuries 188–90

Roth, S.M. 206

rows 60–2

rugby 84–5

Sabo, D. 15

Sale, D.G. 123, 133

satellite cells 149

scheduling of a training program 138–9

Schustin, B.N. 146

Sheppard, J. 156

Shimokochi Y. 196

shin splints 199–200

shoulder injuries 188–9

shuffling 68

Shultz, S.J. 196

single-effort jumps 109–11

size principle for motor units 11

snatch exercises 27–34

soccer 226–81; beginner athletes in 229–40; national-caliber athletes in 240–59; needs analysis for 227–9; test results for 85–6

specificity of training 1, 122–5, 129, 132, 173–4, 217

speed, tests of 76

speed barrier 102

speed training 1, 65–6, 98–104, 157–60, 172–4; for beginner athletes 214–15; for elite athletes 222; for national-caliber athletes 217–19; and needs analysis 137; see also velocity specificity

Spinks, C.D. 166

split-body workouts 151–4

split jerks 34–8

split snatches 33

split squats 43–4

spondylolysis and spondylolisthesis 191

sprains 191

sprint-based conditioning 115–16

sprinting 65–8, 101–4, 158–60; assisted 102–3, 160; needs analysis for 141–4; resisted 103, 158–60; stepwise approach to 116; varied-pace 103–4; while fatigued 160

squat jumps 110

squats 38–47

stabilizing muscles 11

standing long jump 75, 111

standing triple jump 75, 114

Staron, R.S. 7

starting techniques for athletes 67

static stretching 94, 118

statistical models of sports 138

status of an individual athlete 140

stopping techniques 67

strains 191

strength, tests of 72–4

strength training 1, 9–16, 94–7, 123–4, 152–6, 159, 172–4; age-appropriate 204–7; for beginner athletes 214–15;